Commercial and Industrial Law

THE M & E HANDBOOK SERIES

Commercial and Industrial Law

Anne R. Ruff

LLB, LLM, CertEd
Senior Lecturer in Law
Middlesex Polytechnic

THIRD EDITION

MACDONALD AND EVANS

Macdonald & Evans Ltd
Estover, Plymouth PL6 7PZ

First published 1978
Second edition 1981
Third edition 1984

British Library Cataloguing in Publication Data
Ruff, Anne R.
Commercial and industrial law.—3rd ed.—
(The M & E HANDBOOK series, ISSN 0265-8828
1. Commercial law—England
I. Title
344.206'7 KD1629

ISBN 0-7121-0195-0

Typeset by
Mathematical Composition Setters Ltd,
7 Ivy Street, Salisbury

Printed in Great Britain by Hollen Street Press,
Slough, Berks.

Preface to the Third Edition

This HANDBOOK attempts to present the outlines of commercial and industrial law in one volume. The major changes since the last edition have been in the areas of employment and social security legislation, with the passing of the Employment Act 1982, the Social Security and Housing Benefits Act 1982 and the Health and Social Services and Social Security Adjudications Act 1983. The House of Lords decisions on arbitration and interpretation of the employment legislation are the main case-law developments. The Trade Union Bill and the Health and Social Security Bill are likely to receive the Royal Assent this session, and their provisions have been outlined where appropriate.

I have tried to explain these and other changes simply but comprehensively, so that students preparing for examinations in commercial and industrial law will find in this book a useful supplement to the standard textbooks, both for initial learning and for examination revision.

I would like to thank the Institute of Legal Executives, the Institute of Chartered Secretaries and Administrators and the Institute of Cost and Management Accountants for allowing me to reproduce selected questions from their past examination papers. The book is suitable for professional examinations such as the Commercial Law paper in the Fellowship Examination of the Institute of Legal Executives, or the Industrial Law and Practice (formerly Industrial Law) paper for the Institute of Chartered Secretaries and Administrators. It would also be useful for the Business Law paper in the Foundation Stage of the Institute of Cost and Management Accountants, and for the English Business Law paper of the ICSA. Personnel officers, office and factory administrators and owners of small businesses will find a basic introduction to relevant areas of the law within these pages.

The law is stated as at 30th April 1984.

1984 A.R.R.

Contents

Table of Cases

Table of Statutes

PART ONE

COMMERCIAL LAW

CHAPTER I

Agency

THE PRINCIPAL-AGENT RELATIONSHIP

1. The essential characteristic. The essential characteristic of an agent is that he is invested with a legal power to establish contractual relations between his principal and third parties.

2. The creation of the relationship. The relationship of the principal and agent may be created in the following ways.

(*a*) By express appointment.
(*b*) By implication of the law.
(*c*) By subsequent ratification of an authorised act.
(*d*) By statute. *See* II, **11**; V, **10**.

3. Express appointment. Where the principal expressly appoints his agent, and the agent accepts the appointment, the relationship is based on contract and is sometimes known as contractual agency. No particular form of appointment is needed unless the agent is required to enter into contracts under seal, in which case the authority must be given under seal. (An authority given under seal is known as a *power of attorney*; *see* Powers of Attorney Act 1971.)

4. Contractual capacity of an agent. Usually, although not always, the agent incurs no contractual obligations towards the third party. Thus, the general rule is that an agent need not have contractual capacity, although, of course, the principal must have capacity.

NOTE: The European Communities Act 1972, s.9(1) appears to provide that if an agent acting for a company is also one of its "directors", the principal (i.e. the company) may be bound by its agent to contracts that the principal has no power to enter into at all.

5. Kinds of appointed agents. Appointed agents may be divided into three classes.

(*a*) *Special agents*, who are appointed to perform a particular act, after which their authority comes to an end.
(*b*) *General agents*, who have a continuous authority to act in some particular trade or business.
(*c*) *Universal agents*, who have unlimited authority to act for their principals.

6. Implication of the law. The law may infer an agency from the conduct of the parties or from the necessity of the case. The former gives rise to agency by estoppel and the latter to agency of necessity. An example of a case where the court found that an implied agency had risen is *Stockton* v. *Mason* (1979) CA.

7. Agency by estoppel. The effect of the doctrine of agency by estoppel can be seen in three kinds of cases; as follows.

(*a*) Consider the following generalised example: as a result of X's conduct, Y appears to be X's agent, and on faith of this appearance Z contracts with Y and suffers consequent loss. If Z has a cause of action arising from the contract, he may sue X, who will be estopped from denying that Y is his agent and may thus be liable. Thus, no principal-agent relationship may be actually in existence, but by virtue of this doctrine such a relationship is created.
(*b*) A principal-agent relationship may be in existence but the authority may be limited by agreement between the parties. If the agent exceeds his authority thc doctrine of estoppel may operate to bind the principal.
(*c*) The principal-agent relationship may have been determined but an agency by estoppel sometimes arises after the actual authority of an agent has been determined—for if a former agent continues to deal with third parties who believe that the agency still exists, the former principal will be estopped from denying that he is the principal. Thus a principal should be careful to give notice of the determination of his agent's authority to all possible third parties.

Trueman v. *Loder* (1840): A dealt with T on behalf of his principal, P. The agency was determined but notice of this was not given to T. A subsequently dealt with T in his own name. T suffered loss as a result of A's breach of contract and he sued P. HELD: P was estopped from denying that A was still his agent. Damages were awarded against P.

8. Agency of necessity. An authority may be conferred by law in circumstances where property is in jeopardy, and, at the time of the emergency, the instructions of the owner cannot be obtained. In such cases, there is a legal implication that the owner has consented to the creation of an agency, or to the extension of an existing authority. It may be regarded as yet another example of the law giving effect to the presumed intentions of the parties.

An agency of necessity arises when all the following conditions are satisfied.

(*a*) The person claiming to be an agent of necessity must have been driven by a real emergency, and not by mere convenience: *Prager* v. *Blatspiel, Stamp and Heacock Ltd.* (1924).

(*b*) It must be practically impossible to obtain fresh instructions from the owner: *Springer* v. *Great Western Railway Co.* (1921).

(*c*) An agent of necessity must act bona fide in the interests of all concerned, and in particular in the interests of the principal. If he does not, he will be personally liable for his action.

9. Ratification of an unauthorised act. Where A acts in the name of, or professionally on behalf of, B, without B's authority, B may ratify the act and make it as valid as if it had been done with his authority. The result is the same whether A had no authority at all to act for B, or whether A merely acted in excess of an authority conferred by B. Ratification is effective only subject to the following conditions.

(*a*) The only person having power to ratify is the person on whose behalf the act was done: and this person must then:

(*i*) have existed,

(*ii*) have been named or described,

(*iii*) have been competent, and must have remained competent to be principal.

(*b*) There must have been an act capable of ratification.

(*c*) Ratification must take place within a reasonable time.

(*d*) The person ratifying must have full knowledge of all material facts, or be prepared to ratify in any event.

NOTE: Ratification is an expression of intention, and may be express or implied from conduct.

POSITION OF PRINCIPAL AND AGENT WITH REGARD TO THIRD PARTIES

10. Four possible circumstances. Here it is necessary to consider whether a third party (with whom the agent has contracted) is capable of suing, or being sued by, the agent or the principal. On the basis that the agent was authorised to enter the contract, there are four circumstances to examine.

(*a*) *A named principal*—where both the fact of agency and the name or description of the principal are disclosed to the third party.
(*b*) *A disclosed principal*—where the agent discloses the existence of the principal, but not his name or description.
(*c*) *An undisclosed principal*—where the existence of the principal is not disclosed, and the third party believes that he is contracting personally with the agent.
(*d*) *A foreign principal*—where the principal can be any one of (*a*), (*b*) or (*c*) but he does not reside or carry on business in England and Wales.

The class into which the principal falls may affect the personal liability of the agent, and may also affect the rights and duties of the principal under a contract made by the agent with the third party.

11. A named principal. Where the agent discloses the fact of the agency and the name or the description of the principal to the third party, the general rule is that the agent incurs no rights or obligations. The contract is made between the principal and the third party, and it is between these that the rights and obligations are created. The legal effect is the same as if the principal had contracted directly with the third party.

NOTE: This general rule will be modified by any term, express or implied, to the effect that the agent is to be liable to the third party or to the principal. In particular: (1) The agent is always liable on a deed executed in his own name. (2) The agent is always liable on a bill of exchange signed in his own name, without any words showing that he signed as agent. (3) The agent is liable where he is made so by custom of a trade, e.g. in a contract of marine insurance, the broker is always liable to the insurer for the amount of the premium.

12. A disclosed principal. Where the agent clearly contracts as agent, but does not disclose the name or sufficient description of his principal, the third party and the principal are contractually bound. The legal position is the same as where the principal is named. The agent normally drops out when the contract is made unless there is a term, expressed or implied, to the effect that he undertakes liability. In *N. & J. Vlassopoulos* v. *Ney Shipping; The Santa Carina* (1977) the Court of Appeal held that an agent would not be liable on the contract of an insolvent disclosed principal.

13. An undisclosed principal. Where a principal has conferred authority on an agent and the agent subsequently contracts with a third party, but does not disclose the fact of the agency, so that the third party does not know of the existence of the principal, the doctrine of the undisclosed principal will apply. According to this doctrine, the parties have rights as follows.

(*a*) If a cause of action accrues to the third party, he may elect to sue either the agent or the undisclosed principal, if he can find him. A judgment against one is a bar to action against the other.

(*b*) If a cause of action accrues to the undisclosed principal against the third party, his rights will be subject to the following limitations.

(*i*) The agent's authority must have existed at the time of the contract with the third party.

(*ii*) The agent must not have contracted in terms incompatible with the agency, e.g. in a contract of sale or hire, he must not have described himself as "owner": *Humble* v. *Hunter* (1848).

(*iii*) The identity of the agent should not have been material to the third party when entering into the contracts, e.g. the agent's debt to the third party: *Greer* v. *Downs Supply Co.* (1927).

If conditions (*i*), (*ii*) and (*iii*) are not satisfied the undisclosed principal cannot intervene.

(*c*) Only a principal whose existence has been disclosed can ratify: *Keighley Maxsted* v. *Durant* (1901).

14. A foreign principal. It was thought that an agent for a foreign principal contracted personally unless a contrary intention appeared plainly from the contract. However, it now seems settled that the fact that the principal is a foreigner is only one of many circumstances to be taken into account in deciding whether the principal can sue and be sued: *Teheran–Europe Co.* v. *S. T. Belton Ltd.* (1968).

NOTE: Fridman's *Law of Agency* suggests that it might still be argued that a satisfactory solution would be to hold the agent liable as well as the principal.

POSITION AS BETWEEN PRINCIPAL AND AGENT

15. General. The relationship between a principal and his agent is partly contractual and partly fiduciary. The fiduciary element is important. There are always certain rights and obligations existing between the principal and agent, apart from those which clearly stem from their contractual relationship. It must be remembered that the relationship is essentially a confidential one.

16. Obligations of the agent. In addition to his express contractual obligations, an agent is always under the following duties to his principal. These may, of course, be regarded as giving corresponding rights to the principal, who may sue for damages in the event of a breach of duty by the agent.

(*a*) To exercise diligence and whatever skill is professed, e.g. a salesman must sell his principal's property at the best possible price: *Keppel* v. *Wheeler* (1927).

(*b*) To render accounts to the principal as required.

(*c*) Not to let his own interests conflict with his obligations to the principal, e.g. an agent must not become principal as against his own principal.

(*d*) Not to disclose confidential information obtained during the course of his duties as agent.

(*e*) Not to take any secret profit or bribe from any party with whom he deals on behalf of the principal. Where this occurs to the knowledge of the third party, the contract is voidable at the option of the principal.

(*f*) Not to delegate his duties to a sub-agent without authority, expressed or implied: *delegatus non potest delegare* ("a delegate has no authority to delegate").

(*g*) To comply with his principal's instructions and to notify him when compliance becomes impossible.

(*h*) Not to deny the title of the principal to goods, money or land possessed by the agent on behalf of the principal.

17. Obligations of the principal. The principal has always the following duties towards the agent. From these duties the agent derives corresponding rights which he can enforce against his principal.

(*a*) To pay remuneration and expenses as agreed; or failing agreement, as is customary; or failing a custom, to pay what is reasonable, unless the agency relationship can be shown to be gratuitous.

(*b*) To indemnify the agent against losses arising from the execution of his authority.

(*c*) To indemnify the agent against losses and liabilities arising out of an unauthorised act subsequently ratified.

An agent has a lien on goods of his principal lawfully in his possession where the principal has not paid remuneration or expenses properly due.

NOTE: An agent is not entitled to be indemnified against the consequences of his own negligence, default or breach of duty; nor is he entitled to be indemnified against the consequences of an unlawful act except where he is entitled to a contribution towards damages in cases of his liability towards a third party.

BREACH OF WARRANTY OF AUTHORITY

18. The warranty of authority. A person who purports to act as an agent is deemed to warrant that he has his principal's authority. Where a person contracts as agent without any authority, or where an agent contracts in excess of his authority, there is a breach of warranty of authority.

19. Who may bring the action? Any person who has relied on the warranty of authority and has acted upon that reliance and has thereby suffered loss may bring an action for damages against the agent. But no person who knew of the agent's lack of authority, or did not believe him to be an agent, may sue.

NOTE: It is no defence for the agent to plead that he acted in good faith and that he did not know his authority to be at an end. The agent's liability arises independently of fraud or negligence, but where this is present the party who has suffered loss may bring his action for breach of warranty and also in tort in the alternative. However, the amount of damages will depend upon the agent's state of mind and may mean the difference between effective and nominal damages.

TERMINATION OF THE AGENCY RELATIONSHIP

20. Ways in which authority may be ended. The relationship of principal and agent may be terminated by act of the parties or by operation of law as follows.

(*a*) By notice of revocation given by the principal to the agent.

(*b*) By notice of renunciation given to the principal by the agent.

(*c*) By the completion of the transaction, where the authority was given for that transaction only, i.e. in the case of a special agency.

(*d*) By the expiration of the period stipulated in the contract of agency.

(*e*) By mutual agreement, by which the principal discharges the agent from further liability and duty in consideration for a reciprocal discharge from the agent.

(*f*) Generally, by death, mental incapacity, or bankruptcy of the principal or agent.

(*g*) By dissolution, where the principal is a corporation (probably also, where the agent is a corporation).

(*h*) By the destruction of the subject-matter of the agency.

(*i*) By the contract becoming unlawful.

21. Unilateral termination of agency. Where there is a contract of agency, summary unilateral termination, unless within the terms of the contract, will be in breach of contract, and damages may be awarded against the party revoking or renouncing. However, if there is no period of notice stipulated in the contract of agency, either party may give reasonable notice at any time.

> NOTE: Although the general rule is that an agency agreement is always revocable and will not be specifically enforced, where the agency is coupled with an interest, the authority is irrevocable; e.g. if A owes the money to B and subsequently gives him power of attorney to sell certain property and to discharge the debt from the purchase money, the power is coupled with an interest and is, therefore, irrevocable: *Gaussen* v. *Morton* (1830).

22. Ostensible authority. The termination of an agent's actual authority, does not necessarily mean that the principal is not bound by future acts of the former agent. Where notice of revocation has not been given to third parties, they may still regard the former agent as having actual authority to enter contracts for the former principal. If such a third party enters a contract with a former agent, on the faith of his ostensible authority, the former principal will be liable if a cause of action accrues to the third party: *Trueman* v. *Loder* (1840). A prudent principal will therefore give notice of the termination of agency to all who have dealt with his former agent as agent (*see* also **7**(*c*)).

PARTICULAR CLASSES OF AGENTS

23. Mercantile agents. A mercantile agent is one "having, in the customary course of his business as such agent, authority either to sell goods, or to consign goods for the purpose of sale, or to buy goods, or to raise money on the security of goods": Factors Act 1889, s.1. This definition covers factors, brokers, auctioneers and dealers on commission, but it does not cover clerks and servants. Where a mercantile agent sells goods without authority, the buyer gets good title to the goods. This is a statutory exception to the common law principle *nemo dat quod non habet: see* IV, **23**.

24. Factors. A factor is a mercantile agent employed to sell goods which have been placed in his possession or control. He is the apparent owner of the goods in his custody and can sell in his own name. A factor has, in the absence of agreement to the contrary, a lien over his principal's goods in respect of any claim he may have arising out of the agency.

25. Brokers. A broker is an agent employed to make bargains and contracts in matters of trade, commerce and navigation between other parties for a compensation commonly called brokerage. A broker is distinguished from a factor in the matter of possession of goods. A broker does not take his principal's goods into his possession, whereas a factor does. In addition, a broker cannot sue third parties in his own name, whereas a factor may always sue third parties if they are in breach. Finally, a broker may not buy and sell in his own name unless permitted by a custom of his particular branch of trade: a factor may always buy and sell in his own name. Where a broker makes a contract between buyer and seller, he enters the terms into his book and signs it. He then sends a memorandum of the contract to each party—a *bought note* to the buyer and a *sold note* to the seller. He is thus an agent for both the buyer and the seller.

26. Auctioneers. An auctioneer is an agent whose ordinary course of business is to sell goods or real property by public auction. An auctioneer must:

(*a*) disclose his principal,
(*b*) sell to a third person,
(*c*) accept the highest bid made at the sale (unless there is a reserve price which is not reached).

Until the fall of the hammer, the auctioneer is the agent of the vendor, but he becomes the agent of the purchaser for the purpose of signing the memorandum of sale. However, an auctioneer may sue for the price of goods sold and delivered even if his commission has been paid.

27. Del credere agents. A *del credere* agent is a mercantile agent who earns an extra commission (*del credere* commission) in return for giving an undertaking to his principal that third parties shall pay the sums due on their contracts. In the event of default by a third party, the *del credere* agent is bound to pay his principal the sum owed by the third party. (The agent may, of course, sue the third party.) A *del credere* agency may be implied on the grounds of a custom of a trade. A *del credere* agent's undertaking is incidental to the contract between the principal and the third party. It is, therefore, not a guarantee within the meaning of s.4 of the Statute of Frauds.

28. Partners. In a partnership firm every partner is an agent of the firm and his other partners for the purpose of the business of the partnership: Partnership Act 1890, s.5. (*see* II, **11.**)

29. Estate agents. An estate agent is an agent employed, *inter alia*, to find a purchaser for his client's real property (e.g. land, houses, commercial premises). The Estate Agents Act 1979 (EAA 1979) now regulates certain aspects of estate agency work. The Act is enforced by the local weights and measures authority and by the Director General of Fair Trading (*see* IV, **48**). The Act is chiefly concerned with regulating the activities of those persons engaged in estate agency work and with safeguarding clients' money (*see* **30**).

(*a*) *Estate agency work* is defined as "things done" by a person in the course of business, pursuant to instructions received from a client who wishes to dispose of or acquire an interest in land: EAA 1979, s. 1.

(*b*) "*Things done*" must be either for the purpose of introducing the client to a prospective purchaser or seller, or for securing the sale or purchase after such an introduction has been made in the course of business: EAA 1979, s. 1. The definition does not cover the management of rented property, which will not be covered by the Act. "Things done" must go beyond the mere dissemination of information, e.g. advertisements in newspapers.

(*c*) Any person may become an estate agent, although the EAA 1979, s.22 gives the Secretary of State the power to make regulations which will ensure that there is a minimum standard of competence which all estate agents must meet. The Director General of Fair Trading may judge that a person is unfit to practise as an estate agent and in certain circumstances may prohibit that person from doing all or particular aspects of estate agency work, e.g. where he has been convicted of certain criminal offences: EAA 1979, s.3. The Director General of Fair Trading may also issue a warning order where, for example, a person has failed to comply with obligations imposed by the 1979 Act: s.4.

(*d*) The Act does not apply, *inter alia*, to solicitors, credit-brokers, insurance brokers, and surveyors and valuers: EAA 1979, s.1.

30. Problem areas. There are two main problem areas in the relationship between an estate agent and his client (the principal). These are deposits, which are dealt with by the 1979 Act, and commission, which is not dealt with by that Act.

(*a*) *Deposits.* The 1979 Act defines clients' money in terms of contract and pre-contract deposits received by a person engaged in estate agency work: s.12. The estate agent holds the client's money on trust: s.13. This means that the money will not now form part of the agent's assets on his insolvency (*see Sorrell* v. *Finch* (1976) for the type of problem that could arise prior to the Act).

(*b*) *When the estate agent has a right to commission.* Denning LJ in *Dennis Reed Ltd.* v. *Goody* (1950) laid down the following five propositions which are the basis for interpreting an estate agent's contract with his principal.

(*i*) It is the common undertaking of them both that commission is payable out of the purchase price.

(*ii*) The agent is only entitled to receive commission if he succeeds in effecting a sale.

(*iii*) If the agent desires the principal to pay commission on offers to purchase, he must use clear and unequivocal language to that effect.

(*iv*) The agent is not entitled to commission where a binding contract is made, but the purchaser fails to perform the contract.

(*v*) The agent is entitled to commission where a binding contract is made but the vendor fails to complete and the purchaser remains ready, able and willing to complete.

However, some estate agents use contracts with express terms which differ from these propositions, e.g. the agent is entitled to a commission for merely effecting an introduction to a prospective purchaser.

31. Limitations of the Act. The Estate Agents Act 1979 can be criticised for failing to deal with the commission aspect of estate agency work as well as several other contentious areas such as gazumping, sole agency agreements and misdescription of properties. There still seems to be a need for some general scheme, or standard form contract, whereby the rights and liabilities of the estate agent and his principal are clearly stated.

PROGRESS TEST 1

1. What is the essential characteristic of an agent? **(1)**

2. Explain the different ways in which the relationship of principal and agent may be created. **(2–9)**

3. A dealt with B in the course of his (A's) duties as C's agent. The agency relationship has now been brought to an end, but A continues to deal with B. A has always used his own name in his dealings with B, but B knew that he was acting as C's agent. B has not yet been informed of the termination of A's agency. Advise C as to his liabilities towards B. **(7)**

4. D, a carrier, discovers that a consignment of tomatoes owned by E has deteriorated badly before the destination has been reached. Therefore, he sells the consignment for what he can get: this is about one-third of the market price for good tomatoes. E has now brought an action against D for damages, D wishes to know whether he can claim that he was an agent of necessity. Advise him. **(8)**

5. In what circumstances does an agent who has contracted within his authority remain liable on the contract? **(11, 12)**

6. Explain the doctrine of the undisclosed principal. **(13)**

7. What rights and duties exist between principal and agent? **(16, 17)**

8. In what circumstances may an action be brought for breach of warranty of authority? Who may bring the action? **(18, 19)**

9. In what ways may the principal-agent relationship be terminated? **(20, 21)**

10. Distinguish between the actual authority and the ostensible authority of an agent. **(7, 22)**

11. Define a "mercantile agent". **(23)**

12. What special rules apply to (*a*) factors, (*b*) brokers, and (*c*) *del credere* agents? **(24, 25, 27)**

13. To what extent does the Estate Agents Act 1979 regulate the activities of persons working as estate agents? **(29–31)**

CHAPTER II

The Law of Partnership

NATURE OF A PARTNERSHIP

1. Sources of partnership law. The law of partnership was amended and declared in the Partnership Act 1890 (PA). Any study of partnership must, therefore, be based on the Act; but the rules of common law, particularly contract and agency, continue to apply except where the Act provides to the contrary.

2. Definition. "Partnership is the relation which subsists between persons carrying on a business in common with a view of profit": Partnership Act 1890, s.1(1).

3. Differences between partnerships and other forms of enterprise. A partnership may be contrasted with other forms of business enterprise, in particular limited companies and sole traders.

(*a*) A partnership is an unincorporated association, which means that it does not have a separate legal identity or personality from that of each individual partner. Thus as a general rule the partners are ultimately responsible for all partnership activities (*see* **13–22**) and each partner is personally liable without limitation for the partnership debts. Other examples of unincorporated associations are sports clubs, social clubs and trade unions (*see* X, **17**). However, partnerships and trade unions are subject to additional legal provisions which apply to their particular circumstances.

(*b*) A limited company is the most common type of joint stock company. It enables small investors, and others, to acquire shares in the company and to be liable only for the share price. It is a corporation and as such has corporate personality. A limited company has a separate legal identity or personality from that of its shareholders, which means, *inter alia*, that usually any claim against a company cannot be brought against the individual directors or shareholders of the company. The company is liable for its debts up to the value of its assets.

(*c*) Unlike an individual, a company does not have the legal capacity to enter into any kind of contract. This is because the company's powers are limited to carrying out the objects for which it was established. These objects are stated in the memorandum of association, which is one of the documents required when creating a limited company under the Companies Acts 1948-81. Any act done by the company which exceeds these powers is *ultra vires* and the company will not be liable for the act. For example, if a company is set up with the object of running a car hire business, and after several years decides to expand into the air charter business, buying an aircraft for the new venture, it is likely that this purchase would be *ultra vires*. This means, *inter alia*, that the seller would not be able to enforce the contract against the company to recover the purchase price or enforce the carrying out of the contract. However, if the *directors* of the company made the agreement with the seller of the aircraft who was acting in good faith then the contract would not be *ultra vires*: European Communities Act 1972, s.9(1).

(*d*) There are no special rules as to the formation of a partnership (*see* **4**), although there is a limit on the number of partners allowed (*see* **8**), whereas a limited company must be created in a particular manner under the Companies Acts 1948-81.

(*e*) A partnership may be dissolved in various ways (*see* **23**), whereas a limited company is usually dissolved by a procedure called "winding up". This procedure may be compulsory, voluntary or under supervision. Compulsory winding up by court order would arise, for example, where a company is unable to pay its debts. Voluntary winding up could arise in various circumstances, for example, if the members wish to cease trading or the company cannot continue its business because of its liabilities. Winding up under the supervision of the court is uncommon.

(*f*) A sole trader is an individual in business on his own behalf. He is treated by the law like any other person. His business is not regulated by any special rules of law.

4. Formation of partnerships. Partnership agreements may be made with or without formality. They may be oral or written, and may but need not be under seal. The ordinary rules of contract are applied to test whether agreement has been reached. Where a partnership agreement is in writing, the document is called the articles of partnership. Partnership agreements may be varied by subsequent agreement, express or implied, between the partners.

5. Testing the existence of partnership. Where there is a dispute whether a partnership exists the point must be decided in order to know whether the Partnership Act applies. First, the definition in s.1(1) must be used as a test (*see* **2**). Further, the Act provides the following rules which must be used where applicable to determine whether or not a partnership exists.

(*a*) Co-ownership of property does not of itself create a partnership whether or not the co-owners share any profits made by the use of the property.

(*b*) The sharing of gross returns does not of itself create a partnership, whether the persons sharing such returns have or have not a joint or common right or interest in any property from which the returns are derived.

(*c*) The receipt by a person of a share of the profits of a business is prima facie evidence that he is a partner in the business, but this evidence may be rebutted where it can be shown that the purpose of the share of the profits was any of the following.

(*i*) The payment of a debt by fixed instalments.

(*ii*) The remuneration of an employee of the business.

(*iii*) Payment made to the widow or child of a deceased partner.

(*iv*) Payments to the previous owner of a business who has sold the goodwill, i.e. where the consideration for the goodwill is a share in subsequent profits.

(*v*) Payments by way of interest on a loan advanced for use in the business.

Walker West Developments v. *F.J. Emmett* (1978): the question was raised whether the relationship between the parties was a partnership or merely contractual. The Court of Appeal considered that contractual language was not inconsistent with the existence of a partnership. The court found that a partnership existed and that as no provision had been made for loss-sharing, s.24(1) applied (*see* **10**).

6. The firm and the firm-name. Persons who have entered into a partnership with one another are called collectively a firm. The name under which the business is carried on is the firm-name. A firm is not a distinct legal entity and must be clearly distinguished from a corporation. Where partners contract in the firm-name, the contract will take effect as if the names of each and every partner were substituted in the contract for the firm-name. Similarly, partners may sue or be sued in the firm-name.

7. Choice of firm-name. The general rule is that partners may carry on their business under any firm-name they choose. However, this rule is subject to the following provisos.

(*a*) The firm-name must not be such as to raise the implication that the business is connected with another with which it is in competition.

(*b*) The requirements of the Companies Act 1981 must be satisfied. The Act repealed and replaced the Registration of Business Names Act 1916, so ending any form of central registration of business names. The 1981 Act, s.28, provides that where the firm name does *not* consist of the surnames of *all* the partners (forenames or initials may be added) the following requirements must be satisfied:

(*i*) *No misleading names.* The name should not be likely to give the impression that the business is connected with local or central government, nor should the name include any word or expression specified in regulations made under s.31 of the Act which is aimed at controlling the use of prestigious names. The use of such names (there are approximately 90), for example "Royal", must be submitted to a specified government department or other specified body for any possible objections, and then approved by the Secretary of State.

(*ii*) *Disclosure of names and address(es): s.29*

1. All business documents (i.e. letters, written orders for goods or services, invoices, receipts, and debt demands) must state legibly: the name of each partner; and an address within Great Britain for each partner at which service of any document relating to the business (e.g. a writ) will be effective.

> NOTE: This provision does not apply to a partnership of more than twenty persons (*see* **8**) so long as there is a list of all the partners at the firm's principal place of business and the existence and availability of such a list and the address of that principal place of business are given on the business documents. Any person may inspect this list during office hours.

2. A notice containing the above names and addresses must be displayed in a prominent position in the business premises so that it may easily be read by customers and suppliers.

3. Such names and addresses must be given immediately in writing to any business contact who asks for them.

Contravention of the requirements of (*i*) and (*ii*) are criminal offences. In addition civil disabilities are imposed for breach of (*ii*). If a defendant to a claim in contract can show that he had a counterclaim which he was unable to pursue or that he has suffered some financial loss because of the plaintiff's failure to comply with the requirements of (*ii*), then the court must dismiss the plaintiff's claim unless it is just and equitable to allow the case to continue.

8. Number of partners. The Companies Act 1948 provides that no banking partnership consisting of more than ten members may be formed, and that, in the case of any other kind of partnership, the maximum shall be twenty: ss.429 and 434. This provision was amended by the Companies Act 1967. Section 119 of the 1967 Act provides that banking partnerships may consist of not more than twenty persons each of whom is authorised by the Department of Trade to be a member of such a partnership. Section 120 of the 1967 Act provides that partnerships of more than twenty persons may be formed in the case of solicitors, accountants and stockbrokers.

RELATIONSHIPS BETWEEN PARTNERS

9. Partners' rights and duties. The mutual rights and duties between partners are ascertained by:

(*a*) the express and implied terms of the partnership agreement; and

(*b*) the provisions of the Partnership Act.

In either case, the rights and duties may be varied by the consent of all the partners of a firm. Such consent may be express or may be implied from a course of dealing. In ascertaining the terms of the partnership agreement, the ordinary rules of contract apply. In practice, the articles of partnership usually contain detailed terms which determine the mutual rights and obligations of the partners.

However, whatever may be the terms of the agreement, or in the absence of any written agreement at all, the law requires that each partner must observe the utmost fairness and good faith towards his fellow partners.

10. Partnership Act 1890, s.24. This important section of the PA provides the following set of rules which apply subject to any agreement, express or implied, between the partners.

(*a*) *Equal shares.* All the partners are entitled to share equally in the capital and profits of the business, and must contribute equally towards the losses whether of capital or otherwise sustained by the firm. (*See Walker West Developments* v *F. J. Emmet* (1978), referred to in **5**.)

(*b*) *Indemnity*. The firm must indemnify every partner in respect of payments made and personal liabilities incurred by him:

(*i*) in the ordinary and proper conduct of the business of the firm; or

(*ii*) in or about anything necessarily done for the preservation of the business or property of the firm.

(*c*) *Interest on advances*. A partner, making, for the purpose of the partnership, any actual payment or advance beyond the amount of capital which he has agreed to subscribe, is entitled to interest at the rate of five per cent per annum from the date of the payment or advance.

(*d*) *Interest on capital*. A partner is not entitled, before the ascertainment of profits, to interest on the capital subscribed by him.

(*e*) *Management*. Every partner may take part in the management of the partnership business.

(*f*) *Remuneration*. No partner is entitled to remuneration for acting in the partnership business.

(*g*) *Introduction of partners*. No person may be introduced as a partner without the consent of all existing partners.

(*h*) *Internal disputes*. Any difference arising as to the ordinary matters connected with the partnership business may be decided by a majority of the partners, but no change may be made in the nature of the partnership business without the consent of all existing partners.

(*i*) *Books*. The partnership books are to be kept at the place of business of the partnership (or the principal place, if there is more than one), and every partner may, when he thinks fit, have access to and inspect and copy any of them.

11. Partners as agents. Every partner is an agent of the firm and his other partners for the purpose of the business of the partnership: PA, s.5. Thus the general law of agency is incorporated into the law of partnership, and, in this connection, the Act makes specific provision for the following duties.

(*a*) *Uberrima fides*. Partners are bound to render true accounts and full information of all things affecting the partnership to any partner or his legal representative: s.28.

(*b*) No secret profits. Every partner must account to the firm for any benefit derived by him without the consent of the other partners from any transaction concerning the partnership, or from any use by him of the partnership property, name or business connection: s.29.

(*c*) *No competition*. If a partner, without the consent of the other partners, carries on any business of the same nature as, and competing with, that of the firm, he must account for and pay over to the firm all profits made by him in that business: s.30.

12. Partnership property. Partnership property includes the following.

(*a*) Property originally brought into the partnership stock: s.20.
(*b*) Property acquired on account of the firm for the purposes of the partnership business: s.20. Unless the contrary intention appears, property bought with money belonging to the firm is deemed to have been bought on account of the firm: s.21.

Partnership property must be held and applied by the partners exclusively for the purposes of the partnership and in accordance with the partnership agreement: s.20.

RELATIONS OF PARTNERS AND THIRD PARTIES

13. Partnership contracts with third parties. Partnership firms enter into contracts with third parties through the agency of one or more of the partners. Every partner is an agent of the firm and his other partners for the purpose of the business of the partnership; and the acts of every partner who does any act for carrying on, in the usual way, business of the kind carried on by the firm are binding on the firm unless:

(*a*) the partner so acting has in fact no authority to act in the particular matter; and
(*b*) the person with whom he is dealing either:
(*i*) knows that he has no authority to act in the particular matter, or
(*ii*) does not know or believe him to a partner: s.5.

14. A partner's authority. Where a partner enters into a contract with a third party on behalf of his firm, the partner is an agent and the firm (including the partner himself) is the principal. As in the case of any other agent, the partner can bind his principal only to the limit of his actual or apparent authority. An act is within a partner's apparent authority if it is "for carrying on in the usual way business of the kind carried on by the firm". For example, a partner in a firm of house builders will have an apparent authority to enter a contract for the purchase of a quantity of bricks. A partner's apparent authority thus depends upon the nature of the business of his firm.

In the case of a trading partnership (i.e. one in which the principal operations are buying and selling), a partner has the apparent authority to bind his firm in the following kinds of transaction.

(*a*) *Pledging* the partnership goods: *Butchart* v. *Dresser* (1853).
(*b*) *Selling* the partnership goods: *Dore* v. *Wilkinson* (1817).
(*c*) *Buying* goods on the firm's account: *Bond* v. *Gibson* (1808).
(*d*) *Borrowing money* on behalf of the firm.
(*e*) *Paying the firm's debts* so as to give a good discharge to the debtor.
(*f*) Drawing, accepting, indorsing of *negotiable instruments*.
(*g*) *Engaging employees* for the firm.

NOTE: Thc apparent authority of a partner in a *non-trading* firm is considerably narrower than in the case of a trading firm: in particular, he cannot draw, accept or indorse negotiable instruments so as to bind the firm (except ordinary cheques).

The apparent authority of a partner (whether of a trading or a non-trading firm) does not extend to any of the following: (*i*) giving a guarantee, unless this is within the usual business of the firm or there is a trade custom permitting it; (*ii*) submission of a dispute with a third party to arbitration; (*iii*) the execution of a deed on behalf of the firm unless under a power of attorney.

15. Contractual liability of partners to third parties. Every partner in a firm is liable *jointly* with the other partners for all debts and obligations of the firm incurred while he is a partner: s.9.

According, a firm's creditor may sue any or all of the partners; he may not bring a fresh action against the remaining partners in the event of judgment being unsatisfied. In practice, it is advisable to bring an action against the firm in the firm-name, for this has the same effect as if the action were brought against each and every partner.

16. Liability of the firm for torts. Where a partner commits a tort while acting in the ordinary course of the partnership business, the firm is vicariously liable. The firm is similarly liable where a partner commits a tort with the authority of his co-partners. The firm's liability in tort is *joint and several*. This means that an unsatisfied judgment against one or some of the partners is *not* a bar to a further action against the remaining partners.

17. Liability of the firm for crimes. It is possible that in certain circumstances a firm might be liable for a crime committed by one of the partners. In *Parsons* v. *Barnes* (1973) the court decided on the facts, which went considerably beyond the simple relationship of partners, that the partners acted in concert in committing an offence under s.14 of the Trade Descriptions Act 1968. Thus one partner was found guilty although he was not present when the work complained of was done, and had not personally issued the invoice and receipt. However, he was present when the work was discussed with the customer. The court was not prepared to lay down a general proposition that one partner was necessarily responsible for the acts of his co-partner under the legislation.

18. Liability of new partners. The general rule is that an incoming partner is not liable for the firm's debts incurred before he became a partner: s.17. The incoming partner can, however, assume liability by novation. Novation in this case is a tripartite agreement between:

(*a*) a creditor of the firm,
(*b*) the partners existing at the time the debt was incurred, and
(*c*) the incoming partner.

19. Liability of retiring partners. A retiring partner's liability to the firm's creditors depends primarily upon whether debt was incurred before or after retirement.

(*a*) *Debts incurred before retirement.* A partner who retires from a firm does not thereby cease to be liable for partnership debts or obligations incurred before his retirement: s.17. An outgoing partner can be discharged from his liability to the firm's creditors by express release or by novation. In the case of novation the parties are:

(*i*) the retiring partner,
(*ii*) the firm as newly constituted after the retirement, and
(*iii*) the creditor.

(*b*) *Debts incurred after retirement.* Where a person deals with a firm after a change in its constitution, he is entitled to treat all apparent members of the old firm as still being members of the firm until he has notice of change: PA, s.36. A retiring partner must, therefore, ensure that all persons who deal with the firm are given notice of the retirement, or he will be liable to them for debts incurred after he has left the firm. An advertisement in the *London Gazette* is sufficient notice of the retirement to persons who had no dealings with the firm before the retirement.

20. Death or bankruptcy. The estate of a partner who dies, or who becomes bankrupt, or of a partner who, not having been known to the person dealing with the firm to be a partner, retires from the firm, is not liable for partnership debts contracted after the date of the death, bankruptcy, or retirement respectively: PA, s.36.

21. Holding out. Any person who represents himself, or allows himself to be represented, as a partner of a particular firm, is liable as a partner to any person who gives credit to the firm on the faith of the representation, PA, s.14. This is a form of agency by estoppel.

22. Guarantees. A continuing guarantee given either:

(*a*) to a firm, or

(*b*) to a third person in respect of the transactions of a firm, is, in the absence of agreement to the contrary, revoked as to future transactions by any change in the constitution of the firm to which, or of the firm in respect of the transactions of which the guarantee was given: PA, s.18. A guarantee given by a firm is not affected by subsequent changes in the constitution of that firm.

DISSOLUTION OF PARTNERSHIP

23. How a partnership may be dissolved. A partnership may come to an end in any of the following ways.

(*a*) By expiration or notice.
(*b*) By bankruptcy, death or charge.
(*c*) By illegality.
(*d*) By decree of the court.

24. Expiration or notice. Subject to any agreement between the partners, a partnership is dissolved:

(*a*) if entered into for a fixed term, by the expiration of that term;

(*b*) if entered into for a single adventure or undertaking, by the termination of that adventure or undertaking;

(*c*) if entered into for an undefined time, by any partner giving notice to the other or others of his intention to dissolve the partnership: PA, s.32.

25. Bankruptcy or death. Subject to any agreement between the partners, every partnership is dissolved as regards all the partners by the death or bankruptcy of any partner: PA, s.33. It is not usual, however, for a partnership business to come to an end because of the death or bankruptcy of one of the partners. The business is usually continued by the remaining partners. The agreement to continue may be contained in the articles, or the remaining partners may by fresh agreement, express or implied, continue the partnership business: s.33(1).

26. Charge. A partnership may, at the option of the other partners, be dissolved if any partner suffers his share of the partnership property to be charged under the Partnership Act for his separate debt: PA, s.33. The charge referred to here is that provided by s.23 of the Partnership Act, whereby the court may make an order charging the interest of any partner in the partnership property for the payment of a judgment debt. This provision:

(*a*) recognises the undesirability of a partner who cannot pay his judgment debts; and
(*b*) allows the other partners to get rid of him.

27. Illegality. A partnership is in every case dissolved by the happening of any event which makes it unlawful for the business of the firm to be carried on, or for the members of the firm to carry it on in partnership: s.34.

28. Decree of the court. On application by a partner the court may decree a dissolution of the partnership in any of the following cases.

(*a*) When a judge of the Court of Protection is satisfied that, by reason of mental disorder, a partner is incapable of managing his property and affairs, he may order the dissolution of the partnership: Mental Health Act 1983, s.96.
(*b*) When a partner, other than the partner suing, becomes in any way permanently incapable of performing his part of the partnership contract.
(*c*) When a partner, other than the partner suing, has been guilty of such conduct as, in the opinion of the court, regard being had to the nature of the business, is calculated to affect prejudicially the carrying on of the business.
(*d*) When a partner, other than the partner suing, wilfully or persistently commits a breach of partnership agreement, or otherwise so conducts himself in matters relating to the partnership business that it is not reasonably practicable for the other partner or partners to carry on the business in partnership with him.

(*e*) When the business of the partnership can only be carried on at a loss.

(*f*) Whenever in any case circumstances have arisen which, in the opinion of the court, render it just and equitable that the partnership be dissolved: PA, s.35.

NOTE: A salaried partner who has no proprietary interest in the partnership generally has no claim to an order for the winding up of a partnership: *Stekel* v. *Ellice* (1973).

29. Rights of partners on dissolution.

(*a*) Where the partnership is dissolved for fraud or misrepresentation, the partner entitled to dissolve the partnership is also entitled to:

(*i*) a lien or right of retention over the surplus of the partnership assets;

(*ii*) stand in the place of the creditors of the firm for any payment made by him in respect of the partnership liabilities; and

(*iii*) be indemnified against all debts and liabilities of the firm: PA, s.41.

(*b*) If a partnership is dissolved before the expiration of the term, otherwise than by death, the court may order the repayment of any premium unless:

(*i*) the dissolution is wholly or directly due to the misconduct of the partner who paid the premium; or

(*ii*) the partnership was dissolved by an agreement which did not provide for the return of any part of the premium: PA, s.40.

(*c*) After the dissolution of a partnership, the authority of each partner to bind the firm, and the other rights and obligations of the parties, continue so far as may be necessary to wind up the affairs of the partnership and to complete transactions begun but unfinished at the time of the dissolution: PA, s.38.

NOTE: If there are special grounds or if there is dissension between the parties the court may appoint a receiver and, in certain circumstances, a manager.

30. Realisation of assets.

(*a*) One partner is entitled by action in the firm's name to realise the assets, on giving the other partners an indemnity against the costs of the action.

(*b*) Every partner is entitled to have the property of the partnership applied in payment of the debts and liabilities of the firm, and to have the surplus assets applied in payment of what may be due to the partners.

(*c*) The goodwill of a partnership is an asset which, if it exists, should be sold on dissolution as in the case of any other asset. Goodwill is that approbation which has been earned by a business over a period of time. It usually involves the acquisition of a number of regular customers or clients who will remain after a change in the constitution of the firm, or even in the event of the business being sold as a going concern. It has been said that goodwill is merely the probability that the old customers will resort to the old place.

31. Transfer of goodwill. The rights of the vendor and purchaser of goodwill may be defined as follows.

(*a*) *Purchaser's rights.* On the sale of goodwill the purchaser may, unless the terms of the contract of sale provide otherwise,

(*i*) represent himself as continuing the business;

(*ii*) maintain the exclusive rights to the use of the firm-name; and

(*iii*) solicit former customers of the business and restrain the vendors from doing so.

(*b*) *Vendor's rights.* The vendor may enter into competition with the purchaser unless he is prevented by a valid restraint clause in the contract of sale.

32. Settlement of accounts on dissolution. It is provided by the Partnership Act 1890 that in settling accounts between the partners after a dissolution of partnership, the following rules must, subject to any agreement, be observed.

(*a*) The account will start from the last settled account.

(*b*) Profits are ascertained on the basis of sums actually paid out and received in that year.

(*c*) Losses, including losses and deficiences of capital, must be paid first out of profits, next out of capital, and lastly, if necessary, by the partners individually in the proportion in which they were entitled to share profits.

(*d*) The assets of the firm, including the sums, if any, contributed by the partners to make up losses or deficiencies of capital, must be applied in the following manner or order:

(*i*) in paying the debts and liabilities of the firm to persons who are not partners therein;

(*ii*) in paying to each partner rateably what is due from the firm to him for advances as distinguished from capital;

(*iii*) in paying to each partner rateably what is due from the firm to him in respect of capital;

(*iv*) the ultimate residue, if any must be divided among the partners in the proportion in which profits are divisible: PA, s.44.

33. Remaining deficiencies of capital. Where there remains insufficient capital to repay all the partners in full, the general rule (as above) is that the partners are paid rateably each according to his share in the capital. Where, however, the deficiency of capital is attributable to the insolvency of one of the partners, that deficiency must be borne by the other partners in the proportion of their last agreed shares in the capital. This is known as the rule in *Garner* v. *Murray* (1904).

LIMITED PARTNERSHIPS

34. Limited Partnerships Act 1907. Partnerships with limited liability were made possible by the Act of 1907. There are, however, very few limited partnerships in existence today because the advantages accorded to this kind of partnership are more conveniently gained by operating the business in the form of a registered company. The Limited Partnerships Act 1907 contains a number of far-reaching modifications to the general law of partnership.

35. Constitution and registration. The Act of 1907 provides as follows.

(*a*) *Number of partners.* A limited partnership must not consist of more than twenty members or ten in the case of a banking partnership. This provision does not apply in the case of solicitors, stockbrokers or accountants: Companies Act 1967, s.121.

(*b*) *General and limited partners.* Every limited partnership must include at least one general partner and at least one limited partner.

(*i*) General partners are liable for all debts and obligations of the firm and are entitled to take part in the management of the firm.

(*ii*) Limited partners contribute capital or property valued at a stated amount, and are not liable for the debts of the firm beyond that amount. This contribution may not be withdrawn except in the event of dissolution. Limited partners have no rights to share in the management of the firm, nor are they deemed to be the agents of the firm.

(*c*) *Registration.* Every limited partnership must be registered by sending to the Registrar of Companies a statement signed by the partners containing the following particulars.

(*i*) The firm-name.

(*ii*) The general nature of the business.

(*iii*) The principal place of business.

(*iv*) The full name of each of the partners.

(*v*) The term, if any, for which the partnership is entered into and the date of its commencement.

(*vi*) A statement that the partnership is limited, and the description of every limited partner as such.

(*vii*) The sum contributed by each limited partner, and whether paid in cash or how otherwise.

If default is made in registration, the partnership will be deemed a general partnership, and the limited partners will lose the advantage of limited liability and be fully liable for the firm's debts.

PROGRESS TEST 2

1. Define "partnership" and comment on your definition. **(2, 3)**
2. What restrictions are there on the choice of a firm-name? **(6, 7)**
3. Explain fully the legal relationship existing between partners. **(9–11)**
4. In what circumstances may a partner bind his firm in dealing with a third party? **(13–15)**
5. Explain the liability of (*a*) new and (*b*) retiring partners. **(18, 19)**
6. How may a partnership be dissolved? **(23–28)**
7. What are the rights of partners on dissolution? **(29, 30)**
8. What are the rules as to settlement of accounts on the dissolution of a partnership? **(32)**
9. Outline the provisions of the Limited Partnerships Act 1907. **(34, 35)**

CHAPTER III

Negotiable Instruments

INTRODUCTION

1. Characteristics of negotiable instruments. Certain instruments have the special quality of negotiability. Instruments may be made negotiable by statute (e.g. bills of exchange and promissory notes) or by mercantile custom judicially recognised (e.g. bearer debentures and Exchequer bills). However, most negotiable instruments in use today are governed by statute. Any negotiable instrument has the following characteristics.

(*a*) Title to a negotiable instrument passes either (*i*) by mere delivery, or (*ii*) where payable to order by delivery together with indorsement, i.e. signature of the transferor.
(*b*) No notice of the transfer of title is required to be given to any person liable on the instrument.
(*c*) The holder of a negotiable instrument may sue in his own name.
(*d*) The transferee of a negotiable instrument, if he is a holder in due course, takes free from all the equities, i.e. free from any right of counterclaim or set-off which any person might have against the transferor.

2. Classes of negotiable instruments. The most important classes of negotiable instruments are bills of exchange (including cheques) and promissory notes. There are certain other forms of negotiable instruments including:

(*a*) share warrants to bearer;
(*b*) dividend warrants;
(*c*) debentures payable to bearer;
(*d*) bearer bonds;
(*e*) banknotes;
(*f*) bankers' drafts.

BILLS OF EXCHANGE

3. Bills of Exchange Act 1882 (BEA). This Act, together with the Cheques Act 1957, codifies the law relating to bills of exchange (including cheques) and promissory notes.

4. Bills of exchange. A bill of exchange is an unconditional order in writing, addressed by one person to another, signed by the person giving it, requiring the person to whom it is addressed to pay on demand or at a fixed or determinable future time a sum certain in money to or to the order of a specified person, or to bearer: BEA, s.3. Any instrument which does not comply with this definition, or which orders any act to be done in addition to the payment of money, is not a bill of exchange.

NOTE

(1) A bill is an order and not a request. But the use of the word "please" as a form of courtesy will not prevent an instrument from being an order.

(2) The order must be: (*a*) unconditional, (*b*) in writing, (*c*) addressed by one person (the drawer) to another (the drawee), (*d*) signed by the person giving the order (the drawer).

(3) The order must require the drawee to pay a sum certain in money: (*a*) on demand, or (*b*) at a fixed or determinable future time.

(4) The order must require the drawee to make payment: (*a*) to a specified person (the payee), (*b*) to the order of the payee, or (*c*) to bearer.

(5) A bill is not invalid by any of the following reasons: (*a*) that it is not dated; (*b*) that it does not specify the value given, or that any value has been given for it; (*c*) that it does not specify the place where it is drawn or the place where it is payable; (*d*) that it is ante-dated or post-dated, or that it bears the date of a Sunday.

See Korea Exchange Bank v. *Debenhams (Central Buying)* (1979) where the Court of Appeal held that the bill was not expressed to be payable at a fixed or determinable future time, and therefore was not a bill of exchange within the meaning of the Act.

5. Inland and foreign bills. An inland bill is a bill which is or on the face of it purports to be:

(*a*) both drawn and payable within the British Islands, or

(*b*) both drawn and payable within the British Islands upon some person resident therein: BEA, s.4.

Any other bill is a foreign bill: BEA, s.4.

6. Demand bills. A bill is payable on demand which is expressed to be payable on demand, or at sight, or on presentation; or in which no time for payment is expressed. Such bills become payable when presented to the drawee for payment: BEA, s.10.

7. Bills payable at a future time. A bill is payable at a determinable future time which is expressed to be payable (*a*) at a fixed period after date or sight, or (*b*) on or at a fixed period after the occurrence of a specified event which is certain to happen, though the time of happening may be uncertain: BEA, s.11.

NOTE: (1) An instrument expressed to be payable on a contingency is not a bill, and the happening of the event does not cure the defect.

(2) Where a bill is expressed to be payable at a fixed period after date is issued, or where the acceptance of a bill payable at a fixed period after sight is undated, any holder may insert therein the true date of issue or acceptance, and the bill shall be payable accordingly.

(3) Sight refers to the first sighting of the bill by the drawee.

8. Time of payment. Where a bill is not payable on demand, the day on which it falls due is determined as follows.

(*a*) Where a bill is payable at a fixed period after date, or after the happening of a specified event, the bill is overdue when the relevant period has expired. This is determined by excluding the day from which the time is to begin to run and by including the day of payment.

(*b*) Where a bill is payable at a fixed period after sight the time begins to run from the date of acceptance if the bill is accepted, and from the date of noting or protest if the bill be noted or protested for non-acceptance, or for non-delivery.

NOTE: Days of grace are not now added. All bills whose payment falls due on non-business days, i.e. Saturdays, Sundays and bank holidays, are payable on the succeeding business day: BEA, s.14(1).

ACCEPTANCE OF A BILL

9. Definition. The acceptance of a bill is the signification by the drawee of his assent to the order of the drawer: BEA, s.17.

NOTE: (1) The acceptance must be written on the bill and signed by the drawee. But the mere signature of the drawee is sufficient.

(2) It must not express that the drawee will perform his promise by any means other than the payment of money.

(3) Acceptance is incomplete and revocable until the bill is delivered by the drawee to the holder. Upon delivery the drawee becomes liable on the bill, and is then called the acceptor.

10. General acceptance. A general acceptance assents without qualification to the order to the drawer: BEA, s.19.

NOTE: (1) An acceptance to pay at a particular place is a general acceptance, unless it expressly states that the bill is to be paid there only and not elsewhere.

(2) The mere signature of the drawee on the face of the bill constitutes a general acceptance.

(3) In addition to the signature, there may also be written the word "accepted", and/or the date, and/or a statement as to where the bill is payable.

11. Qualified acceptance. An acceptance is qualified which is:

(*a*) *conditional*, i.e. where payment by the acceptor is expressed to be dependent on the fulfilment of a stated condition;

(*b*) *partial*, i.e. an acceptance to pay part only of the amount for which the bill is drawn;

(*c*) *local*, i.e. an acceptance to pay at a particular specified place only;

(*d*) *qualified as to time*, e.g. where the acceptor of a bill drawn as payable one month after date qualifies his acceptance with the words "payable three months after date";

(*e*) *accepted by some, but not all, of the drawees* where there is more than one drawee: BEA, s.19.

12. The effect of acceptance. The drawee is not liable on the bill unless and until he accepts it. By accepting the bill, he engages that he will pay it according to the tenor of his acceptance. If it is a general acceptance, he is fully liable to pay according to the order of the drawer. If it is qualified acceptance, he is liable to pay according to the order of the drawer as qualified by the acceptance.

NOTE: (1) The holder of a bill may refuse to take a qualified acceptance. If he does not get a general acceptance, he may treat the bill as dishonoured.

(2) Where a qualified acceptance is taken, and the drawer or an indorser (a transferor who has signed his name on the back

of the bill) has not authorised the qualified acceptance, or does not subsequently give his assent to it, such drawer or indorser is discharged from liability on the bill. (This provision does not apply to a partial acceptance provided due notice is given by the holder.)

(3) When the drawer or indorser of a bill receives notice of a qualified acceptance, and does not within a reasonable time express his dissent to the holder, he is deemed to have assented to it.

13. Presentment for acceptance. A bill must be presented for acceptance in the following cases.

(*a*) Where a bill is payable after sight, presentment for acceptance is necessary in order to fix the maturity date of the instrument. A holder of such a bill must present it for acceptance or negotiate it within a reasonable time.

(*b*) Where a bill expressly stipulates that it shall be presented for acceptance, it must be presented for acceptance before it can be presented for payment.

(*c*) Where a bill is drawn payable elsewhere than at the residence or place of business of the drawee, it must be presented for acceptance before it can be presented for payment: BEA, s.39.

In no other case is presentment for acceptance necessary in order to render liable any party to the bill. In particular, there is no need to present for acceptance bills drawn payable (*a*) on sight, on demand or on presentation, or (*b*) after date.

14. Rules as to presentment for acceptance. A bill is only presented for acceptance if it is presented according to the following rules.

(*a*) Presentment must be made by the holder (or his agent) to the drawee (or his agent) at a reasonable hour on a business day before the bill is overdue.

(*b*) Where a bill is addressed to two or more drawees, who are not partners, presentment must be made to them all, unless one has authority to accept for all, when presentment may be made to him only.

(*c*) Where the drawee is dead, presentment may be made to his personal representative.

(*d*) Where the drawee is bankrupt, presentment may be made to him or to his trustee.

(*e*) Where authorised by agreement or usage, a presentment through the Post Office is sufficient: BEA, s.41.

15. Excuses for non-presentment. Presentment for acceptance according to the rules is excused, and the bill may be treated as dishonoured by non-acceptance in the following circumstances.

(*a*) Where the drawee is dead or bankrupt, or is a fictitious person or a person not having capacity to contract by bill.

(*b*) Where, after the exercise of reasonable diligence, presentment cannot be effected.

(*c*) Where, although presentment has been irregular, acceptance has been refused on some ground: BEA, s.41.

16. Dishonour by non-acceptance. A bill is dishonoured by non-acceptance:

(*a*) when it is duly presented for acceptance, and acceptance is refused or cannot be obtained; or

(*b*) when presentation for acceptance is excused and the bill is not accepted: BEA, s.43.

NEGOTIATION OF A BILL

17. Definition. A bill is negotiated when it is transferred from one person to another in such a manner as to constitute the transferee the holder of the bill: BEA, s.31.

NOTE: (1) The holder of a bill is either (*a*) the payee or indorsee in possession, or (*b*) the bearer.

(2) A bill payable to bearer is negotiated by delivery.

(3) A bill payable to order is negotiated by the indorsement of the holder completed by delivery.

18. Indorsements. When a holder places his signature on the back of the bill, he is said to indorse the bill. There are several kinds of indorsements, as follows.

(*a*) *Indorsements in blank.* This kind of indorsement specifies no indorsee, i.e. it is no more than the signature of the holder as transferor. A bill so indorsed becomes payable to bearer, i.e. it becomes transferable by mere delivery.

(*b*) *Special indorsement.* A special indorsement specifies the person to whom, or to whose order, the bill is to be payable. A bill so endorsed is further negotiated by indorsement completed by delivery.

(*c*) *Restrictive indorsement.* An indorsement is restrictive which prohibits the further negotiation of the bill or which expresses that it is a mere authority to deal with the bill as directed, and not a transfer of ownership of it, e.g. "Pay D only", or "Pay D for the account of X", or "Pay D or order for collection".

(*d*) *Conditional indorsement.* An indorsement may purport to make payment or transfer subject to some condition. In such cases the condition may be disregarded by the payer, and payment to the indorsee is valid whether the condition has been fulfilled or not.

(*e*) *Indorsement sans recours.* Where the holder of a bill indorses it *sans recours* or "without recourse to me", he negatives his own liability on the bill. A transferee can, of course, refuse to take a bill indorsed in this way.

19. Transfer by delivery. A bill payable to bearer is negotiated by delivery and no indorsement is necessary. In this case, the transferor is called a transferor by delivery; and since he does not sign the bill, he is not subsequently liable as a party to it: BEA, s.58.

NOTE: A bill is payable to bearer in the following circumstances:

(1) where it is expressed to be payable to bearer;
(2) where the last indorsement is in blank;
(3) where it is payable to a fictitious person.

In all other cases, an indorsement is necessary to negotiate the bill.

PAYMENT OF A BILL

20. Presentment for payment. A bill must be duly presented for payment according to the following rules, otherwise the drawer and indorsers are discharged: BEA, s.45.

(*a*) Where the bill is not payable on demand, presentment must be made on the day it falls due.

(*b*) Where the bill is payable on demand, presentment must be made within a reasonable time.

(*c*) Presentment must be made by the holder (or his agent) to the drawee named on the bill (or his agent).

(*d*) Presentment must be made at the proper place.

(*e*) Where authorised by agreement or usage a presentment through the Post Office is sufficient.

21. Excuses for delay or non-presentment. Delay in presentment for payment is excused when caused by circumstances beyond the control of the holder, and not due to his negligence. Presentment for payment is dispensed with in the following circumstances.

(*a*) Where, after the exercise of reasonable diligence, presentment cannot be effected.
(*b*) Where the drawee is fictitious.
(*c*) As regards the drawer where the drawee or acceptor is not bound, as between himself and the drawer, to accept or pay the bill, and the drawer has no reason to believe that the bill would be paid if presented.
(*d*) As regards an indorser where the bill was accepted or made for the accommodation of that indorser and he has no reason to expect that the bill would be paid if presented.
(*e*) By waiver of presentment by a person entitled to notice of dishonour: BEA, s.46.

22. Dishonour by non-payment. A bill is dishonoured by non-payment:

(*a*) when it is duly presented for payment and payment is refused or cannot be obtained; or
(*b*) when presentment is excused and the bill is overdue and unpaid: BEA, s.47.

When a bill is dishonoured by non-payment, an immediate right of recourse against the drawer and indorsers accrues to the holder: BEA, s.47.

23. Notice of dishonour. When a bill has been dishonoured by non-acceptance or non-payment, notice of dishonour must be given to the drawer and each indorser, and any drawer or indorser to whom notice is not given is discharged, provided that:

(*a*) where a bill is dishonoured by non-acceptance and notice of dishonour is not given, the rights of a holder in due course subsequent to the omission are not affected; and
(*b*) where a bill is dishonoured by non-acceptance and notice of dishonour is given, it is not necessary to give notice of a subsequent dishonour by non-payment unless the bill in the meantime has been accepted: BEA, s.48.

NOTE: (1) Notice must be given when the bill is dishonoured, but not before. However, the time of notice is the time of receipt: *Eaglehill Ltd.* v. *Needham Builders Ltd.* (1973).
(2) Notice of dishonour must be given to prior parties to the bill by the holder of the dishonoured bill, or by any indorser who

is liable on the bill. In practice, it is usual for each party to the bill to claim against the party immediately before him (usually his own transferor), so that a chain of notice-giving takes place from the holder, through each indorser, ultimately reaching the drawer. Notice may take any form, i.e. it may be oral or in unsigned writing, or it may take the form of the return of the dishonoured bill.

24. Excuses for non-notice and delay. Delay in giving notice of dishonour is excused where the delay is not caused by default or negligence. Notice of dishonour is dispensed with in the following circumstances.

(*a*) When, after the exercise of reasonable diligence, notice cannot be given or does not reach the drawer or indorser sought to be charged.

(*b*) By waiver by a person entitled to receive notice.

(*c*) As regards the drawer in the following cases:

(*i*) where drawer and drawee are the same person;

(*ii*) where the drawee is a fictitious person or has no contractual capacity;

(*iii*) where the drawer is the person to whom the bill is presented for payment;

(*iv*) where the drawee or acceptor is as between himself and the drawer under no obligation to accept or pay the bill;

(*v*) where the drawer has countermanded payment.

(*d*) As regards the indorser in the following cases:

(*i*) where the drawee is a fictitious person or has no contractual capacity, and the indorser was aware of the fact at the time of indorsing;

(*ii*) when the indorser is the person to whom the bill is presented for payment;

(*iii*) where the bill was accepted or made for his accommodation: BEA, s.50.

25. Noting and protesting. These are two methods of obtaining formal evidence of the dishonour of a bill.

(*a*) *Noting*. A dishonoured bill is noted by a notary public, who must re-present the bill, and then write on the face of the bill that it was dishonoured. The holder of an inland bill which has been dishonoured may arrange for the bill to be noted, but this procedure is not necessary to preserve the recourse against prior parties.

(*b*) *Protesting*. In this case the notary re-presents the bill, and then makes out a formal certificate of dishonour (the protest) containing a copy of the bill. Where the services of a notary cannot be obtained, a householder may sign a certificate attesting the dishonour of the bill: two witnesses must also sign. A foreign bill must be protested for dishonour by non-acceptance or by non-payment. If it is not protested, the drawer and the indorsers are discharged: BEA, s.51.

CONSIDERATION FOR A BILL: HOLDERS

26. What constitutes consideration. Section 27 of the Bills of Exchange Act 1882 provides that valuable consideration for a bill may be constituted by:

(*a*) any consideration sufficient to support a simple contract (*see Thoni GmbH & Co. KG* v. *RTP Equipment* (1979) where the Court of Appeal discussed whether there was any consideration for the bill of exchange in question);

(*b*) an antecedent debt or liability (but the antecedent debt must be owed by the negotiator or drawer of the bill, not a stranger to it): *Oliver* v. *Davis* (1949). A recent example which confirms that a stranger to a bill cannot benefit from s.27 is *Hasan* v. *Willson* (1977).

27. Holder for value. Where value has been given at any time for a bill, the holder is deemed to be a holder for value as regards the acceptor and all parties to the bill who becomes parties prior to such time.

28. Holder in due course. A holder in due course is a holder who has taken a bill, complete and regular on the face of it, under the folllowing conditions.

(*a*) That he became the holder of it before it was overdue, and without notice that it had been previously dishonoured, if such was the fact.

(*b*) That he took the bill in good faith and for value, and that at the time the bill was negotiated to him he had no notice of any defect in the title of the person who negotiated it: BEA, s.29.

In *Jade International Steel Stahl Und Eisen GmbH Co. KG v. Robert Nicholas (Steels)* (1978) the Court of Appeal held that the drawer of a bill of exchange who then derives title from a holder in due course is a holder in due course, and his rights lie to be determined as such and not as drawer.

29. Presumption of value and good faith. In the case of bills of exchange, the following two presumptions exist.

(*a*) Every party whose signature appears on a bill is prima facie deemed to have become a party for value.

(*b*) Every holder of a bill is prima facie deemed to be a holder in due course: BEA, s.30.

30. Holder's rights. The rights and powers of a holder of a bill are as follows.

(*a*) He may sue on the bill in his own name.

(*b*) Where he is a holder in due course, he holds the bill free from any defect of title or prior parties, as well as from mere personal defences available to prior parties among themselves, and may enforce payment against all parties liable on the bill.

(*c*) Where his title is defective:

(*i*) if he negotiates the bill to a holder in due course, that holder obtains a good and complete title to the bill, and

(*ii*) if he obtains payment of the bill, the person who pays him in due course gets a valid discharge for the bill: BEA, s.38.

31. Holder's duties. The general duties of the holder of a bill are as follows.

(*a*) To present the bill for acceptance where necessary according to the rules.

(*b*) To present the bill for payment according to the rules.

(*c*) To give notice of dishonour for non-acceptance or non-payment.

(*d*) In the case of a dishonoured foreign bill, to obtain a protest.

LIABILITY OF PARTIES: DISCHARGE

32. Drawee/acceptor. The drawee of a bill who does not accept it is not liable on the instrument: BEA, s.53. The acceptor engaged that he will pay the bill according to the tenor of his acceptance and is precluded from denying to a holder in due course the existence of the drawer and the genuineness of his signature: BEA, s.54.

33. The drawer. The drawer of a bill:

(*a*) engages that on due presentment it will be accepted and paid, and that, if it be dishonoured, he will compensate any party who is compelled to pay it, provided the requisite proceedings on dishonour be taken;

(*b*) is precluded from denying to a holder in due course the existence of the payee: BEA, s.55.

34. The indorser. The indorser of a bill:

(*a*) engages that on due presentment it will be accepted and paid, and that, if it be dishonoured, he will compensate any subsequent party who is compelled to pay it, provided the requisite proceedings on dishonour be taken;
(*b*) is precluded from denying to a holder in due course the genuineness of the drawer's signature and all previous indorsements;
(*c*) is precluded from denying to any subsequent indorsee that he had a good title to it: BEA, s.55.

NOTE: Judgment against persons liable on a bill may be ordered in a currency other than sterling. Administration of Justice Act 1977, s.4.

35. Transferor by delivery: A transferor by delivery, i.e. one who negotiates the bill without indorsing it, is not liable on the instrument: BEA, s.58. A transferor by delivery warrants to his immediate transferee, being a holder for value, that the bill is what it purports to be, that he has a right to transfer it, and that at the time of transfer he is not aware of any fact which renders it valueless: BEA, s.58.

NOTE: Although a transferor by delivery will not be liable on the bill, he will be liable for breach of contract to his immediate transferee in the event of the bill being dishonoured.

36. Forged signatures. The general rule is that a forged signature on a bill is wholly inoperative: BEA, s.24. The effect of the forgery depends upon which signature has been forged, i.e. whether it is the drawer's, acceptor's or indorser's.

(*a*) Where the drawer's signature is forged the instrument does not satisfy the definition in s.3 of the Act, and it therefore cannot be a bill of exchange. However, the indorsers of such an instrument will be liable as between each other as if the instrument were a valid bill by reason of the rule of statutory estoppel in s.55. In addition, if the instrument has been accepted, the acceptor is likewise estopped from denying to a holder in due course the genuineness of the drawer's signature: BEA, s.54.
(*b*) Where an indorsement is forged, the rights of the parties to the bill prior to the forgery are not affected, but those taking the

bill after the forgery will have rights as between one another as if the bill were valid for them. This is the effect of the rule of statutory estoppel in s.55.

Consider this example: A draws a bill on B payable to C; then C indorses this bill specially to D, who indorses the bill specially to E; then X steals the bill from E and forges E's signature to a special indorsement to F; then F indorses the bill specially to G, who indorses the bill specially to H. Applying the rule in s.24, that the forged signature is totally inoperative, it is clear that the bill remained the property of E after the forgery and that no title to the bill passed to F, G and H. The forgery caused a break in the chain of transference of title. But H can claim against G or F, who will not be allowed to set up the forgery (s.55). If H claims against G, then G in his turn will be able to claim similarly against F. F will not be able to claim against any of the parties prior to the forgery: his only recourse will be against X, if he can find him.

(*c*) A forged acceptance is by virtue of s.24 totally inoperative. The instrument remains a good bill whose legal effect is that of a bill which has not been accepted. The drawer and indorsers are liable according to the usual rules.

(*d*) If a signature on a bill has been forged and the party whose signature it is purported to be gets to know of the forgery he may, if he does not inform the holder within a reasonable time, be estopped from asserting it: *Greenwood* v. *Martins Bank* (1933).

(*e*) The acceptor of a bill by accepting it is precluded from denying to a holder in due course the genuineness of his signature: BEA, s.54.

37. Discharge of a bill. A bill is discharged when no rights and obligations attach to it. A party to a bill is discharged when he is no longer liable on it. Discharge may occur in any of the following ways.

(*a*) *Payment in due course*, i.e. payment made at or after maturity to the holder in good faith: BEA, s.59.

(*b*) *Merger*, i.e. when the acceptor is the holder at or after maturity: BEA, s.61.

(*c*) *Waiver*, i.e. when the holder at or after maturity renounces his rights against the acceptor: BEA, s.62.

(*d*) *Intentional cancellation* of the bill by the holder: BEA, s.63.

(*e*) *Material alteration* without the consent of all parties liable. Examples of material alterations are any alteration of the date or the sum payable. In this case, the bill is avoided except as against any party who has himself made or assented to the alteration and subsequent indorsers. However, where a bill has been materially altered, but the alteration is not apparent, and the bill is in the hands of a holder in due course, such holder may avail himself of the bill as if it had not been altered, and may enforce payment of it according to its original tenor: BEA, s.64.

(*f*) *Statute barred*, i.e. the bill cannot be sued upon more than six years after the date of dishonour.

CHEQUES

38. Definition. A cheque is a bill of exchange drawn on a banker and payable on demand: BEA, s.73. A cheque is a particular kind of bill of exchange to which certain special rules apply. These rules are to be found in Part III of the Bills of Exchange Act 1882, and the Cheques Act 1957. The two Acts must be construed as one.

39. Banker and customer. The relationship between banker and customer is a contractual one.

(*a*) The banker is under a general duty to pay cheques drawn by the customer, provided there is a sufficient credit balance in the customer's account, or up to the amount of an agreed overdraft but not without enquiry in unusual cases. The banker is under a contractual duty to exercise such care and skill as would be exercised by a reasonable banker, and that care and skill includes a duty to enquire if the banker has a deep suspicion that the funds are being misapplied: *Karak Rubber Co. Ltd.* v. *Burden (No. 2)* (1972). For this purpose, the banker may be regarded as the customer's agent, with authority to pay the cheques drawn.

The duty and authority of a banker to pay a cheque drawn on him by his customer are terminated by the following.

(*i*) Countermand of payment. This may be written or oral; but an oral countermand should, in practice, be confirmed in writing: BEA, s.75.

(*ii*) Notice of the customer's death: BEA, s.75.

(*iii*) Notice of the customer's mental disorder.

(*iv*) Notice of the presentment of a bankruptcy petition against the customer.

(*v*) The making of a receiving order against the customer.

(*vi*) The assignment of the customer's credit balance to a third party.

(*vii*) The service of a garnishee order attaching to the

customer's account, i.e. an order forbidding the bank to pay the attached moneys to the customer.

(*viii*) Where the account contains trust funds, notice that the customer is in breach of trust.

(*ix*) Where the credit balance or the agreed overdraft is not sufficient to cover the cheque.

(*x*) Where the cheque is not signed with the customer's usual signature.

(*xi*) Where the customer is a limited company, notice of a petition for compulsory winding up or a resolution for voluntary winding up will terminate the banker's duty to honour cheques.

(*b*) The banker has a qualified obligation not to disclose information concerning the customer's affairs. The bank can be excused for disclosing such information in certain circumstances, for example under s.7 Bankers' Books Evidence Act 1879.

40. Paying banker and collecting banker. Where a customer draws a cheque on his banker, that banker is known as the paying banker with respect to that cheque. Where the holder of a cheque presents it to his banker for credit to his account, the banker's duty is to collect the amount from the drawer's banker (i.e. the paying banker); the holder's banker is known as the collecting banker with respect to that cheque.

41. Crossed cheques. The practice of crossing cheques is intended to reduce the possibility of the wrong person being paid.

Crossings may be general or special and, in either case, may or may not include the words "not negotiable": BEA, s.76.

(*a*) A general crossing is constituted by two parallel transverse lines on the face of the cheque with or without "& Co." between them. This crossing is a direction to the paying banker to pay only to a collecting banker, i.e. not to pay across the counter.

(*b*) *A special crossing* is constituted by the addition across the face of a cheque of the name of a banker. Transverse lines are not essential to a special crossing, but they are usual. This crossing is a direction to the paying banker to pay only to the collecting banker named in the crossing.

(*c*) "*Not negotiable.*" Where a cheque bears these words, it is not a negotiable instrument and the payee or any transferee takes it subject to the equities, i.e. the instrument is assignable but not negotiable: BEA, s.81.

(*d*) "*Account payee.*" These words written across the face of a cheque constitute a direction to the collecting banker to collect for the account of the named payee only. If the cheque has been negotiated, so that the holder is not the payee named, the collecting banker is put on enquiry when the cheque is presented for payment. This crossing originated in banker's custom and is now recognised judicially.

42. Protection of the paying banker. The drawee banker has the benefit of statutory protection which is not accorded to other drawees of bills of exchange. The purpose is to allow bankers to carry out their commercial functions as unhampered as possible. Statutory protection is accorded to a banker who pays a cheque in any of the following circumstances.

(*a*) *Payment to bearer.* Where a banker makes payment to the holder of a cheque in good faith and without any notice of any defect in his title, the banker is freed from all liability. However, the person paid must be the holder, and a person holding an order bill by means of a forged or unauthorised indorsement is not a holder: BEA, s.59.

(*b*) *Forged indorsement.* Where a banker pays a cheque: (*i*) in good faith, and (*ii*) in the ordinary course of business, he is deemed to have paid the cheque in due course (i.e. he is discharged) even though an indorsement has been forged: BEA, s.60. (Any other kind of drawee of a bill would remain liable to the true owner in these circumstances.)

(*c*) *Crossed cheques.* Where a banker on whom a crossed cheque is drawn pays it: (*i*) in good faith, and (*ii*) without negligence, and (*iii*) according to the crossing, he is not liable if payment is made to a person other than the true owner of the cheque: BEA, s.80.

(*d*) *No indorsement/irregular indorsement.* Where a banker: (*i*) in good faith, and (*ii*) in the ordinary course of business, pays a cheque drawn on him which is not indorsed or is irregularly indorsed, he is deemed to have paid it in due course: Cheques Act 1957, s.1. This provision does not give the banker the intended amount of protection, since the Committee of London Clearing Bankers have ruled that banking practice (i.e. the ordinary course of business) requires all cheques to be indorsed except where the account of the payee is credited.

(*See* also *Karak Rubber Co.* v. *Burden* (*No. 2*) (1972) at **39.**)

43. Protection of the collecting banker. Where a banker: (*a*) in good faith, and (*b*) without negligence, receives payment of a cheque for a customer with no title or a defective title, he is not liable to the true owner of the cheque: Cheques Act 1957, s.4. (This section applies also to certain instruments analogous to cheques.)

44. Collecting banker's enquiries. In order to benefit from the Cheques Act 1957, s.4, the collecting banker must not have been negligent. The banker is not expected to be abnormally and perpetually suspicious, but he is expected to be reasonably prudent in circumstances where he is put on enquiry. In particular, he may be negligent if he does not make enquiries when collecting payment in the following circumstances.

(*a*) Where a customer presents a cheque for the credit of his private account, but drawn in favour of his employer.

(*b*) Where a customer presents a cheque drawn in favour of him in his official capacity for the credit of his private account.

(*c*) Where a customer presents a cheque for the credit of his own account, but drawn in favour of his principal or where the cheque is drawn by the customer on behalf of his principal, but in favour of the customer (the agent) personally.

(*d*) Where a customer presents a cheque crossed "Account payee" and he is not the payee named.

If the collecting banker has been negligent, then the banker is prime facie liable in conversion to the true owner. However, the Banking Act 1979 s. 47 provides that the collective banker may raise contributory negligence as a defence to an action in conversion.

PROMISSORY NOTES

45. Definition. A promissory note is an unconditional promise in writing made by one person to another signed by the maker, engaging to pay, on demand or at a fixed or determinable future time, a sum certain in money, to, or to the order of, a specified person or to bearer: BEA, s.83.

NOTE: The fundamental difference between a bill of exchange and a promissory note is that the bill is an order to pay, and a note is a promise to pay.

46. IOUs. An IOU is merely a written admission of indebtedness: it is not a promissory note and is not negotiable.

47. Inland and foreign notes. A note which is, or on the face of it purports to be, both made and payable within the British Isles is an inland note. Any other note is a foreign note: BEA, s.83.

When a foreign note is dishonoured, there is no need for it to be protested as in the case of foreign bills: BEA, s.89.

48. Application of BEA to notes. In applying the provisions of the Bills of Exchange Act 1882 to promissory notes, the maker corresponds with the acceptor of the bill, and the first indorser of a note corresponds with the drawer of an accepted bill payable to drawer's order. However, the provisions relating to acceptance of a bill do not apply to notes: BEA, s.89. Where, in a bill, the drawer and drawee are the same person, or where the drawee is a fictitious person or a person without contractual capacity, the holder may treat the instrument, at his option, either as a bill or as a note: BEA, s.5.

In particular, a note, like a bill, is incomplete and revocable until it has been delivered to the payee or bearer: BEA, ss.5 and 84.

PROGRESS TEST

1. What are the characteristics of a negotiable instrument? Give examples of documents classified as negotiable instruments. **(1, 2)**
2. Analyse the statutory definition of a bill of exchange. What is the difference between an inland bill and a foreign bill? **(4, 5)**
3. What are the rules as to time of payment of a bill? **(8)**
4. Distinguish between general and qualified acceptance. What is the effect of the acceptance? **(9–12)**
5. When must a bill be presented for acceptance? What are the rules as to presentment for acceptance? **(13–15)**
6. Explain fully how a bill may be negotiated. **(17)**
7. What are the rules as to presentment for payment of a bill **(20, 21)**
8. When must notice of dishonour be given? What do you understand by (*a*) noting, and (*b*) protesting a bill? **(23–25)**
9. What constitutes consideration for a bill of exchange? What presumptions are made in connection with consideration? **(26, 29)**
10. Define "holder in due course". What are the rights and duties of a holder of a bill? **(28, 30, 31)**
11. What are the liabilities of (*a*) the drawer, and (*b*) an indorser of a bill of exchange? In what way do the liabilities of a transferor by delivery differ from those of an indorser? **(32–35)**
12. Explain the effect of a forged signature to a bill. **(36)**
13. In what ways may a bill be discharged? **(37)**
14. Define a cheque. In what ways may a cheque be crossed? Explain the legal effects of the different kinds of crossing. **(38, 41)**

15. What is the usual relationship between banker and customer? When is the banker's duty and authority to pay a cheque drawn on him terminated? **(39)**

16. What is the difference between a paying banker and a collecting banker? Outline the statutory provisions designed for the protection of bankers. **(40, 42–44)**

17. Define a promissory note and compare it with a bill of exchange. **(45–48)**

CHAPTER IV

Sale of Goods

INTRODUCTION

1. Sale of Goods Act 1979. The law relating to the sale of goods has been consolidated by the Sale of Goods Act 1979 (SGA). The Act is merely a restatement of the existing statute law, so it does not change the substantive law. The Act does not provide a complete statement of the rights and duties of parties to a contract of sale, as they are also subject to the general principles of contract law, and the common law (*see* for example *Lambert* v. *Lewis* (1981) at **13**(*c*)).

2. Other legislation. It should also be noted that statute law has imposed many obligations on the commercial seller of goods to members of the public, in order to protect the ordinary consumer. The Consumer Protection Act 1961, the Consumer Safety Act 1978, the Unfair Contract Terms Act 1977 and the Trade Descriptions Acts 1968 and 1972 are examples of legislation which aims to prevent misleading descriptions being applied to goods and the sale of unsafe articles. The legislation is often implemented through detailed regulations, e.g. the Nightwear (Safety) Order 1978 (No. 1728) which prohibits the supply of children's nightwear which has been treated with or contains a particular chemical. Breach of the duties imposed by this legislation is a criminal offence.

3. EEC and consumer protection. The European Economic Community (EEC) has become increasingly concerned with consumer protection in recent years, and has, for example, drawn up proposals which, if implemented, would ensure that any individual suffering injury to person or property as a result of a defective article would be entitled to receive compensation from the producer or the importer of the article. It would not be necessary for the individual to prove that the producer or the importer was negligent.

THE CONTRACT OF SALE

4. Definition. A contract of sale of goods is a contract whereby the seller transfers or agrees to transfer the property in goods to the buyer for a money consideration, called the price: SGA, s.2. The contract may be made in writing, or by word of mouth, or both, or it may be implied from the conduct of the parties: SGA, s.4.

5. Sale and agreement to sell. Where under a contract of sale the property in the goods is transferred from the seller to the buyer, the contract is called a sale; but where the transfer of the property in the goods is to take place at a future time or subject to some condition thereafter to be fulfilled, the contract is called an agreement to sell: SGA, ss.2 and 5.

6. Conditional sale and credit sale. Certain conditional sale agreements and credit sale agreements are affected by the provisions of the Hire-Purchase Act 1965. This Act is to be repealed by the Consumer Credit Act 1974, but the relevant provisions are not yet in force. However, the definition of these terms will remain the same, subject to textual amendments.

(*a*) Conditional sale agreements affected by the Acts are those under which the purchase price, or part of it, is payable by instalments and the total purchase price does not exceed £7,500. The property in the goods is to remain with the seller (notwithstanding that the buyer is to be in possession of the goods) until such conditions as to the payment of instalments or otherwise as may be specified in the agreement are fulfilled; and the purchaser is not a body corporate (*see* V, **6**).

(*b*) Credit sale agreements affected by the Acts are those where the purchase price is payable by five or more instalments; the total purchase price exceeds £30 but does not exceed £7,500; the purchaser is not a body corporate; and the agreement is not a conditional sale agreement as defined above. However, the Consumer Credit Act 1974 defines a credit sale agreement as an agreement for the sale of goods under which the purchase price, or part of it, is payable by instalments, but which is not a conditional-sale agreement. In order to come within the provisions of the 1974 Act the total amount of credit should not exceed £7,500 and the debtor should not be a body corporate.

7. Capacity to buy and sell. Capacity to buy and sell is regulated by the general law concerning capacity to contract and to transfer and acquire property. However, where necessaries are sold and delivered to a minor or to a person who by reason of mental incapacity or drunkenness is incompetent to contract, he must pay a reasonable price for the goods. Necessaries are goods suitable to the condition in life of the minor or other person and to his actual requirements at the time of sale and delivery: SGA, s.3.

8. Goods. "Goods" includes all chattels personal other than things in action and money. The term includes emblements (annual agricultural crops), industrial growing crops, and things attached to or forming part of the land which are agreed to be severed before sale or under the contract of sale.

"*Future goods*" are goods to be manufactured or acquired by the seller after the making of the contract of sale: SGA, s.5.

"*Specific goods*" are goods identified and agreed on at the time the contract is made: SGA, s.5.

9. Goods which perish. Where goods which are the subject of a sale perish, the following rules apply.

(*a*) Where there is a contract for the sale of specific goods and the goods, without the knowledge of the seller, have perished at the time when the contract is made, the contract is void: SGA, s.6.

(*b*) Where there is an agreement to sell specific goods, and subsequently the goods, without any fault on the part of the seller or buyer, perish before the risk passes to the buyer, the agreement is thereby avoided: SGA, s.7.

10. Other kinds of contract. Where the substance of the contract is an undertaking to use skill in producing a particular article, the contract may be one for work and materials and not a contract for the sale of goods. The Sale of Goods Act does not apply to contracts for work and materials, contracts of exchange and barter and contracts of hire. However, the Supply of Goods and Services Act 1982 provides that similar implied terms should apply to such contracts. The Act also imposes certain obligations on a supplier acting in the course of business where there is a contract for the supply of services. The supplier is required to exercise reasonable care and skill, to supply the service within a reasonable time (unless otherwise specified) and to charge a reasonable sum (unless otherwise specified).

(*a*) A contract to paint a portrait has been held to be a contract for the exercise of skill and not a contract of sale of goods: *Robinson* v. *Graves* (1935).

(*b*) A contract to make and supply ship's propellers has been held to be a contract of sale of goods, in spite of the skill involved: *Cammell Laird & Co. Ltd.* v. *Manganese Bronze Co. Ltd.* (1934).

DUTIES OF SELLER AND BUYER

11. The duty to deliver the goods. It is the duty of the seller to deliver the goods in accordance with the terms of the contract of sale. Whether it is for the buyer to take possession of the goods or for the seller to send them to the buyer is a question depending in each case on the contract between the parties. Apart from any such contract, express or implied, the place of delivery is the seller's place of business, if he has one, and if not, his residence: SGA, s.29.

NOTE: (1) The time of delivery is the time, if any, fixed in the contract of sale. But where, under the contract of sale, the seller is bound to send the goods to the buyer, but no time for sending them is fixed, the seller is bound to send them within a reasonable time.

(2) Unless otherwise agreed, delivery of the goods and payment of the price are concurrent conditions, that is to say, the seller must be ready and willing to give possession of the goods to the buyer in exchange for the price.

12. The duty to pass good title. Under a contract of sale, the seller transfers, or agrees to transfer, the property in goods to the buyer.

(*a*) In every contract of sale, other than one to which (*b*) below applies, there is:

(*i*) an implied condition on the part of the seller that, in the case of a sale he has a right to sell the goods, and that in the case of an agreement to sell he will have a right to sell the goods at the time when the property is to pass: SGA, s.12(1); and

(*ii*) an implied warranty that the buyer will take the goods free from any charge or encumbrance not disclosed or known to the buyer before the contract is made: SGA, s.12(2)(*a*); and

(*iii*) an implied warranty that the buyer will enjoy quiet possession of the goods subject to any known or disclosed charges or encumbrances: SGA, s.12(2)(*b*).

(*b*) In a contract of sale to transfer only such title as the seller or a third person may have, there is:

(*i*) an implied warranty that all charges or encumbrances known to the seller and not known to the buyer have been disclosed to the buyer before the contract is made: SGA, s.12(4); and (*ii*) an implied warranty that neither the seller, nor a third party nor anyone claiming through or under them, will disturb the buyer's quiet possession of the goods: SGA, s.12(5).

Rowland v. *Divall* (1923): R bought a motor car from D for £334. Two months after the sale, R, who was a motor dealer, sold the car to X for £400. Some two months later, the police took the car from X, as it had been stolen before it came into D's possession. R refunded the £400 to X, and then brought this action to recover the £334 from D. HELD: D was in breach of the condition implied in s.12(1) . There was a total failure of consideration, and R was entitled to recover all the money he had paid. It was immaterial (*i*) that R had possession of the car for two months, and (*ii*) that *restitutio* was not possible.

Microbeads AG v. *Vinhurst Road Markings Ltd.* (1975): In 1966 an English company applied for a patent for road-marking apparatus, which was granted in 1972. In 1970 the defendant buyers had bought three road-marking machines from the plaintiffs, but they were dissatisfied with the machines and withheld payment. The plaintiff brought an action to recover the balance. The defendants claimed that there was a breach by the plaintiff of s.12(1) and s.12(2) of the 1893 Act which correspond to s.12(1) and s.12(2)(*b*) of the 1979 Act. The Court of Appeal HELD: (1) that the sellers were not in breach of s.12(1) because they had a right to sell at the date of sale and had therefore passed a good title; but

(2) the sellers could be in breach of s.12(2) if the buyers' possession and enjoyment were disturbed at a date subsequent to the sale by reason of the publication of the patent specification. It is possible to have a breach of s.12(2) without also a breach of s.12(1).

13. The duty to deliver goods of the right kind. It is the duty of the seller to deliver to the buyer goods which accord with the terms of the contract. In addition, the Sale of Goods Act 1979 provides that the following implied conditions will apply to contracts for the sale of goods.

(*a*) *Correspondence with description.* Where there is a contract for the sale of goods by description, there is an implied condition that the goods will comply with the description: SGA, s.13(1). A sale of goods will not be prevented from being a sale by description by reason only that, being exposed for sale or hire, for example on a supermarket shelf or in a garage forecourt, they are selected by the buyer: SGA. s.13(3).

Varley v. *Whipp* (1900): V contracted to sell W a secondhand reaping machine. W had not seen the machine, and V described it as being new the previous year, and said it had been used to cut about 50 or 60 acres only. When the machine was delivered W discovered that it was a very old machine, so he returned it to V. V brought this action against W for the price of the machine. HELD: there was a contract of sale by description and there was a breach of the implied condition as to correspondence with description in s.13.

NOTE: Criminal liability for false trade descriptions made in the course of a business, is imposed by the Trade Description Acts 1968 and 1972.

(*b*) *Merchantable quality.* Where the seller sells goods in the course of a business, there is an implied condition that the goods supplied under the contract are of merchantable quality, except there is no such condition:

(*i*) as regards defects specifically drawn to the buyer's attention before the contract is made; or

(*ii*) if the buyer examines the goods before the contract is made, as regards defects which that examination ought to reveal: SGA, s.14(2).

Goods of any kind are of merchantable quality within the meaning of the Act if they are as fit for the purpose or purposes for which goods of that kind are commonly bought as it is reasonable to expect, having regard to any description applied to them, the price (if relevant) and all other relevant circumstances: SGA, s.14(6).

Brown & Son Ltd. v. *Craiks Ltd.* (1970): B gave two orders to C for the manufacture of large quantities of rayon cloth to a detailed specification. The buyer intended to use the cloth for making dresses and the seller bona fide thought it was for industrial use. Both orders were accepted and the agreed price was 36.25d. per yard. B, on discovering subsequently that the cloth was not suitable for dressmaking, wrote to C cancelling the contract. Both parties were left with a considerable amount of cloth on their hands which was eventually sold, C obtaining 30d. per yard and B only 15d. per yard. B brought this action against C, claiming that the goods were not of merchantable quality, basing his case on s.14(2). B claimed: (*i*) that there was only one normal use for such cloth at the time of delivery, namely dressmaking, and that there was not any normal use of the cloth of the description ordered for industrial purposes, and (*ii*) that the discrepancy between the contract price (36.25d. per yard) and the price at which C subsequently sold the remaining cloth (30d. per yard) showed that the goods were not of merchantable quality. HELD: (1) the cloth was reasonably capable of being used, was saleable for a number of industrial purposes and was merchantable for these purposes, and

(2) there was not a sufficient abatement in price as to lead to the conclusion that the cloth was not of merchantable quality.

Cehave NV v. *Bremer Handelsgesellschaft mbh; The Hansa Nord* (1975): There was a contract for the sale of 12,000 tons of citrus pulp pellets c.i.f. Rotterdam for use as animal feed. Between payment by the buyers and the arrival of the pellets at the port, their market price had fallen. On discharge much of the pellets in one hold were damaged while pellets in the other hold were in a satisfactory condition. The buyer rejected the whole cargo and claimed repayment of the price on the grounds that they were not in good condition. Arbitration took place in London, and on appeal to the Court of Appeal it was held: (1) that since the damaged pellets were ultimately bought for use in cattle feed they were of merchantable quality and there was no breach of s.14(2); and

(2) the buyers were not entitled to reject the goods, but were entitled to damages for breach of the express term. The damages were the difference in value between the damaged and the sound pellets.

Lee v. *York Coach and Marine* (1977): The plaintiff purchased from the defendants a seven-year-old motor car for £355. The car was supplied with a new MOT certificate. In the two weeks after the purchase the car was twice returned to the garage for repairs, and the defendants refused to carry out further repairs. The plaintiff had used the car for driving her children to school, and for one forty-mile journey. She had the car examined, and it was apparent that an MOT certificate should not have been given. An expert examiner stated that the car was in a dangerous condition, in particular in respect of its braking system and of corrosion of the sub-frame. The Court of Appeal held that the car was neither of merchantable quality nor fit for the purpose intended since, although it had in fact been driven on the road, there was clear evidence that it was not in a condition where it could safely be so driven.

(*c*) *Fitness for a particular purpose.* Where the seller sells the goods in the course of business and the buyer, expressly or by implication, makes known to the seller any particular purpose for which the goods are bought, there is an implied condition that the goods supplied are reasonably fit for that purpose, except where the circumstances show that:

(*i*) the buyer does not rely, or

(*ii*) it is unreasonable for him to rely,

on the skill or judgment of the seller: SGA, s.14(3).

Frost v. *Aylesbury Dairy Co. Ltd.* (1905): The defendant dairy company supplied the plaintiff with milk for the consumption of his family. The book used to record the amount supplied to the plaintiff contained a notice in which the dairy company stated the precautions taken to ensure that the milk supplied was pure. The plaintiff's wife died as a result of being infected with typhoid by milk supplied by the defendants. The plaintiff claimed damages under s.14(3). HELD: the defendants knew, by implication, the purpose for which the plaintiff bought the milk, i.e. for domestic consumption. The plaintiff had relied on the skill of the defendants. As the milk was not reasonably fit for domestic consumption, the defendants were in breach of the implied condition in s.14(3). Thus the liability is absolute.

Kendall v. *Lillico & Sons Ltd.* (1968): G bought ground nuts from K. G's purpose was to resell in smaller quantities for compounding as food for cattle and poultry—this purpose being known to K. The nuts were in fact toxic and unfit for poultry. G sold some of the nuts to S, knowing that S required them for compounding into food for pigs and poultry. S compounded the nuts into food which was then bought by H, who fed it to his pheasants, which consequently died. S (who admitted liability to H) sued G, who sued K. The claim was for breach of the implied conditions of fitness for purpose under s.14(3) and of merchantable quality under s.14(2). HELD: (1) *As between G and S.* The compounding into foodstuffs was a "particular purpose" within s.14(3) and S had relied on G's skill or judgment. G was liable to S. (2) *As between K and G.* The purpose for which G required the goods was sufficiently "particular" to be within s.14(3) and K was liable for breach of the implied condition of fitness for purpose.

Ashington Piggeries v. *Christopher Hill* (1971): The defendants were two mink companies concerned with the breeding of mink and with the supply of equipment and foodstuffs to other mink breeders. The plaintiffs, who manufactured compounds for animal feeding, entered an agreement with the defendants for the manufacture of a mink food to be called King Size. The formula was supplied by the defendants, and the plaintiffs had made it clear that they knew nothing about the nutritional requirements of mink. The plaintiffs did, however, suggest, as a variation in the formula, the substitution of herringmeal for fishmeal. For about a year King Size was used by about 100 mink farms without complaint. But in March 1961, the plaintiffs bought a large consignment of herringmeal which had been contaminated by a chemical known as DMNA, toxic to mink, but harmless to other animals. The inclusion of contaminated herringmeal in the manufacture of King Size resulted in serious losses on some mink farms. The plaintiffs claimed payment for King Size containing the contaminated meal and the defendants counterclaimed for damages for breach of contract. HELD: (1) there was a breach of the condition implied by s.14(3) of the Sale of Goods Act 1893, that the goods were reasonably fit for their purpose, the buyers having relied on the skill and judgment of the sellers, even though that reliance was only partial; (2) the sellers were also in breach of the condition implied by s.14(2) that the goods were of merchantable quality.

Lambert v. *Lewis* (1980): This case illustrates that in practice a contract for the sale of goods may not only be subject to the Sale of Goods Act 1979, but may involve other areas of law. A was injured in a road accident caused by a trailer becoming detached from the vehicle towing it, because the towing hitch was defective in design. The trailer was owned by B, but was being driven by C, his employee at the time of the accident. B had purchased the towing hitch from D, who were retailers. D had obtained the hitch from one of their suppliers, X. The hitch was produced by E, reputable manufacturers, whose literature stated that it was foolproof and that it needed no maintenance. A brought an action (*i*) for negligence (in tort), and (*ii*) under the Fatal Accidents Acts (A's husband and son were killed in the accident) against B and C. B claimed that D were in breach of s.14 as they had supplied him with a towing hitch which was neither fit for the purpose for which it had been supplied nor of merchantable quality. D claimed damages from E for negligent misrepresentation and breach of warranty (under general principles of contract law). The Court of Appeal HELD: (1) that B was negligent (in tort) as he had not noticed that the towing hitch was defective nor had he ensured that the towing hitch was regularly checked; (2) that D were liable to indemnify B because the damage sustained was a natural consequence of D's breach of warranty under SGA, s.14; (3) that D could not recover damages from E (under the law of contract) because the statements in E's literature did not form part of any collateral contract between D and E, nor did D purchase the hitch from the suppliers, X, in reliance on those statements; and (4) D could not recover damages from E (for tort of negligence) because although E had been negligent in producing a defective towing hitch, D had only suffered economic loss (the obligation to indemnify B) not physical injury to person or property as a result of E's negligence. D appealed to the House of Lords against decision (2) above. The House of Lords HELD: that B was not entitled to be indemnified by D, so reversing the Court of Appeal's decision on this point.

(*d*) *Sale by sample.* In the case of a contract for sale by sample there is an implied condition that:

(*i*) the bulk will correspond with the sample in quality;

(*ii*) the buyer will have a reasonable opportunity of comparing the bulk with the sample; and

(*iii*) the goods will be free from defect rendering them unmerchantable, which would not be apparent on reasonable examination of the sample: SGA, s.15.

14. The duty to deliver the right quantity. It is the duty of the seller to deliver the quantity of goods he agreed to sell to the buyer. A stipulated quantity is part of the description of the goods. There is, therefore, an implied condition that the quantity delivered corresponds with the quantity contracted for.

(*a*) *Delivery of too little.* Where the seller delivers to the buyer a quantity of goods less than he contracted to sell, the buyer may reject them, but if the buyer accepts the goods as delivered, he must pay for them at the contract rate: SGA, s.30(1).

(*b*) *Delivery of too much.* Where the seller delivers to the buyer a quantity of goods larger than he contracted to sell, the buyer may accept the goods included in the contract and reject the rest, or he may reject the whole: s.30(2). If the buyer accepts the whole of the goods so delivered, he must pay for them at the contract rate: s.30(3).

(*c*) *Delivery of mixed goods.* Where the seller delivers to the buyer the goods he contracted to sell mixed with goods of a different description, not included in the contract, the buyer may accept the goods which are in accordance with the contract, and reject the rest, or he may reject the whole: s.30(4).

15. The duty to accept the goods. It is the duty of the buyer to accept the goods in accordance with the terms of the contract of sale. The buyer is deemed to have accepted the goods when he intimates to the seller that he has accepted them, or when after the lapse of a reasonable time, he retains the goods without intimating to the seller that he has rejected them: s.35.

NOTE: However, where goods are delivered to the buyer, which he has not previously examined, he is not deemed to have accepted them unless and until he has had a reasonable opportunity of examining them for the purpose of ascertaining whether they are in conformity with the contract: s.34. In *Algemene Oliehandel International BV* v. *Bunge SA* (1978) seventeen days was considered to give the buyers of crude maize oil a reasonable opportunity of examining the oil.

16. The duty to pay the price. It is the duty of the buyer to pay for the goods according to the terms of the contract. The price in a contract of sale may be fixed by the contract, or may be left to be fixed in a manner thereby agreed, or may be determined by the course of dealing between the parties. Where the price cannot be determined in this way, the buyer must pay a reasonable price: s.8.

EXCLUSION OF LIABILITY

17. Implied terms.

(*a*) In the case of a contract for the sale of goods, any term which attempts to exclude the provisions of s.12 of the 1979 Act will be void. The Unfair Contract Terms Act 1977 (UCTA), s.6(1) provides that liability for breach of obligations arising from s.12 cannot be excluded or restricted by reference to any contractual term.

(*b*) As against a person dealing as a consumer, liability for breach of the obligations arising from ss.13, 14 or 15 of the 1979 Act cannot be excluded or restricted by reference to any contract terms: UTCA, s.6(2). As against a person dealing other than as a consumer this liability can be excluded or restricted by reference to a contract term, but only in so far as the term satisfies the requirement of reasonableness: UCTA, s.6(3).

NOTE: *See* also provisions of the Fair Trading Act 1973 in **50**.

18. Express terms. A party to a contract may attempt to exclude by an express term of the contract, any liability arising from, for example, failure to perform the contract or breach of contract. The validity of such an exemption clause is determined by the principles of the law of contract. However, where a party to a contract deals as a consumer or on the other's written standard terms of business, the other party cannot rely on an exemption clause, unless the clause is reasonable, to exclude, restrict, alter or avoid his contractual obligations: UCTA, s.3.

19. Dealing as a consumer. A party to a contract "deals as a consumer" in relation to another party if:

(*a*) he neither makes the contract in the course of a business nor holds himself out as doing so; and

(*b*) the other party does make the contract in the course of a business; and

(*c*) in the case of a contract governed by the law of sale of goods (or hire-purchase or certain other contracts) the goods passing under or in pursuance of the contract are of a type ordinarily supplied for private use or consumption.

It is for those claiming that a party does not deal as a consumer to show that he does not. However, on a sale by auction or by competitive tender the buyer is not in any circumstances to be regarded as dealing as a consumer.

20. The reasonableness test. The contract term must have been a fair and reasonable one having regard to the circumstances which were, or ought reasonably to have been, known or in the contemplation of the parties when the contract was made. The Act provides guidelines for determining what is "reasonable" under s.6. Examples of the factors which should be taken into account are the strength of the bargaining positions of the parties relative to each other, and whether the customer knew or ought reasonably to have known of the existence of the term: s.11.

21. Third parties. The 1977 Act, s.5, provides that liability arising from the sale or supply of goods ordinarily supplied for private use or consumption cannot be excluded by a term of the contract. This section does not apply to the parties to the contract, but to where a third party suffers loss or damage because the goods are defective, or as a result of the negligence of the manufacturer or distributor of the goods. Thus, liability under the tort of negligence cannot be excluded by a manufacturer's guarantee. John buys an opaque bottle of ginger beer for his wife Mary. She drinks the ginger beer before finding the remains of a decomposed snail at the bottom of the bottle. Mary is violently sick and suffers nervous shock as the result of the manufacturer's negligence in failing to ensure that the bottles are thoroughly cleaned before being filled with ginger beer. In this case the manufacturer cannot expressly exclude his liability.

TRANSFER OF OWNERSHIP

22. Transfer of property. The following rules apply as between buyer and seller and must be read subject to **23**. Where there is a contract for the sale of unascertained goods, no property in the goods is transferred to the buyer unless and until the goods are ascertained: SGA, s.16. Unascertained goods are goods of a specified class, but which have not yet become identified as the goods which are to pass under the contract: *Re Wait* (1927).

Otherwise, the general rule is that property passes when the parties intend that it shall pass: for the purpose of ascertaining the intention of the parties, regard will be had to the terms of the contract, the conduct of the parties, and the circumstances of the case: SGA, s.17.

In cases where it is not possible to ascertain the intention of the parties in this way, the rules set out in s.18 should be applied. These are as follows.

Rule 1. Where there is an unconditional contract for the sale of specific goods, in a deliverable state, the property in the goods passes to the buyer when the contract is made, and it is immaterial whether the time of payment or the time of delivery, or both, be postponed.

Rule 2. Where there is a contract for the sale of specific goods and the seller is bound to do something to the goods for the purpose of putting them into a deliverable state, the property does not pass until such things be done and the buyer has notice thereof.

Rule 3. Where there is a contract for the sale of specific goods in a deliverable state, but the seller is bound to weigh, measure, test, or do some other act or thing with reference to the goods for the purpose of ascertaining the price, the property does not pass until such act or thing be done and the buyer has notice thereof.

Rule 4. When goods are delivered to the buyer on approval or "on sale or return" or other similar terms the property therein passes to the buyer:

(*a*) when he signifies his approval or acceptance to the seller or does any other act adopting the transaction;

(*b*) if he does not signify his approval or acceptance to the seller but retains the goods without giving notice of rejection, then, if no time has been fixed for the return of the goods, on the expiration of a reasonable time. What is a reasonable time is a question of fact.

Rule 5. (1) Where there is a contract for the sale of unascertained or future goods by description, and goods of that description and in a deliverable state are unconditionally appropriated to the contract, either by the seller with the assent of the buyer, or by the buyer with the assent of the seller, the property in the goods thereupon passes to the buyer. Such assent may be expressed or implied, and may be given either before or after the appropriation is made.

(2) Where in pursuance of the contract, the seller delivers the goods to the buyer or to a carrier or other bailee (whether named by the buyer or not) for the purpose of transmission to the buyer, and does not reserve the right of disposal, he is deemed to have unconditionally appropriated the goods to the contract.

NOTE: *The passing of risk.* Unless otherwise agreed, the goods remain at the seller's risk until the property therein is transferred to the buyer, but when the property therein is transferred to the buyer, the goods are at the buyer's risk: s.20. However, if delivery is delayed through the fault of one party the goods are at risk of that party if there is loss which would not otherwise have occurred, and liability can still exist as a bailee of the goods of the other party.

23. Transfer of title. Title to goods is the right of ownership with respect to them. It is possible to include a reservation of title clause in the contract of sale. This is most likely to be found where payment for the goods is subsequent to delivery and means that the seller has the right to the goods if the buyer fails to pay for them (*see* **24**). As to the passing of title from seller to buyer, the general rule is that where goods are sold by a person who is not the owner thereof, the buyer acquires no better title to the goods than the seller had: s.21. This principle is often expressed by the use of the maxim *nemo dat quod non habet.*

EXCEPTIONS:

(1) *Sale by agent.* Where goods are sold by a person who is not the owner thereof, and who sells them under the authority or with the consent of the owner, the buyer acquires good title to the goods: s.21.

(2) *Sale by estoppel.* Where the original owner by his statements or conduct leads the innocent purchaser to believe that the

unauthorised seller in fact has the right to sell the goods, the owner is precluded from denying the seller's authority to sell and the buyer acquires a good title to the goods: *Henderson & Co.* v. *Williams* (1895). (However, this rule is rarely applied: *see Central Newbury Car Auctions* v. *Unity Finance Ltd.* (1957).) In *Moorgate Mercantile Co. Ltd.* v. *Twitchings* (1976) a finance company, owners of a car, were not estopped from recovering the car from a third party who had searched at H.P. Information and found no evidence of the car being the subject of a hire-purchase agreement. Lord Edmund Davies in the House of Lords considered that there was no legal duty on the owner not to be careless, in this case by failing to register the hire-purchase agreement.

(3) *Sale under statutory provisions.* This enables the apparent owner of goods to dispose of them as if he were the true owner thereof. For example: (*a*) Sale by mercantile agent without authority. Where a mercantile agent is, with the consent of the owner, in possession of goods or of the documents of title to goods, any sale or other disposition of the goods, made by him when acting in the ordinary course of business of a mercantile agent will be as valid as if he were expressly authorised by the owner to make the same: Factors Act 1889, s. 2. (*b*) Sale by the possessor (debtor) of a motor vehicle bailed under a hire-purchase agreement. Where the debtor disposes of the vehicle, before the property in the vehicle has become vested in him, to a private purchaser that disposition will have effect as if the creditor's title to the vehicle had been vested in the debtor immediately before that disposition. This will also be the case where the debtor similarly disposes of the vehicle to a trade or finance purchaser, if the person who is the first private purchaser of the motor vehicle after that disposition is a purchaser of the vehicle in good faith without notice of the relevant agreement. In *Stevenson* v. *Beverley Bentinck* (1976) the Court of Appeal held that the protection afforded to a private purchaser would not apply to a person who in his spare time carried on the business of a car dealer, even though he was employed full-time in another job, and the car in question was for his own private use. The Act is concerned with the status and not the capacity of the purchaser.

(4) *Sale in market overt.* Where goods are sold in market overt, according to the usage of the market, the buyer acquires good title to the goods, provided he buys them in good faith and without notice of any defect or want of title on the part of the seller: s.22(1). Market overt occurs in all shops in the City of

London, and in all markets where the usage is established. A sale in a shop in the City of London is deemed to be a sale in market overt when (*a*) the sale takes place in business hours on a business day between sunrise and sunset (*Reid* v. *Metropolitan Police Commissioner* (1973); (*b*) the entire transaction takes place in the part of the shop which is open to the public; (*c*) the goods are of a class usually sold in that shop; and (*d*) the shopkeeper is the seller, i.e. he must not be the buyer.

(5) *Sale under a voidable title.* When the seller of goods has a voidable title thereto, but his title has not been avoided at the time of the sale, the buyer acquires a good title to the goods, provided he buys them in good faith and without notice of the seller's defect of title: s.23. The same rule applies where there is any other kind of disposition of goods under a voidable title, e.g. where goods are pawned.

(6) *Seller in possession after the sale.* Where a person having sold goods continues or is in possession of the goods or of the documents of title to the goods, the delivery or transfer by that person, or by a mercantile agent acting for him, of the goods and/or documents of title under any sale, pledge or other disposition thereof, to any person receiving the same in good faith and without notice of the previous sale, will have the same effect as if the person making the delivery or transfer were expressly authorised by the owner of the goods to make the same: s.24. According to this rule, if X sells goods to Y, so that Y has the property in the goods but the actual possession is retained by X, and X sells and delivers the same goods to Z, who takes them in good faith, Z gets good title. Y will be left with an action for damages against X, for he cannot recover the goods from Z.

(7) *Buyer in possession after the sale.* Where a person having bought or agreed to buy goods obtains, with the consent of the seller, possession of the goods or the documents of title to the goods, the delivery or transfer by that person, or a mercantile agent acting for him, of the goods or documents of title, under any sale, pledge, or other disposition thereof, to any person receiving the same in good faith and without notice of any lien or other right of the original seller in respect of the goods, will have the same effect as if the person making the delivery or transfer were a mercantile agent in possession of the goods or documents of title with the consent of the owner: s.25(1). In *Worcester Works Finance Co. Ltd.* v. *Cooden Engineering Co. Ltd.* (1972) A sold a car to B who sold it to C. A took possession of the car after B's cheque was not honoured, and while B was

selling the car to C. The court held that the retaking of the car by A constituted a delivery of the car by B under a disposition and so A had an interest under s.25(1).

RIGHTS OF UNPAID SELLER AGAINST THE GOODS

24. Unpaid seller's rights. Notwithstanding that the property in the goods may have passed to the buyer, the unpaid seller of goods, as such, has by implication of law the following rights.

(*a*) A lien on goods for the price while he is in possession of them.
(*b*) In case of the insolvency of the buyer, a right of stopping the goods in transit after he has parted with possession of them.
(*c*) A right of resale: s.39(1).

If the contract of sale includes a reservation of title clause, then where the buyer fails to pay for the goods the seller may be entitled to recover the goods not just from the buyer but also from subsequent purchasers. (*See Aluminium Industrie Vaassen BV* v. *Romalpa Aluminium Ltd.* (1976).)
Where property in goods has not passed to the buyer, the unpaid seller has also a right of withholding delivery similar to and co-extensive with his rights of lien and stoppage in transit where the property has passed to the buyer.

25. Unpaid seller's lien. The unpaid seller of goods who is in possession of them is entitled to retain possession of them until payment or tender of the price in the following cases, namely:

(*a*) where the goods have been sold without any stipulation as to credit;
(*b*) where the goods have been sold on credit, but the term of credit has expired;
(*c*) where the buyer becomes insolvent: s.41.

NOTE: The seller loses his lien (1) when he delivers the goods to a carrier or other bailee for the purpose of transmission to the buyer without reserving the right of disposal of the goods; or (2) when the buyer or his agent lawfully obtains possession of the goods; (3) by waiver: s.43(1). Also, the seller ceases to have a right of lien when the price is paid or tendered.

26. Stoppage in transit. When the buyer of goods becomes insolvent, the unpaid seller who has parted with the possession of the goods has the right of stopping them in transit, that is to say, he may resume possession of the goods so long as they are in the course of transit, and may retain them until payment or tender of the price: s.44.

NOTE: (1) *Documents of title.* The right of stoppages will be defeated by the prior right of a person to whom the buyer transferred documents of title relating to the goods, provided they were received in good faith and for value: ss.47 and 25(1).

(2) *Duration of transit.* Goods are deemed to be in course of transit from the time when they are delivered to a carrier or other bailee for the purpose of transmission to the buyer, until the buyer or his agent takes delivery of them from such carrier or other bailee: s.45. There is no right of stoppage after transit is at an end.

(3) *How stoppage is effected.* The unpaid seller may exercise his right of stoppage in transit either: (*a*) by taking actual possession of the goods, or (*b*) by giving notice of his claim to the carrier or other bailee in whose possession the goods are: s.46(1).

27. Right of resale. An unpaid seller's right to resale may arise either from an express contractual reservation, or from the provisions of the Sale of Goods Act 1979, or from the common law generally.

(*a*) *Express reservation.* Where the seller expressly reserves a right of resale in case the buyer should make default, the seller may resell the goods. Where the seller exercises this right, the original contract is rescinded but he is not deprived of any claim for damages he may have against the original buyer: s.48(4).

(*b*) *Statutory right of resale.* The Act provides that an unpaid seller may resell the goods:

(*i*) where the goods are of a perishable nature; or

(*ii*) where the unpaid seller gives notice to the buyer of his intention to resell, and the buyer does not, within a reasonable time, pay or tender the price: s.48(3).

Where the seller exercises his statutory right of resale, the original contract is rescinded because the seller has put it out of his power to perform his contract: *R. V. Ward* v. *Bignall* (1967).

(*c*) *Resale at common law.* Where the buyer has repudiated the contract of sale, the unpaid seller may have a right of resale. This right arises because a repudiation by one party has the effect of allowing the other party to elect to treat himself as discharged from further liability.

SELLER'S PERSONAL REMEDIES

28. Seller's remedies. Where the buyer is in breach of contract, the seller may bring either:

(*a*) an action for the price of the goods, or
(*b*) an action for damages for non-acceptance,
according to the nature of the breach.

29. Action for the price. The seller's right to action arises in either of the following circumstances.

(*a*) Where, under a contract of sale, the property in the goods has passed to the buyer, and the buyer wrongfully neglects or refuses to pay for the goods according to the terms of the contract.
(*b*) Where, under a contract of sale, the price is payable on a certain day irrespective of delivery, and the buyer wrongfully neglects or refuses to pay such price: s.49.

30. Ascertainment of price. The price of goods may be:

(*a*) fixed by the contract; or
(*b*) left to be fixed in a manner agreed between the parties; or
(*c*) determined by the course of dealing between the parties; or
(*d*) a reasonable price, which is payable:
(*i*) when the price is not fixed by the contract, or in a manner agreed between the parties; or
(*ii*) where there is an agreement to sell at a valuation, and no valuation is made, and the goods have been delivered to, and appropriated by, the buyer: ss.8 and 9.

31. Damages for non-acceptance. Where the buyer wrongfully neglects or refuses to accept and pay for the goods, the seller may maintain an action against him for damages for non-acceptance: s.50(1). The measure of damages for non-acceptance is:

(*a*) the estimated loss directly and naturally resulting, in the ordinary course of events, from the buyer's breach of contract: s.50(2); and
(*b*) any further loss due to special circumstances outside the ordinary course of events, but which the buyer had knowledge of, actual or imputed: s.54 (*see also Victoria Laundry Ltd.* v. *Newman Industries Ltd.* (1949)).

NOTE: The seller should take reasonable steps to mitigate the loss. Usually he will sell the goods to a third person.

32. The prima facie rule. Where there is an available market for the goods in question, the measure of damages is, prima facie, to be ascertained by the difference between the contract price, and the market or current price at the time or times when the goods ought to have been accepted or, if no time was fixed for acceptance, then at the time of refusal to accept: s.50(3). This means that the seller should sell the goods for what he can get and then claim for damages to recover the difference between the market price and the contract price. The court may disregard this rule wherever it would not produce a just result: *W. L. Thompson Ltd.* v. *R. Robinson (Gunmakers) Ltd.* (1955).

Campbell Mostyn v. *Barnett* (1954): The buyer agreed to buy 500 tons of tinned ham, and when the seller attempted to deliver 350 tons, the buyer refused to accept. The seller then resold the 350 tons at a price higher than the original contract price. But at the date of the original buyer's refusal to accept delivery, the market price was below the contract price. The seller brought the action against the buyer for damages for non-acceptance. HELD: the measure of damages should be the difference between the contract price and the market price at the time of the refusal to accept. The subsequent rising of the market price was immaterial.

Charter v. *Sullivan* (1957): The buyer agreed to buy a Hillman "Minx" motor car, and later wrote to the seller telling him that he no longer intended to complete the sale. A few days later, the seller sold the car to another buyer, for at the time he could sell all Hillman "Minx" cars he could get. HELD: the seller was entitled to nominal damages only.

Lazenby Garages v. *Wright* (1976): The plaintiff was a dealer in second-hand cars. He purchased a second-hand BMW 2002 on 14th February 1974 for £1,325. On 19th February the defendant agreed to purchase the car from the plaintiff for £1,670. The car was to be delivered on 1st March, but on 20th February the defendant repudiated the contract in full. The plaintiff resold the car on 23rd April for £1,770, but brought an action for breach of contract claiming damages calculated as representing the difference between the amount the plaintiff had paid for the car and what the defendant had agreed to pay. The Court of Appeal held that second-hand cars are by their nature unique and the appropriate test for assessing damages was what would reasonably have been expected to have been in the contemplation of the parties as a natural consequence of the breach. The defendant could not have contemplated that the plaintiff would sell one car less out of a total of second-hand car sales. Since the plaintiff sold the car for more than the price agreed with the defendant, they suffered no loss, and the defendant's appeal was allowed. (*W. L. Thompson Ltd.* v. *R. Robinson (Gunmakers) Ltd.* (1955) was distinguished.)

BUYER'S PERSONAL REMEDIES

33. Buyer's remedies. Where the seller is in breach of contract, one or more of a number of remedies may be available to the buyer. The remedies are as follows.

(*a*) An action for damages for non-delivery.
(*b*) Rejecting the goods and treating the contract as repudiated.
(*c*) An action for damages for breach of warranty.
(*d*) Setting up breach of warranty as a defence to an action for the price.
(*e*) An action for money paid on a consideration which has wholly failed.
(*f*) An action for specific performance.

The remedies available in any case will depend upon the circumstances.

34. Damages for non-delivery. Where the seller wrongfully neglects or refuses to deliver the goods to the buyer, the buyer may maintain an action against the seller for damages for the non-delivery: s.51(1). The measure of damages for non-delivery is:

(*a*) the estimated loss directly and naturally resulting, in the ordinary course of events, from the seller's breach of contract: s.51(2); and
(*b*) any further loss due to special circumstances outside the ordinary course of events, of which the seller had knowledge, actual or imputed: s.54 and *Victoria Laundry Ltd.* v. *Newman Industries Ltd.* (1949).

NOTE: *Mitigation of loss.* The buyer should take reasonable steps to mitigate the loss. Generally, this means that he should buy similar goods from a third person.

35. The prima facie rule. Where there is an available market for the goods in question, the measure of damages is, prima facie, to be ascertained by the difference between the contract price and the market or current price of the goods at the time or times when they ought to have been delivered, or, if no time was fixed, at the time of refusal to deliver: s.51(3). This means that the buyer should buy similar goods at the current price obtaining, and claim damages to recover the difference between the current price and the contract price. This is a prima facie rule, and the court may disregard it where it so wishes.

36. Right to treat the contract as repudiated. Where the seller is in breach of a condition, express or implied, the buyer may reject the goods and treat the contract as repudiated: s.11.

NOTE: (1) The Act does not define "condition". But a condition is generally regarded as being a term of contract which is identified with the main purpose of the contract. "Warranty" is defined in s.61(1) as being collateral to the main purpose of a contract.

(2) The buyer loses the right of rejection where the contract is not severable and he has accepted the goods, or part of them. By s.35 the buyer is deemed to have accepted the goods when he intimates to the seller that he has accepted them, or, except where s.34 applied (buyer's right of examining the goods), when the goods have been delivered to him, and he does any act in relation to them which is inconsistent with the ownership of the seller, or when, after the lapse of a reasonable time, he retains the goods without intimating to the seller that he has rejected them.

37. Damages for breach of warranty. Where there is a breach of warranty by the seller, or where the buyer elects, or is compelled, to treat any breach of condition on the part of the seller, as a breach of warranty, the buyer may maintain an action for damages for the breach of warranty: s.53. The buyer is not entitled to reject the goods.

NOTE: (1) *Definition.* Warranty means an agreement with reference to goods which are the subject of a contract of sale, but collateral to the main purpose of such contract. But whether a term in a contract of sale is a condition or a warranty depends in each case on the construction of the contract.

(2) *Breach of warranty ex post facto.* The buyer may elect to treat the seller's breach of condition as a breach of warranty, i.e. he may waive his right to treat the contract as repudiated, accept delivery of goods, and bring an action for damages for breach

of warranty *ex post facto*. In addition, where a contract of sale is not severable, and the buyer has accepted the goods, or part of them, the breach of any condition by the seller can only be treated as a breach of warranty, and not as a ground for rejecting the goods and treating the contract as repudiated, unless there is a term of the contract to that effect.

(3) *Measure of damages*. The measure of damages for breach of warranty is:

(*a*) the estimated loss directly and naturally resulting in the ordinary course of events, from the breach of warranty: s.53(2); and

(*b*) any further loss due to special circumstances outside the ordinary course of events, of which the seller had knowledge, actual or imputed: s.54 and *Victoria Laundry Ltd.* v. *Newman Industries Ltd.* (1949).

Jackson v. *Chrysler Acceptances; Minories Garages (Third Party)* (1978): A garage sold a car to the plaintiff on hire-purchase. The car was not of merchantable quality (*see* **13**(*b*)). The Court of Appeal stated that for the purpose of assessing damages, regard should be had to what would have been the market value of the car at the time of contracting, if the defects had been known. Thus the damages were the difference between the actual price paid for the car and this market value.

AUCTION SALES

38. The fall of the hammer. A sale by auction is complete when the auctioneer announces its completion by the fall of the hammer, or in other customary manner. Until such announcement is made, any bidder may retract his bid: s.57(2).

39. Seller's right to bid. A right to bid may be expressly reserved by or on behalf of the seller. Where a right to bid is expressly reserved, but not otherwise, the seller, or any *one* person on his behalf, may bid at the auction: s.57.

40. Reserve price. A sale by auction may be notified to be subject to a reserve price: s.57(3). Where there is such notification, every bid is a "conditional offer subject to its being up to the reserve price" and where an auctioneer inadvertently knocks down to a bidder who has bid less than the reserve price, there is no contract of sale: *McManus* v. *Fortescue* (1907).

41. Illegal bidding agreement. A knockout, i.e. an agreement by which an intending bidder undertakes to abstain from bidding, is not illegal at common law, but the position was altered by the Auctions (Bidding Agreements) Acts 1927 and 1969 which provide that:

(*a*) where a person who buys goods at an auction has been a party to an agreement between potential bidders not to bid for the goods, and one of the parties to the agreement was a dealer, then the seller may avoid the contract under which the goods were sold; and

(*b*) the dealer is guilty of a criminal offence.

42. Mock auctions. It is a criminal offence to promote or conduct a mock auction at which one or more lots are offered for sale: Mock Auctions Act 1961. A mock auction is one where either the bidder pays less for the article than his highest bid, or the right to bid is restricted to persons who have bought or agree to buy one or more articles, or where any articles are given away. However, the Act only applies to "auctions" of certain prescribed articles, e.g. household articles, or numerical and scientific instruments or apparatus.

INTERNATIONAL TRADING CONTRACTS

43. Commercial practice. The English courts are frequently required to adjudicate on international contracts for the sale of goods. These contracts are often based on standard forms commonly used by the international trading community. Such forms include standard terms and conditions, the most usual of which are discussed below. It should also be noted that these contracts sometimes include a term which states that any disputes between the parties should be referred to arbitration (*see* VI).

The expressions c.i.f. (cost, insurance, freight), f.o.b. (free on board) and f.a.s. (free alongside ship) are generally used in commerce, and are useful in that they give a general indication of the terms of the contracts they describe. The expressions do not, however, indicate with precision the details of the contract. In order to avoid confusion, many traders make use of "incoterms 1953" which are standardised interpretations of these expressions.

44. C.i.f. contracts. The duties of the parties under a c.i.f. contract are usually as follows.

(*a*) *Seller's duties*

(*i*) To obtain any export licence required.

(*ii*) To arrange for the carriage of the goods to the port of destination and to pay the freight charges.

(*iii*) To arrange the loading of the goods at the port of shipment.

(*iv*) To procure a policy in insurance to cover the goods during transit for the benefit of the buyer.

(*v*) To furnish the buyer with a bill of lading, the invoice of the goods, and the insurance policy.

(*b*) *Buyer's duties.*

(*i*) To pay the contract price on delivery of the documents.

(*ii*) To pay all unloading, lighterage and wharfage charges at the port of destination.

(*iii*) To pay all customs and import duties.

45. F.o.b. contracts. The duties of the parties under an f.o.b. contract are usually as follows.

(*a*) *Seller's duties.*

(*i*) To deliver the goods on board the ship named by the buyer.

(*ii*) To notify the buyer immediately the goods have been delivered on board.

(*b*) *Buyer's duties.*

(*i*) To arrange for the contract of affreightment.

(*ii*) To give the seller sufficient notice of the name of the ship, its loading berth, and the time for delivery to the ship.

(*iii*) To pay all charges and to bear all risks from the time the goods have passed the ship's rail.

46. F.a.s. contract. The duties of the parties under an f.a.s. contract are usually as follows.

(*a*) *Seller's duties.*

(*i*) To deliver the goods alongside the ship.

(*ii*) To notify the buyer immediately the goods have been delivered alongside.

(*b*) *Buyer's duties.*

(*i*) To arrange for the contract of affreightment.

(*ii*) To give the seller sufficient notice of the name of the ship, its loading berth, and the time for delivery alongside.

(*iii*) To pay all charges and to bear all risks from the time the goods are delivered alongside.

47. International sales. The Uniform Laws on International Sales Act 1967 incorporates into the law of the United Kingdom the uniform laws on the international sale of goods which govern the obligations of the seller and buyer arising from a contract of sale, but only to the extent that the parties have chosen it as the law applicable to their contract.

DIRECTOR GENERAL OF FAIR TRADING

48. Functions. The Fair Trading Act 1973 provided for the appointment of a Director General of Fair Trading who was given responsibility for the administration and enforcement of laws designed to foster competition, and a variety of functions related to the protection of consumers. The Office of Fair Trading was also established in 1973 and it operates in the following four main areas:

(*a*) consumer affairs;
(*b*) consumer credit (*see* V);
(*c*) monopolies and mergers;
(*d*) restrictive trade practices (*see* VII).

The Director General is required to submit to the Secretary of State annual reports on his activities which provide a detailed account of the work done by the Office of Fair Trading.

49. Consumer affairs. The Director General is closely concerned with consumer protection. His powers and duties include the following.

(*a*) Proposing new laws to end unfair trading practices. The Director General makes a reference to the Consumer Protection Advisory Committee (CPAC) asking them to consider the undesirable effects of a particular trading practice. These references are released to the national press together with details of the particular practice. The CPAC must usually report to the Secretary of State within three months of the reference. If they agree with the Director General's proposals, or make modified proposals, the Secretary of State can give them legal effect by an Order approved by Parliament. Any breach of the Order would make a person liable to criminal proceedings, which on conviction would be punishable by a fine or imprisonment, or both. An example of such an order is the Consumer Transactions (Restrictions on Statements) Order 1976 which, *inter alia*, makes it a criminal offence for a shop to put up a notice purporting to deprive a customer of his legal rights, e.g. credit given where goods are unsatisfactory, but no cash refund. A recent example which has caused some difficulty in interpretation is the Price Marking (Bargain Offers) Order 1979 as amended.

(*b*) Dealing with manufacturers and traders who persistently commit criminal offences or breach their civil obligations to the detriment of the public.

(*c*) Encouraging trade organisations to produce codes of practice for members to follow when dealing with consumers. Codes of practice have been drawn up to apply to the sale of shoes, cars and electrical goods.

(*d*) Publishing information and advice for consumers. Such information and advice is usually available from the Office of Fair Trading, Citizens Advice Bureaux and local Trading Standards or Consumer Protection departments.

50. Unfair trading. Part III of the Fair Trading Act 1973 gives the Director General additional functions for the protection of consumers. Where a manufacturer or trader persistently commits criminal offences, e.g. under the trade descriptions legislation, or breaches civil obligations, e.g. implied terms (*see* **13**), then the Director General can ask the manufacturer or trader to give a written assurance that he will refrain from continuing this course of conduct. If the manufacturer or trader refuses to give such an assurance, or fails to comply with its terms, legal proceedings can be brought which may lead to a court order forbidding him to continue this conduct. Any breach of that order would be a contempt of court, and could result in a fine or a prison sentence.

The Consumer Affairs Division of the Office of Fair Trading maintains a central register of convictions under consumer legislation, including offences under the Trade Descriptions Acts.

PROGRESS TEST 4

1. Define a contract of sale of goods. **(4, 8)**
2. Distinguish between (*a*) a contract of sale of goods, (*b*) an agreement to sell, (*c*) a conditional sale agreement, (*d*) a credit sale agreement, and (*e*) a contract for work and materials. **(5, 6, 10)**
3. What is the effect on a contract of sale of goods if the goods perish? **(9)**
4. What are the duties of a seller under a contract of sale of goods? **(11–14)**
5. Examine the implied duties of a seller under the Sale of Goods Act 1979, using cases to illustrate these duties. **(13)**

6. What are the duties of a buyer under a contract of sale of goods? **(15, 16)**

7. Consider whether and in what circumstances it is possible for a seller to exclude his liability under these implied terms and duties. **(17–20)**

8. Summarise the law relating to the transfer of ownership of goods under a contract of sale. **(22, 23)**

9. The general rule is that where goods are sold by a person who is not the owner of them the buyer acquires no better title than the seller had (*nemo dat quod non habet*). State seven exceptions to this general rule. **(23)**

10. Explain the rights of the unpaid seller against the goods. **(24–27)**

11. In what circumstances may a seller sue the buyer for the price of the goods? How is the price ascertained? **(29, 30)**

12. In what circumstances may a seller sue the buyer for damages? What is the measure of damages? **(31, 32)**

13. List the remedies available to the buyer in the event of the seller's breach. Explain how damages are assessed. Mention the circumstances in which the buyer may treat the contract as repudiated, and accordingly reject the goods. **(33–37)**

14. What special rules are applicable to sales of goods by auction? **(38–42, 19)**

15. Outline the duties of the parties under c.i.f., f.o.b. and f.a.s. contracts. **(44–46)**

16. What are the functions of the Director General of Fair Trading? **(48)**

17. What impact does the work of the Office of Fair Trading have on contracts of sale of goods? **(49, 50)**

CHAPTER V

Hire-Purchase and Consumer Credit

INTRODUCTION

1. Consumer Credit Act 1974. This Act is the most far-reaching reform of consumer credit law ever carried out in the United Kingdom. The Act establishes for the protection of the consumer a new system of credit control administered by the Director General of Fair Trading. It is replacing the previous legislation relating to hire-purchase, moneylending and pawnbroking. For the first time similar rules will apply to all kinds of credit and hire transactions. The Act is mainly concerned with credit or hire transactions of individuals, including sole traders and partnerships but not limited companies, where the credit provided does not exceed the value of £5,000. The monetary limit is to be increased to £15,000 from 20th May 1985. The hire-purchase provisions have not yet come into force (hire-purchase transactions are still governed by the common law, or the Hire-Purchase Act 1965) but when they do on 19th May 1985, hire-purchase will be one of the most common forms of consumer credit transactions. Other examples of such transactions are bank loans and the use of credit card facilities.

HIRE-PURCHASE AT COMMON LAW

2. The nature of hire-purchase. A contract of hire-purchase is a bailment of goods coupled with an option to purchase. The option to purchase may or may not be exercised, and there is no contract of sale unless and until the option is exercised. The hirer is not a person who has agreed to buy goods and the Sale of Goods Act 1979 does not apply: thus the hirer cannot pass title to a third party under s.25 (but *see* IV **23**, exception (3)(*b*)). Moreover, in case of bankruptcy of the hirer, the owner can recover the goods

3. The parties. The parties to a contract of hire-purchase are:

(*a*) *the owner*, who undertakes to let out the goods on hire with an option to purchase when all payments have been made; and (*b*) *the hirer*, who undertakes to pay the hire-purchase charges according to the agreement.

The usual commercial procedure is for the dealer to sell the goods to a finance company which then enters the hire-purchase agreement with the customer. The financing company is the owner of the goods and the customer is the hirer. The dealer or shopkeeper is not usually a party to any contract with the hirer at common law, and therefore he cannot be sued for breach of the implied terms (*see* IV, **13**): *Drury* v. *Buckland* (1941). However, the dealer may be liable in negligence, and under a collateral contract: *Andrews* v. *Hopkinson* (1957).

4. The dealer as agent. Disputes have occurred as to the extent of the authority of the dealer as agent of the finance company. The position is often complicated by the insertion in the contract of hire-purchase of a clause to the effect that the dealer is *not* an agent of the company.

In *Financings Ltd.* v. *Stimson* (1962), Lord Denning MR said that "if we take, as we should, a realistic view of the position, the dealer is in many respects, and for many purposes, the agent of the finance company. I am aware, of course, that the finance companies often put clauses into their forms in which they say that the dealer is not their agent. But these clauses are often not worth the paper they are written on. Nobody can make an assertion of that kind in an agreement so as to bind the courts if it is contrary to the facts of the case."

The agency of the dealer must be decided on the facts of each case. (But where the contract of hire-purchase is governed by statute the dealer is deemed to be an agent of the owner: *see* **10**.)

HIRE-PURCHASE ACT 1965

5. The purpose of the Act. The Act of 1965, which consolidates previous enactments, is designed to protect the interests of a hirer under a hire-purchase agreement and the buyer under a credit-sale agreement. The Act applies to:

(*a*) hire-purchase agreements,
(*b*) conditional sale agreements, and
(*c*) credit sale agreements,

under which the hire-purchase price, or total purchase price as the case may be, does not exceed £7,500. The Act does not apply to contracts in which the hirer or buyer is a body corporate.

6. The agreements defined. For the purposes of the Act, the agreements covered are defined as follows.

(*a*) *Hire-purchase agreement* means an agreement for the bailment of goods under which the bailee may buy the goods or under which the property in the goods will or may pass to the bailee.

(*b*) *Conditional sale agreement* means an agreement for the sale of goods under which:

(*i*) the purchase price is payable by instalments, and

(*ii*) the property in the goods is to remain in the seller (notwithstanding that the buyer is to be in possession of the goods) until such conditions as to the payment of instalments or otherwise as may be specified in the agreement are fulfilled.

(*c*) *Credit sale agreement* means an agreement for the sale of goods, not being a conditional sale agreement, under which the purchase price exceeds £30 and is payable by five or more instalments.

These will be examples of regulated agreements under the Consumer Credit Act 1974 (*see* **16**). It should be noted that the 1974 Act provides its own definitions of these transactions (*see* (*a*), (*b*) below) but the definition of a conditional sale agreement remains the same.

(*a*) "*Hire-purchase agreement*" means an agreement, other than a conditional sale agreement, under which goods are bailed in return for periodical payments by the person to whom they are bailed and the property in those goods will pass to that person if the terms of the agreement are complied with and one or more of the following occurs:

(*i*) the exercise of an option to purchase by that person,

(*ii*) the doing of any other specified act by any party to the agreement,

(*iii*) the happening of any other specified event.

(*b*) "*Credit sale agreement*" means an agreement for the sale of goods, under which the purchase price or part of it is payable by instalments, but which is not a conditional sale agreement, e.g. the property in the goods passes to the buyer.

7. Statutory requirements: hire-purchase and conditional sales. The Act provides as follows.

(*a*) *Statement of cash price.* Before any hire-purchase agreement (or conditional sale agreement) is entered into, the owner (or the seller) must state in writing the cash price. It is sufficient if the hirer (or buyer) has seen the cash price on a price ticket or in a catalogue.

(*b*) *Written agreement.* A hire-purchase agreement (or conditional sale agreement) is unenforceable by the owner (or seller) unless the agreement is signed by the hirer (or buyer) and by or on behalf of all other parties. The agreement must contain:

(*i*) a statement of the hire-purchase price (or total purchase price) and the cash price and the amount of each instalment and when payable,

(*ii*) a list of the goods,

(*iii*) a copy of the statutory notice setting out the hirer's (or buyer's) rights under the contract.

Failure to comply with the statutory requirements means that the owner (seller) is not entitled to enforce the agreement. This means that the owner cannot enforce any contract of guarantee relevant to the agreement, any security given by the hirer or buyer, and any right to recover the goods from the hirer or buyer. The court has a limited discretion to dispense with the statutory requirements, where failure to comply with them has not prejudiced the hirer or buyer.

8. Statutory requirements: credit sales. The Act provides as follows.

(*a*) *Statement of cash price.* Before making any credit-sale agreement the seller must state in writing to the prospective buyer the cash price of the goods. It is sufficient if the buyer has seen the cash price on a price ticket or in a catalogue.

(*b*) *Written agreement.* A credit sale agreement is not enforceable by the seller unless the agreement is signed by the buyer and by or on behalf of the seller.

Failure to comply with the statutory requirements means that the seller is not entitled to enforce the agreement. This means that the seller cannot enforce any contract of guarantee relevant to the agreement, and any security given by the buyer. As in **7** the court has a limited discretion with these requirements.

9. The right of cancellation. Where a person signs a hire-purchase agreement, a conditional sale agreement, or a credit sale agreement and the document is signed at a place other than appropriate trade premises, a right to serve notice of cancellation arises in favour of the hirer or buyer. Notice of cancellation operates to rescind the agreement, which is then deemed never to have had effect.

NOTE: (1) *Appropriate trade premises* means premises at which either the owner or seller normally carries on a business, or goods of the description to which the agreement relates are normally offered for sale in the course of a business carried on at these premises.

(2) *Time limit.* The right of cancellation may be exercised at any time between signing the agreement and the end of the period of four days beginning with the day on which the hirer (or buyer) receives the second statutory copy of the agreement.

10. The dealer as agent. The 1965 Act has clarified the position of the dealer as agent (*see* **4**). The Act provides that where a dealer makes any representation to the hirer (or buyer) with respect to goods to which a hire-purchase, conditional sale or credit sale agreement relates, such representations will be deemed to have been made with him as agent of the owner or seller. It is provided that representations include any statement or undertaking whether constituting a condition or warranty or not. The dealer is also deemed to be an agent for the purpose of receiving notice of cancellation.

11. Implied terms. The Supply of Goods (Implied Terms) Act 1973, ss.8–12 applied the implied terms of the Sale of Goods Act 1893 (now 1979) to transactions governed by the Hire-Purchase Act 1965, and hire-purchase at common law (*see* IV, **13** and **14**). The 1973 Act has been amended in this respect by the Consumer Credit Act 1974, but the provisions are similar subject only to changes in terminology.

12. Right to end the agreement. A hirer is, at any time, entitled to determine the agreement by giving notice of termination in writing to any person entitled, or authorised to receive the sum payable. Where a hirer terminates the agreement, he is liable to pay the amount, if any, by which one-half of the hire-purchase price exceeds the total of the sums paid and the sums due in respect of the hire-purchase price immediately before the termination, or such less amount as may be specified in the agreement.

The buyer under a conditional sale agreement has a similar right to end the agreement (*see* **30**(*i*)).

CONSUMER CREDIT ACT 1974

13. Hire-purchase under the 1974 Act. The Hire-Purchase Act 1965 is to be replaced by the Consumer Credit Act 1974 on 19th May 1985. However, the basic principles will be largely re-enacted and will apply to other consumer credit agreements all of which, including hire-purchase, will be subject to the provisions of the 1974 Act.

14. Provisions of the Act. The Consumer Credit Act 1974 makes provision for the following.

(*a*) A system of control over regulated agreements.
(*b*) The licensing of credit and hire businesses.
(*c*) A public register.
(*d*) Certain rights for consumers.
(*e*) The imposition of certain duties on the Director General of Fair Trading.
(*f*) The enforcement of the Act.

REGULATED AGREEMENTS

15. New concepts. The Consumer Credit Act 1974 introduces the concepts of a "consumer credit agreement" and a "consumer hire agreement". These concepts cover all forms of credit or hire where the amount does not exceed £5,000 (£15,000 from 20th May 1985).

16. Regulated consumer credit agreements. This is an agreement under which credit is provided to an individual where the amount of credit does not exceed £5,000 (£15,000 from 20th May 1985) and the agreement is not an exempt agreement (*see* **17**): s.8. Credit agreements regulated by the Act are divided into two kinds:

(*a*) debtor-creditor-supplier agreements; and
(*b*) debtor-creditor agreements.

NOTE: (1) "*Credit*" includes a cash loan or any other form of financial accommodation including hire-purchase, credit sale and conditional sale agreements.

(2) "*Individual*" includes a partnership or any other unincorporated body of persons not consisting entirely of bodies corporate.

17. Exempt consumer credit agreements. The Act does not regulate consumer credit agreements where the creditor is a local authority, a building society, a body corporate, a charitable organisation or an employers' or workers' organisation. The Secretary of State has power to make orders exempting certain credit agreements from the requirements of the Act. Examples of other exempt credit agreements are as follows.

(*a*) Normal trade credit where payment is made in one instalment or where the credit relates to a particular transaction and payment is required in no more than four instalments. This exemption will not apply to.

(*i*) hire-purchase agreements;
(*ii*) conditional sale agreements;
(*iii*) an agreement secured by an article taken in pawn.

(*b*) Low cost credit.
(*c*) Finance of foreign trade.
(*d*) Land transactions repayable in four instalments or less.
(*e*) Bankers are exempt from most of the formalities required by Part V of the Act, that is ss.55–74, for entry into a credit or hire agreement. They are subject to s.56 (*see* **23**, **24**, **25**(*c*), **30**(*f*) and (*g*)).

18. Debtor-creditor-supplier agreement. This will arise where the creditor is connected in some way with the transaction to be financed by the credit, and can mean that the creditor and the supplier are the same person. If the creditor and the supplier are different people the agreement will be debtor-creditor-supplier only if there are arrangements between them under which the creditor is prepared to finance the transaction between the supplier and the customer: s.12 e.g. hire-purchase agreement.

NOTE: Where the debtor has a claim against the supplier in respect of any misrepresentation or breach of contract, he will have a similar claim against the creditor: s.75. A buys goods from B using C company's finance to pay for them and the goods are defective, if A has a remedy against B he also has a remedy against C.

19. Debtor-creditor agreement. This will arise where there are no arrangements between the creditor and any supplier, e.g. a customer obtains an overdraft from his bank to spend as he wishes: s.13.

20. Regulated consumer hire agreement. This is an agreement made by a person with an individual (the "hirer") for the bailment of goods which:

(*a*) can last for more than three months; and
(*b*) is not a hire-purchase agreement; and
(*c*) does not require the hirer to make payments exceeding £5,000 (£15,000 from 20th May 1985); and
(*d*) is not an exempt agreement: s.15.

21. Exempt consumer hire agreements. These will arise where:

(*a*) the owner is a body corporate authorised by statute to supply electricity, gas or water and the subject of the agreement is a meter or metering equipment; or

(*b*) the owner is the Post Office or the Kingston upon Hull City Council: s.16(6).

22. Variation of agreements. A regulated agreement, whether credit or hire, may provide that the agreement can be varied or supplemented. Where an agreement (a "modifying agreement") varies or supplements an earlier agreement, the modifying agreement shall be treated as:

(*a*) revoking the earlier agreement; and

(*b*) containing provisions reproducing the combined effect of the two agreements.

The old agreement is treated as being revoked and any obligations outstanding under it are treated as outstanding under the new agreement. If the earlier agreement was a regulated agreement, the modifying agreement will usually be treated as a regulated agreement: s.82.

If the creditor or owner has the power to vary a regulated agreement, he has a duty to notify the debtor or hirer.

23. Failure to execute a regulated agreement. Sections 60–63 are concerned with the form and content of a regulated agreement (*see* **30**(*f*)). Section 65 provides that a regulated agreement which is not properly executed is enforceable against the debtor or hirer on an order of the court only. The retaking of goods will be regarded as enforcing the agreement, unless the person in possession of the goods consents to them being taken.

The court should grant an application for an order unless it appears just to do otherwise, bearing in mind the prejudice caused to any person by the contravention in question, the degree of culpability for that contravention, and the powers of the court to vary the agreement and impose conditions on the parties. The court can compensate a debtor or hirer for any prejudice suffered as a result of the contravention.

In the following cases the court must not make an enforcement order of an improperly executed agreement.

(*a*) Where there is no one document containing all the prescribed terms signed by the debtor or hirer.

(*b*) Where there was a failure to supply a copy of the unexecuted agreement as required by s.62, before the commencement of enforcement proceedings.

(*c*) Where there was a failure to supply a copy of the executed agreement as required by s.63, before the commencement of enforcement proceedings.

(*d*) Where there was a failure to give notice of cancellation rights under s.64.

24. Rights of a debtor or hirer under a regulated agreement. The Consumer Credit Act 1974 provides that a debtor or hirer has the following rights under a regulated agreement.

(*a*) Right of withdrawal from a prospective regulated agreement: s.57. This has the same effect as when a regulated agreement is cancelled.

(*b*) Right of cancellation (*see* **30**(*g*)). The effect of cancellation is as follows.

(*i*) Any sum paid by the debtor or hirer is repayable by the person to whom it was paid.

(*ii*) No further sums are payable by the debtor or hirer.

(*iii*) The debtor or hirer has a lien on any goods in his possession for any sum repayable to him.

(*iv*) Where the total charge for credit includes an item in respect of a sum payable to a credit-broker, that sum less £1 is repayable: s.70.

(*v*) Where the debtor has already received the whole or part of the credit, and then cancels the agreement (i.e. before the end of the cooling-off period), except in certain circumstances the agreement remains in force as regards the repayment of credit and the payment of interest. However, if the debtor repays the credit loaned within one month after the cancellation, or before the date on which the first instalment is due, *no* interest is payable on the amount repaid. If the debtor does not repay the loan within this period he must repay the money over the original repayment period, whether he has received part or all of the credit: s.71.

(*vi*) Where the debtor or hirer has already received the goods before the cancellation of the agreement, in most cases the possessor of the goods is under a duty to keep possession of the goods, to take reasonable care of them and to restore the goods to the person from whom he obtained them: s.72.

(*vii*) Where the debtor or hirer gave goods in part-exchange under a regulated agreement which he then cancels, the debtor or hirer is entitled to the return of those goods within ten days of cancellation, or if they are not so returned, to a sum equal to the part-exchange value. Until the goods are returned the debtor or hirer has a lien in respect of goods in his possession under the regulated agreement: s.73.

(*c*) Right to make early payment (*see* **30**(*h*)).

(*d*) Right to end a regulated hire-purchase or conditional-sale agreement (*see* **30**(*i*)).

(*e*) Rights in respect of extortionate credit bargains (*see* **30**(*j*)).

25. Liabilities of a creditor or owner under a regulated agreement. The Consumer Credit Act 1974 provides that a creditor *or* owner will be subject to the following restrictions.

(*a*) The creditor or owner is not entitled to take certain action as a result of any breach by the debtor or hirer of a regulated agreement, unless he first serves a default notice. The action which is so restricted includes terminating the agreement, demanding the early payment of any sum of money, terminating, restricting or deferring any rights conferred on the debtor, or enforcing any security: s.87.

(*b*) The creditor is not entitled to recover possession of goods from a debtor, except on an order of the court, where:

(*i*) the debtor is in breach of a regulated hire-purchase or a regulated conditional sale agreement, and

(*ii*) the debtor has paid to the creditor one-third or more of the total price of the goods, and

(*iii*) the property in the goods remain in the creditor: s.90.

If the creditor does retake in contravention of s.90, the regulated agreement is terminated. This means that the debtor is released from all liability under the agreement and is entitled to recover from the creditor all sums paid by the debtor under the agreement: s.91. The creditor cannot enter property to take possession of goods subject to certain regulated agreements without a court order (*see* **30**(*m*)).

(*c*) The creditor or owner will be liable to the debtor or hirer for any term of the contract and for any misrepresentations made by them in the course of antecedent negotiations. In addition the creditor will be liable for such terms and misrepresentations which have been made by a negotiator, e.g. a supplier, as his agent: s.56 (*see* **10**).

(*d*) Where there is a debtor-creditor-supplier agreement the creditor is jointly liable for any misrepresentation or breach of contract if the supply company is so liable: s.75 (*see* the note to **18**). However, the liability of the creditor does not extend to non-commercial agreements, or to single items which have a cash price of £100 or under, or more than £10,000 (£30,000 from 20th May 1985).

NOTE: Where any sum has been paid by the creditor to the supplier under a debtor-creditor-supplier agreement which is cancelled, the sum should be repaid to the creditor.

(*e*) A term in a regulated agreement is void if it is inconsistent with a provision for the protection of the debtor or hirer contained in the Act or in regulations under the Act: s.173. However, where something may only be done with the order of a court or the Director General, it can be done at the time if the person concerned so consents, e.g. removal of goods (*see* **23**). Refusal of such consent will not give rise to any liability.

(*f*) Schedule 4 of the 1974 Act amends the terminology of ss.8–12 of the Supply of Goods (Implied Terms) Act 1973 which make the creditor, under a hire-purchase agreement, liable to the debtor for a breach of the implied terms under the Sale of Goods Act 1979. (*See* IV, **13** and **14** and note that s.12 has in effect been repealed by the Unfair Contract Terms Act 1977.)

LICENSING PROVISIONS

26. Licensing of credit and hire businesses. All businesses connected with the granting of credit, the hiring of goods, or other ancillary credit activities will need a licence from the Director General of Fair Trading. The business may be a sole trader, a partnership, a limited company or any other corporate or unincorporated association.

A standard licence lasts for ten years.

27. Which businesses need a licence? Section 21 of the Consumer Credit Act 1974 answers this question by stating that a licence is required to carry on a consumer credit business or consumer hire business, but that there are two main exceptions. These are that a local authority does not need a licence to carry on a business and a body corporate empowered by a public general Act naming it to carry on a business does not need a licence to do so.

A licence is required for the following activities.

(*a*) *Consumer credit business.* This is any business so far as it comprises or relates to the provision of credit under regulated consumer credit agreements.

(*b*) *Consumer hire business.* This is any business so far as it comprises or relates to the bailment of goods under regulated consumer hire agreements.

(*c*) *Credit brokerage.* This is the introduction of individuals seeking credit or goods on hire to one or more of the following types of business:

(*i*) consumer credit business;

(*ii*) consumer hire business;

(*iii*) any business which provides credit secured on land (credit up to any amount): s.145(2).

NOTE: (1) It is not credit brokerage to introduce people to sources of credit which are made available under agreements which are covered by the normal trade exemption (*see* **17**(*a*)).

(2) In the case of a business providing credit secured on land (*see* (*iii*) above) which does not fall within (*i*) above, it is credit brokerage only if the client seeks the credit to acquire a dwelling to be occupied by himself or his relative.

(*d*) *Debt adjusting and debt counselling.* The debts must arise under a credit or hire agreement whether regulated or exempt. Debt adjusting consists of:

(*i*) negotiating with the creditor or owner, on behalf of an individual, terms for the discharge of his debt; or

(*ii*) taking over, in return for payment by an individual, his debt; or

(*iii*) any similar activity connected with the liquidation of a debt: s.145(5).

Debt counselling consists of the giving of advice to individuals about the liquidation of their debts: s.145(6).

(*e*) *Debt collecting.* This consists of the taking of steps to procure the payment of debts due under consumer credit agreements or consumer hire agreements: s.145(7).

(*f*) *Credit reference agency.* This is a business comprising the furnishing of persons with information relevant to the financial standing of individuals, being information collected by the agency for that purpose: s.145(8).

NOTE: There is also a group licence which can be issued by the Director General of Fair Trading only if it appears to him that it would be in the public interest to do so. Examples where group licences have been issued are to the Law Society, for solicitors, and to the National Association of Citizens Advice Bureaux (NACAB) for Citizens Advice Bureaux.

For the effect of failure to obtain a licence *see* **34**(*a*), **35**(*a*), (*b*) and (*c*).

28. The fitness test. A licence will be granted on the application of any person if he satisfies the Director General of Fair Trading that:

(*a*) he is a fit person to engage in activities covered by the licence; and
(*b*) the name or names under which he applies to be licensed is or are not misleading or otherwise undesirable.

In determining whether an applicant is such a person, the Director General will have regard to any circumstances appearing to him to be relevant, and in particular any evidence tending to show that the applicant has been concerned with certain breaches of the law or unfair or improper business practices.

An applicant can make representations to the Office of Fair Trading before a licence is refused. There is a right of appeal against the Director General's decision to the Secretary of State for Prices and Consumer Protection, and on points of law to the High Court.

PUBLIC REGISTER

29. The register. The Director General is under a duty to establish and maintain a register which will contain details of:

(*a*) licence applications;
(*b*) licences;
(*c*) revocations, suspensions or variations of licences;
(*d*) other licensing decisions by the Director General under the Act, and the outcome of any appeals from those decisions;
(*e*) various other matters, such as exemptions from certain parts of the Act and orders in respect of agreements by unlicensed traders: s.35.

CONSUMER PROTECTION

30. New rights for consumers. The Act introduces new safeguards and maintains existing protection for consumers (*see also* **24**, **25**). For the purpose of this legislation a consumer is an individual (*see* **16**, note (2)) who is or could be a debtor or hirer in a regulated agreement (*see* **15**). Examples of these rights are as follows.

(*a*) *Advertisements.* These will have to convey a fair and reasonably comprehensive indication of the nature of the credit or hire facilities offered by the advertiser and of their true cost to the person using them: s.44.

Regulations provide more detailed requirements which have to be satisfied by advertisers. Advertisements are divided into three groups, simple, intermediate and full, for which different standards have been set. The format of advertisements is also prescribed. Certain advertisements are exempt from these provisions, e.g. where the credit or hire facilities are solely for the purposes of a person's business.

(*b*) *Canvassing*. It is an offence to canvas debtor-creditor agreements off trade premises: s.49.

(*c*) *Credit-brokers' fees*. Credit-brokers (*see* **27**(*c*)) may charge consumers for their services, but cannot retain more than £3.00 as a fee or commission if the consumer does not enter into an agreement for the credit or hire within six months of the credit-broker's introduction to a prospective source: s.155.

(*d*) *Right to a quotation*. Regulations provide that the consumer is entitled, upon request, to obtain a written quotation setting out the terms on which a creditor, an owner of goods available for hire, or a credit-broker is prepared to do business. Generally, any person offering credit or consumer hire arrangements is obliged to give such a quotation.

(*e*) *Total charge for credit*. Regulations provide that a debtor should be informed of the true cost of the credit, that is the annual percentage rate of charge. The information should be provided in credit advertisements, quotations and written agreements. There are exceptions to this requirement, e.g. it does not apply to a life insurance policy used to repay a loan.

(*f*) *The agreement*. The Secretary of State has made regulations (1983) as to the form and content of regulated agreements and in particular to ensure that the debtor or hirer is aware of:

(*i*) the rights and duties conferred or imposed on him by the agreement,

(*ii*) the amount and the rate of the total charge for credit, and

(*iii*) the protection and remedies available to him under the Acts: s.60.

In addition a regulated agreement is not properly executed unless these requirements and all the terms of the agreement are incorporated into a document which is signed by the debtor/hirer and the creditor/owner. The debtor/hirer will be entitled to receive a copy of the agreement: ss. 60–63 (*see also* **23**). Certain agreements, for example non-commercial ones, are not subject to these regulations. The form and content of guarantees and indemnities given by third parties as security for a regulated agreement are also prescribed by the regulations.

(*g*) *Cooling-off period*. An agreement signed off trade premises will usually be subject to a cooling-off period of five days from the day on which the debtor/hirer received a copy of the agreement or from when he received notice through the post of his right to cancel (where applicable), or in certain cases a cooling-off period of fourteen days following the day on which he signed the agreement: s.68. This allows the consumer to change his mind and cancel the agreement within the prescribed period (*see also* **24**(*a*)). Regulations (1983) also deal with these provisions, and in particular state when it is not necessary for a notice to be sent through the post.

(*h*) *Early payment by the debtor.* The debtor under a regulated consumer credit agreement is entitled at any time to discharge his indebtedness under the agreement: s.94. The Secretary of State is empowered to make regulations (and has done so in 1983), providing for the allowance of a rebate of charges where the debtor exercises his right to complete payments ahead of time: s.95.

(*i*) *Right to terminate.* The debtor under a regulated hire-purchase or regulated conditional sale agreement is entitled to terminate the agreement by giving notice to any person entitled or authorised to receive the sums payable under the agreement: s.99. (This is similar to the provision in the Hire-Purchase Act 1965 (*see* **12**).) The hirer under a regulated consumer hire agreement has similar rights: s.101. Regulations (1983) have prescribed the form and in certain cases the content of the required documents and notices.

(*j*) *Extortionate credit bargains.* If the court finds a credit bargain extortionate it may reopen the credit agreement so as to do justice between the parties. A credit bargain is extortionate if it requires the debtor (or a relative) to make payments which are grossly exorbitant, or if it otherwise grossly contravenes ordinary principles of fair dealing: ss.137–140.

(*k*) *Right to information.* The debtor or hirer is entitled to know the name and address of any credit reference agency which has been consulted as to his creditworthiness: s.157. Where a credit reference agency receives a request in writing, a non-returnable fee of £1.00 and a reasonable amount of information to enable them to identify the file, it must within seven working days of receiving the request give the consumer a copy of the file relating to him kept by the agency: s.158. A consumer can require the agency either to remove or to amend an incorrect and prejudicial entry: s.159. If the applicant is a business consumer, e.g. a sole trader or partnership, then he may only have the right to receive certain information included in or based on entries in the file: s.160. Disputes about the content of a file can be referred to the Director General of Fair Trading for settlement.

(*l*) *Liability of creditor for breaches by supplier* (*see* note to **18** and **25**(*d*)).

(*m*) A creditor or owner of goods cannot enter property to snatch back, i.e. take possession of, goods subject to a regulated hire-purchase or conditional-sale agreement or a regulated consumer hire agreement without a court order: s.92.

(*n*) *Credit-tokens.* Regulations (1983) govern the particulars which have to be contained in a credit-token agreement. There is an upper limit of £50 on a debtor's liability for loss to the creditor following misuse of the credit-token (*see also* **34**(*d*)).

ADMINISTRATION AND ENFORCEMENT PROVISIONS

31. Primary duties of the Director General of Fair Trading. The Consumer Credit Act 1974 gave the Director General responsibilities additional to those under the Fair Trading Act 1973 (*see* IV, **48**). The 1974 Act is being brought into effect in stages by the Secretary of State, but it is administered by the Director General, who has a number of duties under the Act. These are as follows.

(*a*) To administer the licensing system.

(*b*) To adjudicate over the issue, renewal, variation, suspension and revocation of licences and other matters.

(*c*) Generally to superintend the working and enforcement of the Act, and regulations made under it.

(*d*) Where necessary or expedient, to take steps himself to enforce the Act and regulations made under it.

(*e*) So far as is practicable to keep under review and from time to time advise the Secretary of State about social and commercial developments relating to the provision of credit or bailment and related activities.

32. Other duties of the Director General. These include the duty to establish and maintain a public register containing information about licence applicants and holders (*see* **29**); to exclude certain activities from various provisions of the Act (*see* **29**(*e*)); and to act as a final arbiter in disputes between a consumer and a credit reference agency about the correctness of information held by the agency on the consumer (*see* **30**(*k*)).

33. Enforcement authorities. The following authorities have a duty to enforce the Act and regulations made under it:

(*a*) the Director General;

(*b*) the local weights and measures authority.

These enforcement authorities will be mainly concerned with breaches of the criminal law under the Act, although the Director General may take account of any matter which appears to him to constitute a breach of the Act whether or not any sanction for that breach is provided for under the Act: s.170. An example of where this might arise is where an applicant applies for a licence or for the renewal or variation of an existing licence.

Consumers will also be protected by certain provisions of the Act when they are involved in civil actions.

However, a breach of any requirement made by or under the Act will generally incur no civil or criminal sanction except as expressly provided by or under the Act: s.170.

34. Criminal provisions. In certain cases a breach of the Act will result in a person being liable to prosecution at the instigation of one of the enforcement authorities. Examples of such breaches are as follows.

(*a*) Engaging in activities requiring a licence when not a licensee: s.39(1).

(*b*) False or misleading advertisements: s.46(1).

(*c*) Canvassing debtor-creditor agreements off trade premises: s.49(1).

(*d*) Delivering or sending by post an unsolicited credit-token, e.g. a credit card: s.51(1). (*See Elliott* v. *Director General of Fair Trading* (1980).)

(*e*) Failure to supply the debtor with a statement of the amount required to discharge the agreement: s.97(3).

(*f*) Failure of the credit reference agency to disclose or correct filed information: ss.158(4) and 159(6).

35. Civil provisions. In some cases the consumer may have the right to sue a creditor, or the creditor may find that his contract is unenforceable. Examples of these provisions are as follows.

(*a*) Any regulated agreement made by the creditor or the owner while unlicensed is unenforceable against the debtor or hirer, except where the Director General orders otherwise: s.40.

(*b*) Any regulated agreement is rendered unenforceable where the debtor or hirer was introduced to the creditor or owner by an unlicensed credit-broker, except where the Director General orders otherwise: s.149.

(*c*) An agreement for the services of a credit-broker, debt-adjuster, debt-collector, or credit reference agency cannot be enforced if the business is unlicensed, except where the Director General orders otherwise: s.148.

(*d*) An agreement purporting to bind a debtor or hirer to enter into a future regulated agreement is void: s.59.

(*e*) A regulated agreement which is not properly executed is enforceable on an order of the court only: s.65 (*see* **23**).

(*f*) Where a regulated agreement is cancelled, or where a party withdraws from a prospective regulated ageement, the Act provides for the recovery of money paid by the debtor or hirer, the repayment of credit already advanced to the debtor, the return of goods, and the return of goods given in part-exchange or their worth in money: ss.70–73 (*see* **24**).

(*g*) *See also* the note to **18** and **30**(*j*).

PROGRESS TEST 5

1. When the relevant provisions of the Consumer Credit Act 1974 come into force, how will this affect hire-purchase agreements? **(1, 13, 16, 18)**.
2. Explain the nature of hire-purchase. **(2–4)**
3. Define (*a*) a hire-purchase agreement, (*b*) a conditional sale agreement, and (*c*) a credit sale agreement to which the Hire-Purchase Act 1965 applies. How are these definitions affected by the Consumer Credit Act 1974? **(5, 6)**
4. In what circumstances are contracts rendered unenforceable by one of the parties under the Hire-Purchase Act? What is the effect of this unenforceability? **(7, 8)**
5. Describe the right of a person to cancel a hire-purchase, conditional sale or credit sale agreement. Compare this with the right of cancellation under the 1974 Act. **(9, 24(*b*))**
6. Who is liable for any representations with respect to goods subject to a hire-purchase, conditional sale or credit sale agreement? Compare similar provisions under the 1974 Act. **(10, 25(*c*))**
7. Consider the implied terms applicable to hire-purchase agreements. **(11)**
8. What is the purpose of the Consumer Credit Act 1974? **(1, 14)**
9. Which agreements are subject to the provisions of the 1974 Act? **(16, 17, 20, 21)**
10. Describe the two kinds of regulated consumer credit agreements. **(18, 19)**

11. What is the effect if a regulated agreement is not properly executed? **(23)**

12. What are the rights of a debtor under a regulated agreement? **(24)**

13. What are the rights of a hirer under a regulated agreement? **(24)**

14. What are the liabilities of a creditor under a regulated agreement? **(25)**

15. What are the liabilities of an owner under a regulated agreement? **(25)**

16. Which businesses needs a licence if they wish to grant credit, hire goods or engage in other ancillary credit activities? **(26, 27)**

17. Who must be satisfied that the applicant for a licence is a fit person and what does the fitness test entail? **(28)**

18. Consider the ways in which the Act protects the interests of consumers. **(30)**

19. Which requirements must be satisfied for a regulated agreement to be properly executed? **(30(*f*))**

20. Describe the duties of the Director General of Fair Trading under the Consumer Credit Act 1974. **(31, 32)**

21. Who is under a duty to enforce the 1974 Act? Will this enforcement be under the criminal or civil law? Does the Act create any forms of civil liability? **(33–35)**

CHAPTER VI

Commercial Arbitration

REFERENCE TO ARBITRATION

1. Settlement of disputes. Arbitration is the inquiry into, and settlement of, disputes other than in a court of law. The inquiry is conducted and the award made by one or more arbitrators, an umpire or an official or special referee, according to the circumstances. The reference of a dispute to arbitration may be made:

(*a*) by order of the court;
(*b*) by the provisions of an Act of Parliament; or
(*c*) by consent out of court

2. Order of the court. The Rules of the Supreme Court give the court authority to refer matters arising from any hearing to an official or special referee. The matter referred may be the entire dispute or a specific issue within it.

(*a*) *Official referees.* An official referee is an officer of the court to whom matters are referred which require a prolonged investigation into books of account or other documents.

(*b*) *Special referees.* A special referee is one whom the parties to the dispute have agreed to, and who is remunerated by the parties at a rate determined by the court. The court may refer an issue to a special referee in cases where a special technical or local knowledge is required.

3. Statutory arbitration. An Act of Parliament may provide that specified kinds of disputes must be determined by some particular arbitral tribunal. Where this occurs, the arbitral tribunal has exclusive jurisdiction.

EXAMPLES:

(1) *Employment Protection (Consolidation) Act 1978 (see* VIII, **33**). This Act together with detailed regulations govern the jurisdiction, composition, practice and procedure of industrial tribunals and the Employment Appeal Tribunal (*see* XI),

(2) *Social Security Act 1975 (as amended).* Disputes over claims for social security benefits are referred to social security appeal tribunals (*see* XI, **34**).

(3) *Lloyd's Act 1871.* Section 20 provides a statutory arbitration procedure where disciplinary proceedings are brought against a member of Lloyd's of London, the insurance market. *See Moran* v. *Lloyd's (a statutory body)* (1980).

4. Consent out of court. Where two or more parties are in dispute, e.g. whether there has been a breach of contract, they may agree to refer their dispute to an arbitrator. This is an alternative to litigation. The reference to arbitration must be made by a party to the contract, not merely by an interested third party. The agreement to refer to arbitration may be oral or in writing. In cases of disputes over a contract, the arbitration agreement may have been incorporated into the original contract, or it may be made after the dispute has arisen. Arbitration clauses are a common feature of international trading contracts (*see* IV, **43**).

An agreement to refer disputes to arbitration is a contract, and as such is subject to the ordinary law of contract. As a general rule any provision purporting to oust the jurisdiction of the courts is void, as being contrary to public policy. However, there is no objection to a clause which makes reference to arbitration a condition precedent to a right of action. Furthermore, the Arbitration Act 1979 does permit parties to a reference to arbitration to exclude judicial review of arbitration awards in certain cases (*see* **16**).

NOTE: (1) *Written agreements.* Where the arbitration agreement is in writing, the Arbitration Acts 1950 and 1979 apply: *see* below.

(2) *Oral agreements.* Where the arbitration agreement is oral, the Acts apply only if the parties have agreed that they shall apply.

(3) *Valuation distinguished.* An arbitration agreeement by consent out of court is not the same as a valuation. Where parties agree to appoint a valuer and accept his valuation, the purpose is to avoid a dispute. When the valuer makes his valuation, there is no question of dispute between the parties. On the other hand, an arbitration is always concerned with a dispute between the parties.

5. Advantages of arbitration. Businessmen often prefer to settle their disputes by arbitration rather than in open court. This is because the following advantages are often to be gained.

(*a*) Arbitration may be quicker and lead to an earlier settlement of the dispute.
(*b*) Arbitration may be less expensive than litigation.
(*c*) The parties may have their dispute settled by a person with knowledge of some special branch of commerce.
(*d*) Arbitration proceedings may always be conducted in private hearings, thus avoiding the publicity of open court.

However, prior to the Arbitration Act 1979 parties to a dispute often preferred not to refer the case to arbitration in England, because of the readiness with which the English courts exercised their jurisdiction over arbitration agreements and awards, thus diminishing to a certain extent the advantages of going to arbitration. The 1979 Act has attempted to limit the jurisdiction of the courts (*see* **13–18**).

ARBITRATION AGREEMENTS

6. Effect of an arbitration agreement. Here it is necessary to consider the extent to which a party is bound by his agreement to submit to arbitration. In particular, it is necessary to consider whether a party to an arbitration agreement can bring a dispute before the court, notwithstanding the agreement.

7. Legal proceedings. A party to an arbitration agreement may always commence legal proceedings in spite of the arbitration agreement. However, the other party may ask the court to *stay* the proceedings so that the dispute may be heard by an arbitrator according to the agreement: Arbitration Act 1950, s.4. The court will then decide whether or not to grant the stay. A stay will be granted if the following conditions are satisfied.

(*a*) If the matter in dispute is within the scope of the arbitration agreement.
(*b*) If the applicant for the stay has delivered no defence, nor taken any other step in the legal proceedings.
(*c*) If the applicant has always been ready and willing to do everything necessary for the proper conduct of the arbitration according to the agreement.
(*d*) If there is no sufficient reason why the dispute should not be referred to the arbitrator, e.g. the court proceedings would serve no useful purpose, or where they would not be helpful or desirable: *Camilla Cotton* v. *Granadex* (1976).

NOTE: (1) An English court may stay proceedings where one party proves that an arbitration agreement is in existence. This applies to foreign as well as domestic agreements: Arbitration Act 1975, s.1.

(2) The court will generally grant a stay where there is an exclusion agreement (*see* **16**).

8. The court's discretion. It is within the discretion of the court to grant or refuse a stay. In any case, the court will look to the party opposing the stay to show some good reason why arbitration should not take place according to the agreement. The court may refuse a stay for the following reasons.

(*a*) If there is reason to suspect that the appointed arbitrator may be biased.

(*b*) If the question of fraud has arisen. (The court will wish to determine whether any party has been fraudulent.)

(*c*) If the only issue in dispute is a point of law.

(*d*) If reference to arbitration would not provide an effective remedy, for example because the plaintiff seeks an injunction, or is too impoverished to implement the arbitration procedure, but could apply for legal aid for civil proceedings.

(*e*) If this may avoid a multiplicity of actions.

9. Validity of the arbitration agreement. The validity of an arbitration agreement is determined according to the general rules of contract. Where the arbitration agreement is a clause operating within a contract between the parties, the dispute may be either:

(*a*) whether the contract is binding (in which case the arbitrator has no power to determine the issue), or

(*b*) whether there is a breach of contract, the parties agreeing that their contract is binding (in which case the arbitrator has power to determine the case, subject to the discretion of the court).

See Bremer Vulkan Schiffbau und Maschinenfabrik v. *South India Shipping Corporation* (1981) and *Paal Wilson & Co.* v. *Partenreederei* (1982) on the effect of delay in bringing the dispute to arbitration. Arguably, there is need for legislation giving either arbitrators or the courts a discretionary power to dismiss an arbitration claim for want of prosecution.

10. Implied terms in arbitration agreements. In every arbitration agreement which is governed by the Arbitration Act 1950, as amended by the 1979 Act, the following terms are implied unless expressly excluded.

(*a*) Reference must be made to a single arbitrator.

(*b*) The court has the power to appoint an arbitrator in certain circumstances.

(*c*) Where reference is to two arbitrators, then they may appoint an umpire at any time.

(*d*) Where the arbitrators cannot agree, they must appoint an umpire immediately.

(*e*) The parties must submit to examination on oath and produce all documents called for by the arbitrator(s).

(*f*) In the event of non-compliance with an order made by him, the arbitrator can obtain from the High Court the powers of a judge, which would enable him, among other things, to dismiss a claim for want of prosecution: 1979 Act, s.5.

(*g*) The award of the arbitrator(s) will be final and binding.

11. Arbitrator's duties. It is the duty of the arbitrator to make an inquiry into the dispute and then to make an award. The arbitrator should fix the time and place for the hearing and give due notice to the parties and witnesses. He is entitled to use his own knowledge of any commercial matter in connection with the dispute. The arbitrator is generally immune from an action for negligence based on the way he resolved the dispute between the parties and reached his decision.

12. The award. An award is valid, final and binding on the parties if it satisfies the following conditions.

(*a*) It must decide a matter within the arbitration agreement and not something outside its scope.

(*b*) It must be certain.

(*c*) It must be reasonable and possible, e.g. it must not order a party to do something which is clearly beyond his ability or power.

(*d*) It must dispose of every matter referred.

13. Judicial review of arbitration awards. A new procedure has been introduced by the Arbitration Act 1979. This provides for an appeal on a preliminary point of law (*see* **14**), together with an appeal on a question of law arising out of the award (*see* **15**). The parties may exclude this method of judicial review. The courts will not be able to consider questions of fact. It is not always easy to state whether a particular question is one of fact or of law.

14. Preliminary points of law. The High Court has jurisdiction to determine any question of law arising in the course of a reference to arbitration. The arbitrator or the parties to the arbitration must consent to the court determining the question of law. The High Court should only entertain such an application where substantial savings in costs to the parties might be produced, where the determination could substantially affect the rights of one or more of the parties to the arbitration agreement, and where no exclusion agreement is in existence (*see* **16**). An appeal against the decision of the High Court may be made only where the High Court or the Court of Appeal gives leave, and where the High Court certifies that the question of law involved is either one of general public importance or one which for some other special reason should be considered by the Court of Appeal.

15. Appeal against the award. An appeal lies to the High Court on any question of law arising out of an arbitration award. All the parties to the agreement must consent to the appeal or the High Court must have granted leave to appeal. The High Court may only grant leave:

(*a*) where the determination of the question of law concerned could substantially affect the rights of one or more parties to the arbitration agreement; and
(*b*) where no exclusion agreement is in existence (*see* **16**).

The High Court may order the arbitrator concerned to state the reasons for the award in sufficient detail to enable the court to consider any questions of law which might arise out of the award. Unless there was a special reason the arbitrator should have been notified before the award was made that a reasoned award would be required. Conditions may be attached to the leave to appeal. An appeal against the decision of the High Court is subject to the same requirements as an appeal in **14**.

In *The Nema: Pioneer Shipping Ltd.* v. *B.T.P. Tioxide Ltd.* (1981) the House of Lords laid down guidelines as to when leave to appeal should be granted. The House stressed that one of the aims of the 1979 Act was the speedy resolution of disputes sent to arbitration and the avoidance of lengthy court proceedings. The House drew a distinction between "one-off" cases, where either the point of law or the facts were of importance only to the parties, and cases of wider importance, where either the point of law is of general importance (e.g. the interpretation of a clause in a commonly used standard form contract) or the facts are of a general character (e.g. the Iran and Iraq war) which affect similar transactions between many other persons engaged in similar kinds of commercial activity. In the one-off cases leave to appeal should only be granted where it was clearly and immediately apparent to the judge that the arbitrator's reasoning was obviously wrong, because the arbitrator either misdirected himself in law or the decision was one that no reasonable arbitrator could reach. In the cases of wider importance, leave to appeal should be granted only in two situations. First, on a point of law if a strong prima facie case had been made out that the arbitrator had been wrong in his construction and a decision by the court on this point would add significantly to the clarity and certainty of English law. Secondly, leave to appeal should be granted where the judge considered that the arbitrator's conclusion concerning the facts of a general character was "not right" and that in the interests of legal certainty there should be some uniformity in the decisions of the arbitrators.

16. Exclusion agreements. The parties to a reference to arbitration may, by an agreement in writing, exclude:

(*a*) judicial review of the arbitration award (*see* **15**);
(*b*) the power of the court to order the arbitrator to state the reasons for the award (*see* **15**);
(*c*) judicial review of preliminary points of law (*see* **14**).

If the dispute arises out of a domestic arbitration agreement (*see* **17**), the Admiralty jurisdiction of the High Court, a contract of insurance, or a commodity contract, then the exclusion agreement must have been entered into after the commencement of the reference to arbitration. However, if the award or question of law relates to a non-domestic arbitration agreement or to a contract governed by foreign law this requirement does not have to be satisfied.

17. Domestic arbitration agreement. The 1979 Act defines a domestic arbitration agreement as follows:

(*a*) the agreement does not provide for arbitration in a foreign state; and
(*b*) the parties to the agreement are neither nationals nor habitually resident in a foreign state.

In the case of a body corporate (e.g. a limited company, *see* II, **2**) it should not be incorporated, controlled and managed in a foreign state.

In other words, where an agreement provides for arbitration in a foreign state, and where the parties to the agreement are nationals of, or habitually resident in, or corporate bodies based in, a foreign state, then there is a non-domestic arbitration agreement.

In the case of a dispute arising from a domestic arbitration agreement, where the question arises whether any party has been guilty of fraud, the High Court may quash the arbitration agreement.

18. Effect of the 1979 Act. The Arbitration Act 1979 by allowing exclusion agreements has brought English law into line with that of other countries. Prior to the 1979 Act London had become less popular as an arbitration centre because of the ease with which parties to an arbitration agreement could resort to the courts. This ease, in effect, defeated one of the reasons for going to arbitration (*see* **5**).

However, the Arbitration Act 1979 states that an exclusion agreement should not:

(*a*) prohibit or restrict access to the High Court;
(*b*) restrict the jurisdiction of that court;
(*c*) prohibit or restrict the making of a reasoned award;
(*d*) apply to statutory arbitration (*see* **3**).

19. Enforcement of an award. Where a party is reluctant to comply with the order of the arbitrator in the award, the other party may seek to enforce the award in one of the following two ways.

(*a*) *As a judgment.* With the leave of the court, which is usually granted, the award may be enforced in the same way as a judgment: Arbitration Act 1950, s.26. However, this method of enforcement would not be suitable where, for example, the award was not in writing, or where the award was merely declaratory as to one aspect of a contract.

(*b*) *Action.* An award may be enforced by bringing an action on it. The action is in the nature of an action for breach of contract, since it is founded on the agreement to comply with the award.

NOTE: An award made in pursuance of an arbitration agreement made in a state, other than the United Kingdom, which is a party to the New York Convention on the Recognition and Enforcement of Foreign Arbitral Awards is enforceable in England and Wales in the same manner as a domestic arbitration agreement: Arbitration Act 1975, s.3. However, an English court can refuse to enforce the agreement in certain cases, for example where the arbitration agreement is not valid under the law to which the parties are subjected, or where it would be against public policy.

20. Remission to arbitrator. The court has power to remit an award for reconsideration by the arbitrator: s.22 of the 1950 Act. Examples of where this power may be used are as follows.

(*a*) Misconduct on the part of the arbitrator.

(*b*) Fresh evidence has come to light which could not have been discovered prior to the making of the award.

(*c*) The arbitrator has acted under a mistake when putting his award into writing.

21. Setting an award aside. The court has power to set an award aside in any of the following circumstances.

(*a*) Where there has been misconduct of the arbitrator, e.g. where there has been an irregularity of proceedings, or where the arbitrator was biased.

(*b*) Where the award is uncertain in its terms: s.23(2) of the 1950 Act.

PROGRESS TEST 6

1. Define "arbitration". Explain how a reference to arbitration may be made (*a*) by order of the court, (*b*) under the provisions of a statute, and (*c*) by consent out of court. Which type of arbitration is most relevant to commercial law? **(1–4)**

2. What are the advantages of arbitration? **(5)**

3. In what circumstances will the court grant a stay when legal proceedings have been commenced by a party to the arbitration agreement? **(6–8)**

4. How is the validity of an arbitration agreement determined? **(9)**

5. In what circumstances are there implied terms in an arbitration agreement? What are these implied terms? **(4,10)**

6. What are the duties of an arbitrator? When is the award of an arbitrator binding on the parties? **(11, 12)**

7. In what circumstances may a party to a reference to arbitration appeal to the High Court on a preliminary point of law? **(14)**

8. When may a party appeal (*a*) to the High Court, and (*b*) to the Court of Appeal on a question of law arising out of an arbitration award? **(15)**

9. Can an appeal be made either to the High Court or to the Court of Appeal on a question of fact? **(13–15)**

10. In what respects may the jurisdiction of the court be excluded by agreement between the parties to an arbitration agreement?

What form must the exclusion agreement take? When must the exclusion agreement be made in the case of a domestic arbitration agreement? **(16–17)**

11. How does the 1979 Act attempt to limit the use of widely phrased exclusion agreements which could oust the jurisdiction of the courts? **(4, 18)**

12. How may an arbitrator's award be enforced? **(19)**

13. Explain the court's power of (*a*) remission, and (*b*) setting aside the award. **(20, 21)**

CHAPTER VII

Restrictive Trade Practices

RESTRICTIVE AGREEMENTS GENERALLY

1. Legislation. The Restrictive Trade Practices Act 1976 consolidated the enactments relating to restrictive trade practices, including the Restrictive Trade Practices Act 1956. The 1976 Act, which has been slightly amended by the Restrictive Trade Practices Act 1977 and the Competition Act 1980, provides that:

(*a*) certain agreements are required to be registered with the Director General of Fair Trading; and

(*b*) when an agreement is registered the Director General must submit it to the Restrictive Practices Court.

The aim of this legislation is to protect the public interest by ensuring free competition between the manufacturers and suppliers of goods and services. Free competition is thought to lead to greater efficiency, lower prices and better services for the customer. Thus price-fixing between manufacturers of the same goods whereby they all sell their goods at the same price, and monopolies in private industry are generally presumed to be not in the public interest.

The Competition Act 1980, *inter alia*, provides for a two-stage investigation by the Director General of Fair Trading and the Monopolies and Mergers Commission of suspected anti-competitive practices. They may already investigate monopolies in the supply of goods and services, under the Fair Trading Act 1973. The 1980 Act gives additional powers to investigate public sector industries such as nationalised companies.

2. Registered agreements. Agreements which must be registered are as follows.

(*a*) Agreements as to the production, supply, processing or manufacture of goods which restrict:

(*i*) the prices; or
(*ii*) the terms or conditions; or
(*iii*) the quantities or descriptions; or

(*iv*) the processes of manufacture of those goods; or
(*v*) the persons who may obtain those goods; or
(*vi*) the area in which those goods may be obtained: s.6.

(*b*) information agreements as to goods which provide for the furnishing of certain information such as:

(*i*) the prices of goods;
(*ii*) the terms or conditions of supply or acquisition of goods;
(*iii*) the quantities or descriptions of goods;
(*iv*) the costs incurred in producing, supplying or acquiring goods;
(*v*) the processes of manufacture applied to goods;
(*vi*) the persons to whom the goods are supplied, or from whom they are acquired;
(*vii*) the areas in which the goods are to be supplied, or from where they have been acquired: s.7.

(*c*) Agreements as to the supply of services which restrict:

(*i*) the charges for, or
(*ii*) the terms or conditions of, or
(*iii*) the extent or scale of, or
(*iv*) the form or manner of those services, or
(*v*) the persons or areas who or which can obtain or supply these services: s.11.

(*d*) Information agreements as to the supply of services which provide for the furnishing of certain information such as:

(*i*) the charges for, or
(*ii*) the terms or conditions of, or
(*iii*) the extent or scale of, or
(*iv*) the form or manner of, or
(*v*) the costs incurred in providing those services, or
(*vi*) the persons or areas who or which can obtain or supply these services: s.12.

NOTE: Article 85 of the Treaty of Rome provides that all agreements between undertakings, decisions by associations of undertakings and concerted practices (which may affect trade *between* Member States and which have as their object or effect the prevention, restriction or distortion of competition within the Common Market), are void unless exemption is granted by the European Economic Community. In the case of a conflict with UK law, EEC law prevails.

3. Exempt agreements. The Restrictive Trade Practices Act 1976, s.28, provides that the Act does not apply to the following agreements.

(*a*) Agreements expressly authorised by an Act of Parliament or by a statutory instrument.

(*b*) Agreements constituting part of a scheme for rationalising industry under the Income and Corporation Taxes Act 1970.

(*c*) Agreements for the supply of goods between two persons (neither of whom is a trade association) under which *no* such restrictions are made, or information provided as described in **2**(*a*) and (*b*).

(*d*) Agreements between two persons (neither of whom is a trade association) for the exchange of information relating to the operation of processes of manufacture, unless in conflict with **2**(*a*) and (*b*)

(*e*) Certain agreements authorising the use of a trade mark.

(*f*) Certain licences or assigments of a patent or registered design, or an agreement for such a licence or assignment.

(*g*) Agreements as to goods supplied, produced or acquired outside the United Kingdom. If acquired outside the United Kingdom they should not be imported into the United Kingdom for home use.

(*h*) Certain agreements for the exclusive supply of services by one person to another.

(*i*) Agreements between two persons (neither of whom is a services supply association) for the exchange of information relating to techniques or processes to be applied in the provision of designated services.

(*j*) Agreements for supplying services outside the United Kingdom.

4. Other exempt agreements. Other examples of exempt agreements are as follows.

(*a*) Agreements important to the national economy, on the order of the Secretary of State: s.29.

(*b*) Agreements for holding down prices may be approved and so exempt from registration for a specified period: s.30.

(*c*) An agreement which has an authorisation given for the purpose of any provision of the European Coal and Steel Community Treaty relating to restrictive trade practices.

(*d*) Participation agreements which provide for majority state participation in UK offshore petroleum: Participation Agreements Act 1978.

(*e*) Certain undertakings obtained as a result of reports by the Monopolies and Mergers Commission: Competition Act 1980, s.29.

(*f*) Copyright agreements: Competition Act 1980, s.30.

5. The Restrictive Practices Court. The Restrictive Trade Practices Act 1956 set up by the Restrictive Practices Court, which is now governed by the Restrictive Practices Court Act 1976. The court is a superior court of record, i.e. it has the status of the High Court. It consists of five judges assisted by up to ten lay members. When the court sits, it usually does so in divisions consisting of one judge assisted by two lay members. However, in the case of proceedings involving only issues of law these may be heard by one judge sitting alone. The lay members have equal voice with the judge in questions of fact, but on questions of law the opinion of the judge prevails. An appeal by way of case stated may be made on a question of law to the Court of Appeal.

For a case illustrating the court's powers to control restrictive trade agreements by large fines for contempt of court, *see In re an agreement between members of the British Concrete Pipe Association* (1980). *See also: Re Association of British Travel Agents Agreement* (1984).

6. The eight gateways. The court considers agreements which have been placed on the register by the Director General of Fair Trading. In any hearing, the onus is on the parties to the agreement to satisfy the court that the agreement is not contrary to the public interest. If the relevant provisions are found by the court to be contrary to the public interest they will be regarded as void, that is having no effect. Under the 1976 Act the provisions were void from the moment of the court's declaration, but the Competition Act 1980 provides that a minimum of twenty-one days will elapse before the provisions are regarded as void, and the court has the discretion to suspend the operation of all or part of their declaration for up to a total period of nine months.

By ss.10 and 19 of the Restrictive Trade Practices Act 1976 a restriction or an information provision (*see* **2**) in a registrable agreement is deemed to be contrary to the public interest unless the court is satisfied of any one or more of the following eight circumstances (sometimes known as "the eight gateways").

(*a*) That the restriction or information provision is reasonably necessary, having regard to the character of the goods or services to which it applies, to protect the public against injury (whether to persons or premises) in connection with the consumption or installation of those goods, or the use of those goods or services.

(*b*) That the removal of the restriction or information provision would deny to the public as vendors, purchasers or consumers of any goods, or as users of any goods or other property or any services, other specific benefits or advantages enjoyed or likely to be enjoyed by them as such, whether by virtue of the restriction itself or of any arrangements of operations resulting therefrom.

(*c*) That the restriction or information provision is reasonably necessary to counteract measures taken by any one person not party to the agreement with a view to preventing or restricting competition in or in relation to the trade or business in which the persons party thereto are engaged.

(*d*) That the restriction or information provision is reasonably necessary to enable the persons party to the agreement to negotiate fair terms for the supply of goods or services to, or the acquisition of goods or services from, any one person not party thereto who controls a preponderant part of the trade or business of acquiring such goods or supplying such goods or services, or for the supply of goods or services to any person not party to the agreement and not carrying on such a trade or business who, either alone or in combination with any other such person, controls a preponderant part of the market for such goods or services.

(*e*) That, having regard to the conditions actually obtaining or reasonably foreseen at the time of the application, the removal of the restriction would be likely to have a serious and persistent adverse effect on the general level of unemployment in an area, or in areas taken together, in which a substantial proportion of the trade or industry to which the agreement relates is situated.

(*f*) That, having regard to the conditions actually obtaining or reasonably foreseen at the time of the application, the removal of the restriction or information provision would be likely to cause a reduction in the volume of earnings of the export business which is substantial either in relation to the whole export business of the United Kingdom or in relation to the whole business of the said trade or industry.

(*g*) That the restriction or information provision is reasonably required for purposes connected with the maintenance of any other restriction accepted or information provision made by the parties, whether under the same agreement or under any other agreement between them, being a restriction or information provision which is found by the court not to be contrary to the public interest upon grounds other than those specified in this paragraph, or has been so found in previous proceedings before the court.

(*h*) That the restriction or information provision does not directly or indirectly restrict or discourage competition to any material degree in any relevant trade or industry and is not likely to do so.

The court must be further satisfied that the restriction or information provision is not unreasonable having regard to the balance between those circumstances and any detriment to the public, or to persons not parties to the agreement, resulting or likely to result from the operation of the restriction or information provision.

The court has a discretion whether to exercise its jurisdiction or not if it appears right to do so having regard to the operation of any directly applicable Community provision or to the purpose and effect of any authorisation or exemption granted in relation to such a provision: Restrictive Trade Practices Act 1976, s.5.

7. Failure to register. The consequences of failure to register a restrictive or an information agreement within the time stipulated by the Restrictive Trade Practices Act 1976 are as follows.

(*a*) The agreement is void in respect of all restrictions accepted or information provisions made thereunder.

(*b*) It is unlawful for any person who is a party to the agreement and who carries on business within the United Kingdom to give effect to or to enforce the agreement.

(*c*) Any party who enforces or gives effect to a restriction is liable in damages at the suit of anyone suffering a consequential loss.

(*d*) The court may, upon the Director General's application, make up an order in the nature of an injunction restraining any party from giving effect to or enforcing the restriction or information provisions: s.35.

RESALE PRICE MAINTENANCE

8. Price maintenance of goods. Resale price maintenance agreements are those by which manufacturers of goods seek to control the *retail* prices of their manufactured goods. Such agreements are usually made between manufacturer and wholesaler, the latter giving an undertaking not to sell to a retailer except upon an undertaking by the retailer not to sell below the manufacturer's list prices. At common law, this kind of agreement was not enforceable by the manufacturer against the retailer on grounds of privity of contract.

Dunlop Pneumatic Tyre Co. Ltd v. *Selfridge & Co. Ltd.* (1915): D sold motor tyres to X, a wholesaler, in terms that X would not sell the tyres to a retailer, except under a contract whereby the retailer promised to sell at D's list prices. X sold some of these tyres to S, who undertook not to sell below D's list prices.

Subsequently, S sold tyres below the list prices. D brought this action against S claiming an injunction and damages. HELD: by the House of Lords that there was no contract between D and S. S's contract was with X, and D was a stranger to this contract, and the action failed.

The common law doctrine of privity of contract as applied to resale price maintenance is now affected by the Restrictive Trade Practices Act 1956 and the Resale Prices Act 1964. The relevant provisions of these Acts have been consolidated by the Resale Prices Act 1976.

9. Collective enforcement.

(*a*) Section I of the Resale Prices Act 1976 provides that it is unlawful for any two or more persons carrying on business in the United Kingdom as *suppliers* of any goods to make or carry out any agreement or arrangement by which they undertake:

(*i*) to withhold supplies of goods for delivery from dealers who resell or have resold goods in breach of any condition as to the price at which those goods may be resold;

(*ii*) to refuse to supply goods for delivery to such dealers except on terms and conditions which are less favourable than those applicable in the case of other dealers carrying on business in similar circumstances;

(*iii*) to supply goods only to persons who undertake either to withhold supplies of goods as described in (*i*) or to refuse to supply goods as described in (*ii*); or

(*iv*) to authorise the recovery of penalties from dealers who resell or have resold goods in breach of any such condition as is described in (*i*).

(*b*) Section 2 of the 1976 Act provides that it is unlawful for any two or more persons carrying on business in the United Kingdom as *dealers* in any goods to make or carry out any agreement or arrangement by which they undertake:

(*i*) to withhold orders for supplies of goods for delivery from suppliers who supply or have supplied goods otherwise than subject to any condition as to the price at which these goods may be resold, or who refrain or have refrained from taking steps to ensure compliance with such conditions in respect of goods supplied by them;

(*ii*) to discriminate in the handling of goods against goods supplied by such suppliers; or (*iii*) to authorise the recovery of penalites from such suppliers, or the conduct of any domestic proceedings in connection therewith.

Contravention of these provisions will not result in criminal proceedings. However, these sections are enforceable by civil proceedings on behalf of the Crown or by any person affected by a contravention: s.25.

10. Individual enforcement. Section 9 of the 1976 Act provides that any term or condition of a contract for the sale of goods by a supplier to a dealer, or any agreement between a supplier and a dealer relating to such a sale, is void insofar as it purports to establish or provide for the establishment of minimum prices to be charged on the resale of goods in in the United Kingdom.

In addition it is unlawful for a supplier of goods to include such a term in a contract for sale, or to require the inclusion of such a term in a contract, as a condition of supplying goods to a dealer, or to publish in relation to any goods a price stated or calculated to be understood as the minimum price which may be charged on the resale of goods.

Section 11 of the 1976 Act provides that it is unlawful for a supplier to withhold supplies of any goods from a dealer seeking to obtain them for resale in the United Kingdom on the ground that the dealer has sold, or is likely to sell, at a price below the resale price, goods obtained either directly or indirectly from that supplier, or has supplied or is likely to supply such goods, either directly or indirectly, to a third party who had done so, or who would be likely to do so.

Contravention of these provisions will not result in criminal proceedings. However, these sections are enforceable by civil proceedings on behalf of the Crown or by a person affected by a contravention: s.25.

11. Exemption of goods. The Restrictive Practices Court may make an order directing that goods of any class shall be exempted goods for the purposes of individual enforcement: s.14. An application to the court may be made by:

(*a*) the Director General of Fair Trading;
(*b*) any supplier of goods of the class in question; or
(*c*) any trade association whose members consist of or include such suppliers.

12. Exemption orders. The court may make such an order if it appears that in default of a system of maintained minimum resale prices applicable to those goods:

(*a*) the quality of the goods available for sale, or the varieties of goods so available, would be substantially reduced; or

(*b*) the number of establishments in which goods are sold by retail would be substantially reduced; or

(*c*) the prices at which goods are sold by retail would in general and in the long run be increased; or

(*d*) the goods would be sold by retail under conditions likely to cause danger to health in consequence of their misuse by the public; or

(*e*) any necessary services actually provided in connection with or after the sale of goods by retail would cease to be so provided or would be substantially reduced; and

(*f*) in any such case that the resulting detriment to the public as consumers or users of the goods in question would outweigh any detriment to them resulting from the maintenance of minimum resale prices in respect of the goods.

PROGRESS TEST 7

1. What agreements must be registered and with whom? **(1)**
2. What agreements are exempt from the registration provisions of the Restrictive Trade Practices Act 1976? **(3–4)**
3. How can the parties to an agreement satisfy the Court that a registrable agreement is not contrary to the public interest? What is the effect on the agreement if they fail to satisfy the court? **(6)**
4. What is the effect if the parties to a registrable agreement fail to register it? **(7)**
5. Define, and give an example of, a resale price maintanance agreement. **(8)**
6. When will an agreement be contrary to the provisions of the Resale Prices Act 1976? How will the provisions in respect of an agreement between two or more persons be enforced? **(9)**
7. What protection does the Resale Prices Act 1976 give to an individual? Are there any limits on this protection? **(10–12)**

PART TWO

INDUSTRIAL LAW

CHAPTER VIII

The Employer and Employee Relationship

THE CONTRACT OF EMPLOYMENT

1. A voluntary relationship. The relationship between employer and employee (which has replaced the former terminology of master and servant) is based on a voluntary agreement.

In *Nokes* v. *Doncaster Amalgamated Collieries Ltd.* (1940), it was argued that a statute gave a power to transfer the employees of one company into the service of another company without any need to obtain the consent of the employees affected. In firmly rejecting this argument, Lord Atkin said: "I confess it appears to me astonishing that apart from over-riding questions of public welfare, power should be given to a court or to anyone else to transfer a man without his knowledge and possibly against his will, from the service of one person to the service of another. I had fancied that ingrained in the personal status of a citizen under our laws was the right to choose for himself whom he would serve and that this right of choice constituted the main difference between a servant and a serf."

The voluntary nature of the relationship between employer and employee keep it within the general law of contract, the agreement being called the contract of employment, or contract of service. (But *see* X, **20–26** on collective agreements.)

2. Promise to give service. The essential characteristic of a contract of employment is the consideration given by the employee, namely a promise to give service. This concept of service must not be confused with that of work. It is necessary to look at the terms of the contract to discover what is involved by the employee's promise to give service. In *Gorse* v. *Durham County Council* (1971), it was held that a schoolteacher was entitled to his salary for the three-and-a-half days during which he was under temporary suspension from work. (*See also* **28**(*c*).)

3. The "control" test. It sometimes becomes necessary to determine the question whether a contract is one of service or for services. This reflects the distinction between the employee and the independent contractor. The distinction is always important, because the legal incidents to the contract of service are quite different from the incidents to the contract for services. Usually it is not difficult to say whether a particular contract to do work is a contract of service or a contract for services, but sometimes there is ambiguity.

In *Yewens* v. *Nokes* (1880), Bramwell LJ said that: "A servant is a person subject to the command of his master as to the manner in which he shall do his work." This statement indicates that the control test is decisive as to whether a person is an employee or an independent contractor. This test is, however, difficult to apply in cases where the employee is a highly qualified professional man, or in other cases where the employer has little or no power to control the manner in which the work is done. Nevertheless, in these circumstances, the relationship may still be one of employer and employee.

Cassidy v. *Minister of Health* (1951): A patient went into hospital for surgical treatment to cure the stiffness of the third and fourth fingers of his left hand. After the operation he came away with four stiff fingers, his hand being practically useless. It was held by the Court of Appeal that the prima facie case of negligence on the part of the surgeons and nurses had not been rebutted and that the defendant was liable. Somervell and Singleton LJJ decided on the footing of vicarious liability, flowing from the fact that there was a contract of service between each of the surgeons and each of the nurses, in the one case, and the hospital authority in the other. (Denning LJ was in agreement with the other two judges, but he based his decision on other grounds.)

Morren v. *Swinton and Pendlebury BC* (1965): A local authority, wishing to have certain sewerage works carried out, appointed an independent consultant engineer to supervise the execution of the works. The agreement between the local authority and the consultant engineer provided that the local authority should appoint and pay a resident engineer, to be approved by the consultant, to supervise the works under the consultant's instructions. Accordingly, the local authority, with the approval of the consultant, appointed a resident engineer at a salary and the authority had the right to dismiss him. He was paid a subsistence allowance and he was paid for holidays. Employer's national insurance contributions were paid in regard to him and there was a provision for a one-month period of notice. HELD: the resident engineer was employed by the local authority under a contract of service (not a contract for services) notwithstanding that his instructions were given to him by the consultant engineer. Lord Parker CJ said: "The cases have over and over again stressed the importance of the factor of superintendence and control, but that it is not the determining test is quite clear. In *Cassidy* v. *Minister of Health*, Somervell LJ, referred to this matter and instanced, as did Denning LJ, in the later case of *Stevenson, Jordan & Harrison Ltd.* v. *Macdonald & Evans* (1952), that clearly superintendence and control cannot be the decisive test when one is dealing with a professional man, or a man of some particular skill and experience. Incidences of that have been given in the form of a master of a ship, an engine driver, a professional architect or, as in this case, a consulting engineer. In such cases there can be no question of the employer telling him how to do the work; therefore, the absence of control and direction in that sense can be of little, if any, use as a test." But when a professional man in private practice agrees to give his professional services, the relation between him and his client is not one of employee and employer: *Clayton* v. *Woodman Ltd.* (1962).

Ready Mixed Concrete (South East) Ltd. v. *Minister of Pensions and National Insurance* (1968): A company, whose business was the making and selling of concrete, operated a system of delivery by owner drivers. In May 1965, one Latimer entered into a contract with the company for the carriage of concrete. He obtained his lorry by means of a hire-purchase agreement and arranged for it to be painted in the company's colours. The contract between the company and Latimer contained a declaration that Latimer was an independent contractor and provided as follows: (1) that the lorry was to be available exclusively to the company at all times; (2) that the company could require Latimer to drive the lorry himself for the maximum hours permitted by law; (3) that Latimer had a restricted right to employ relief drivers; (4) that Latimer should maintain the lorry and pay all running costs; (5) that the company should pay Latimer at fixed rates for the concrete carried subject to a fixed minimum annual total; (6) that Latimer should wear the company's uniform; and (7) that he should carry out all reasonable instructions "as if he were an employee of the company". Mackenna J considered that a contract of service exists if the following three conditions are fulfilled: (*i*) The employee agrees that in consideration of a wage or other remuneration he will provide his own work and skill in the performance of some service for his employer. (*ii*) He agrees, expressly or impliedly, that in the performance of that service he will be subject to the other's control in a sufficient degree to make that other master. (*iii*) The other provisions of the contract are consistent with its being a contract of service. On the facts before him in this case Mackenna J concluded that the terms of the contract were more consistent with a contract of carriage than with a contract of service.

Market Investigations Ltd. v. *Minister of Social Security* (1969): A part-time interviewer was engaged by the appellants on the basis that when the company were making a survey she would be asked if she was willing to do a number of days' work within a fixed period. She received detailed instructions as to interviewing methods to be used, and additional instructions for particular assignments when she agreed to do them. She might be asked to attend the company's briefing meetings or receive instructions from the company's supervisor. She was paid for the number of days which the company estimated that the interviews would take and expenses, but she was free to work for others in her spare time. The question was whether she was an employed person in insurable employment for the purposes of the National Insurance Acts. Cooke J held that since control, although a matter for consideration, was not decisive, the fundamental test in determining whether a person was performing services under a contract of service or for services was whether the person engaged to perform those services was performing them as a person in business on his own account and thus under a contract for services. He considered that in the present case the extent of control exercised by the company was so extensive as to be consistent with the interviewer being employed under a contract of service, and that she was not in business on her own account. Thus she was an employed earner.

Ferguson v. *John Dawson & Partners (Contractors) Ltd.* (1976): The plaintiff was injured whilst removing scaffolding from a roof and claimed damages from the defendants for being in breach of their statutory duty to provide a guard rail. The question arose whether the plaintiff has been employed by the defendants or had been an independent contractor. When the plaintiff had been taken on by the defendants their site agent had told him "there were no cards, we were purely working as a lump labour force". The defendants did not make deductions in respect of income tax from their weekly payments to the plaintiff, nor any payments in respect of national insurance contributions. The Court of Appeal held that, notwithstanding the label which the parties had put on their relationship to the effect that the plaintiff was "a self-employed labour only sub-contractor", there were other terms which could be implied into the contract from the evidence, including the ability of the defendant's site agent to dismiss the workmen, move them from site to site, tell them what work to do, and that the men were employed on an hourly basis. These terms indicated that the reality of the relationship between the defendants and the plaintiff had been that of employer and employee.

4. Attributes other than control. Mackenna J in the *Ready Mixed Concrete Ltd. case* (*see* **3**) recognised that the control test was inadequate by including the third condition that the provisions of the contract must be consistent with its being a contract of service. Since the control test is sometimes of little or no value, it becomes necessary to inquire further into the nature of the employer and employee relationship to discover whether there are any other attributes besides control which are peculiar to the contract of service and may accordingly provide a more satisfactory test.

(*a*) *Organisation test*. In the *Macdonald & Evans case*, Denning LJ said: "one feature which seems to run through the instances is that, under a contract of service, a man is employed as part of the business, and his work is done as an integral part of the business; whereas under a contract for services, his work, although done for the business, is not integrated into it, but is only accessory to it." In a later case, Denning LJ said that "the test of being a servant does not rest nowadays on submission to orders. It depends on whether the person is part and parcel of the organisation": *Bank voor Handel en Scheepvaart NV* v. *Slatford* (1953).

(*b*) *Other possible factors*. However, in *Market Investigations Ltd.* v. *Minister of Social Security* (1969) Cooke J considered that the fundamental test in determining whether a person was performing services under a contract of service or for services was whether the person was performing those services as a person in business on his own account, but that no exhaustive list had been compiled and perhaps no exhaustive list could be compiled of the considerations which are relevant in determining the question. Factors, apart from control, which may be important are such matters as whether the man performing the services provides his own equipment, whether he hires his own helpers, what degree of financial risk he takes, what degree of responsibility for investment and management he has, and whether and how far he has an opportunity of profiting from sound management in the performance of his task.

(*c*) *Important to consider all factors.* Perhaps the best comment is that of Atiyah in a passage in his *Vicarious Liability in the Law of Torts*, which was cited with approval in *Construction Industry Training Board* v. *Labour Force Ltd.* (1970). He said that it is not possible to lay down "a number of conditions which are both necessary to, and sufficient for, the existence of a contract of service. The most that can profitably be done is to examine all the possible factors which have been referred to in these cases as bearing on the nature of the relationship between the parties concerned. Clearly not all of these factors will be relevant in all cases, or have the same weight in all cases. Equally clearly no magic formula can be propounded for determining which factors should, in any given case, be treated as the determining ones. The plain fact is that in a large number of cases the court can only perform a balancing operation, weighing up the factors which point in one direction and balancing them against those pointing in the opposite direction. In the nature of things it is not to be expected that this operation can be performed with scientific accuracy."

5. Statutory definition of employee. An employee means an individual who has entered into or works under a contract of employment: Employment Protection (Consolidation) Act 1978, s.153. A contract of employment is defined as a contract of service or apprenticeship, whether express or implied, and (if it is express) whether it is oral or in writing. It is a question of fact whether a particular worker is an employee. In *Nethermere (St. Neots) Ltd.* v. *Taverna* (1984) women part-time home workers were held to be "employees" for the purposes of the Act.

Davis v. *New England College of Arundel* (1977): The applicant was a self-employed freelance lecturer who was engaged by the college in 1971 on an annual contract with similar terms to the annual contracts of other members of staff. The applicant wished to be treated as self-employed for tax and social security purposes. He was not re-engaged after May 1974. The point raised was whether he was employed under a contract of service, and so entitled to the protection of the Trade Union and Labour Relations Act 1974, or not. The Employment Appeal Tribunal held that in determining whether an applicant is engaged under a contract of service it is necessary to look at the circumstances objectively. On that basis, the relationship between the applicant and the college was that of an employer and employee. Neither the fact of the applicant's request to be treated as self-employed nor the fact that for fiscal purposes the college treated him as self-employed altered the contractual relationship between the parties.

6. Vicarious liability. One of the legal incidents which results from there being a contract of service rather than a contract for services, is that as a general rule where an employee commits a tort in the course of his employment, the employer is liable to any person who has thereby suffered loss or damage.

7. Course of employment. It is sometimes a matter of difficulty to determine whether an act was done during the course of employment. Any of the following factors may be taken into account. (*See also* XI, **20, 21.**)

(*a*) *Manner of working.* Where an employee commits a tort by performing an act of a kind which he is not employed to perform the employer is not liable, but where the employee merely adopts a wrongful method of doing his work, the employer is liable.

Century Insurance Co. Ltd. v. *Northern Ireland Road Transport Board* (1942): An employee struck a match to light a cigarette while he was carrying out his task of transferring petrol from a lorry to an underground tank. The lighted match caused an explosion and a fire. HELD: the employers were liable because the employee was carrying out his authorised duty in an unauthorised manner.

(*b*) *Prohibition.* Where an employer expressly prohibits his employee from performing certain acts, the prohibition will not protect the employer from liability if its purport is merely to forbid an employee from doing his work in a certain manner. But where an employer's prohibition sets a limit to the sphere of employment, he will not be liable if the employee commits a tort while engaged in the forbidden employment.

Rose v. *Plenty* (1976): A milkman was employed by a dairy company to deliver milk to their customers. There was a notice at the milk depot which expressly prohibited milkmen from employing children in the performance of their duties and from giving lifts on their milk floats. Contrary to these prohibitions the defendant milkman invited the plaintiff, a boy of thirteen, to assist him in the milk round in return for payment. Whilst riding on the milk float the plaintiff was injured when the milkman drove negligently. The plaintiff brought an action against the milkman and his employers. The Court of Appeal held (Lawton LJ dissenting) that the employer's instructions only affected the milkman's mode of conduct within the scope of his employment and did not limit or define the scope of the employment. It followed that, although the milkman's acts of employing the plaintiff and carrying him on the float were prohibited, they had been performed by the milkman within the scope of his employment having been performed for the purposes of the employer's business. (*Twine* v. *Bean's Express Ltd.* (1946) and *Conway* v. *George Wimpey & Co. Ltd.* (1951) were distinguished.)

(*c*) *Time and place of the tort.* An employer will not usually be liable for an employee's tort committed outside working hours, or at a place other than where he is authorised to be during working hours. But there is no hard and fast rule on this point, e.g. where an employee negligently left a tap running shortly after working hours had ended, the employer was held to be liable to a neighbour whose property was damaged by flooding: *Ruddiman* v. *Smith* (1889).

In cases where an employee's work involves travelling, any tort committed will usually be within the course of employment. But where the tort is committed while the employee was on an unauthorised detour, difficulties may arise.

The rule was stated in *Joel* v. *Morrison* (1834) by Parke B as follows: "If he was going out of his way, against his master's implied commands when driving on his master's business, he will make his master liable: but if he was going on a frolic of his own, without being at all on his master's business, the master will not be liable." Whether or not an employee is on a "frolic of his own" will depend on the circumstances of each case.

(*d*) *Emergency measures.* An employee has authority to take emergency measures to protect his employer's property when he has reason to believe that it is in danger. Even where the measures taken by the employee are excessive, the employer may be vicariously liable. But where the employee's conduct is outrageous, it will not be within the course of his employment, and the employer will not be liable.

Poland v. *John Parr & Sons* (1927): An employee, seeing a boy tampering with a bag of sugar which was lying on the employer's waggon, struck the boy with his hand. The boy fell under the moving wagon wheel and was seriously injured. HELD: the blow given by the employee was excessive, but not sufficiently excessive to take the act outside the scope of his employment. The employer was, therefore, vicariously liable for the employee's tort.

Warren v. *Henly's Ltd* (1948): An employee, a garage attendant, accused a customer of trying to leave the garage without paying for his petrol. The language used was violent, and, subsequently, the attendant struck the customer a blow. HELD: there was no evidence that the assault was so connected with the acts which the employee was authorised to do as to be a mode of doing those acts.

(*e*) *Criminal conduct.* In certain circumstances criminal conduct on the part of an employee will be regarded as being in the course of his employment. Where this occurs, the employer will be liable for any loss caused to a third party.

Lloyd v. *Grace, Smith & Co.* (1912): S, a solicitor's managing clerk, was authorised to carry out all the conveyancing work of the firm. During the course of his duties, he persuaded L to transfer to him the benefit of a mortgage of which L was the mortgagee, and also the freehold of certain property held by her. S then realised the mortgage and sold the property and kept the proceeds for himself. S's employer, the sole member of the firm, knew nothing of this criminal conduct at the time, nor did he derive any benefit from it. L brought this action against the firm in detinue for the title deeds of the property and for the moneys received by S in respect of the mortgage. HELD: the firm was liable because the fraud was committed in the course of the clerk's employment.

8. Terms of contract of employment. These terms can be found in any of the following.

(*a*) Express agreement between employer and employee.
(*b*) Terms implied by the common law, e.g. the duty of fidelity (*see* **30**).
(*c*) Terms implied by statute, e.g. terms embodying wages council orders (*see* **9**(*c*)).
(*d*) Collective agreements, e.g. as in *National Coal Board* v. *Galley* (1958) (*see* X, **20, 21**).

(*e*) Work rules.
(*f*) Custom and practice.

DUTIES OF THE EMPLOYER

9. Remuneration. It is the duty of the employer to pay his employee according to the terms of the contract of service. However, the following statutes are designed to protect the interests of employees.

(*a*) *Truck Acts 1831-1940.* These Acts apply to workmen only, i.e. employees engaged in manual labour. The Truck Acts provide that a contract of service between an employer and a workman is illegal and null where there is a term to the effect that wages shall be paid otherwise than in current coin of the realm (including banknotes), and where there is a term purporting to govern the manner in which wages shall be spent. In other words, it is an employer's statutory duty to pay his workmen fully in cash. He may not even deduct previous overpayments of wages.

EXCEPTIONS: (1) *Deductions.* The 1831 Act permits an employer to deduct the cost of food supplied and eaten on his premises, medical attention, tools used by miners and the rent of dwellings occupied by the workman.

(2) *Statutory deductions.* An employer should deduct income tax and social security contributions.

(3) *Independent contract.* There is nothing to prevent the employer and employee from entering a separate contract whereby the workman undertakes to pay the employer for services or goods, provided that the amount is not directly deducted, but is paid by the workman from his full pay.

(4) *Debts to third parties.* An employer may, at the request of the workman, deduct from his wages a debt to a third party owed by the workman. The maximum deductible is one-third of the wages. Thus, where there is a contributory pension or sick fund, the employer may make deductions from his wages, provided payment is made to a third party, e.g. a trustee, and the workman has agreed to the deduction.

(5) *Fines.* An employer may deduct a fair and reasonable amount where there has been some act or omission on the part of the workman likely to cause loss to the employer. However, this is permitted only where provision for the fine is made in a contract in writing signed by the workman or where there is a notice to this effect in some prominent and easily accessible

place. Similar provisions may be made where a workman spoils materials or goods by bad workmanship.

(6) *Attachment of earnings.* The Attachment of Earnings Act 1971 provides that a court may make an attachment of earnings order requiring the debtor's employer to make periodical deductions from the debtor's earnings and to pay them to the collecting officer of the court. The order must specify a rate of protected earnings below which the earnings actually paid to the employee should not fall. Such orders may be made by the county court in respect of judgment debts of £5 or more, administration orders and maintenance orders. The High Court may make such orders only to enforce maintenance orders.

(*b*) *Payment of Wages Act 1960.* This amends the Truck Acts by providing that, in certain specified circumstances, payments of wages by a workman may be made (*i*) into the workman's bank account, (*ii*) by money order, (*iii*) by postal order, (*iv*) by cheque drawn by the employer.

However, payment in these four ways may be made only in the circumstances provided in the Act for 1960. In particular:

(*i*) the workman must make a written request for payment to be made in one of these ways and the employer must have expressed his agreement to the request;

(*ii*) the employer must give with each payment a written notice setting out any deductions that have been made;

(*iii*) no charge or deductions may be made where payment is made as allowed by the Act.

The Act also provides that where a workman is absent from his usual place of work and the employer believes that this is due to sickness or that the workman is away on some duty, payment may be made by postal order unless the workman objects in writing.

(*c*) *Wages Councils Act 1979.* This Act consolidates the law relating to wages councils, which was previously found in the Wages Councils Act 1959. Wages councils have been established in industries where there was no adequate regulation of the payment of workers, usually because there was no satisfactory trade union organisation able to carry on free collective bargaining with the employers. There are approximately forty wages councils in existence. The majority are found in the retail, catering and hairdressing trades, for example the Retail Trade and Allied Trades Wages Council. In deciding whether to set up such a council in a particular industry the Secretary of State may, either on his own initiative or on a joint application from organisations of employers and workers which habitually take part in the settlement of wages and conditions, refer the question to the Advisory, Conciliation and Arbitration Service (ACAS). It is also possible for the Secretary of State to establish a wages council on his own initiative, but it is more usual for him to accept any recommendations made by ACAS as to whether a wages council should be established.

It is the function of wages councils to make orders regarding (*i*) the remuneration (including holiday pay), (*ii*) the holidays to be allowed, and (*iii*) any other terms and conditions, for the workers in relation to whom the council operates, subject to the publication of draft orders and the consideration of any representations made to it as a result of this publication. The orders become part of the individual employee's contract of employment.

10. Written statement of terms. Employers are required, within thirteen weeks of the start of employment, to give all employees normally employed for sixteen hours or more a week, written information about the main terms of their employment, so that they have a clear understanding of their rights and obligations under their contract of employment: Employment Protection (Consolidation) Act 1978, s.1.

The written information must include the following.

(*a*) Names of the employer and employee.

(*b*) Date when the employment started and whether any employment with a previous employer counts as part of a continuous employment with the current employer, and if so the starting date of the previous employment.

(*c*) Title of the job and full details of pay, hours, holidays, sick pay, pension scheme and notice to terminate the contract. (Reference can be made to relevant wages council orders, or to collective agreements.)

(*d*) Details of disciplinary rules, grievance procedures, and personnel.

Alternatively the employer may refer the employee to some document which the employee has reasonable opportunities of reading in the course of his employment, or which is made reasonably accessible to him in some other way.

EXCEPTIONS: Written information is not required in the case of dockworkers, seamen, civil servants, where the employee is a spouse and where an employee is working less than sixteen hours a week.

11. Itemised pay statement. Employees, with certain exceptions, are entitled to an itemised pay statement before or at the time of any payment of wages. This statement must contain particulars of the gross pay, any variable and fixed deductions, and the net pay. The employer may issue a standing statement of fixed deductions, but only if any alterations are notified to the employees when they are made, and it is reissued at least once a year: Employment Protection (Consolidation) Act 1978, ss.8 and 9.

12. The provision of work. Provided an employer continues to pay his employee, he is not generally bound to provide work for him: *Turner* v. *Sawdon* (1901).

(*a*) However, in *Langston* v. *AUEW* (1974) Lord Denning MR suggested that a man has a right to work, and that an employer, when employing a skilled man, is bound to provide him with work when it is available.

(*b*) In *Breach* v. *Epsylon Industries* (1976) the Employment Appeal Tribunal considered that there are circumstances when an obligation to provide work may be implied into a contract of employment.

(*c*) In *Bosworth* v. *Jowett* (1977) an industrial tribunal held that by informing the applicant that he would not be permitted to carry out his duties as sales director for the remaining months of his fixed-term contract, the respondents had repudiated an implied term in the applicant's contract of employment that he had a right to work in conformity with the discipline of the company when work was available. Such action amounted to a dismissal in law, notwithstanding that the respondent had continued to pay the applicant's salary and treat him in other respects as if he were still employed during this period. However, it should be noted that the applicant's service agreement provided for payment of bonus based upon net profits to which he would not be able to contribute by his own efforts as sales director (*see* Exception (1) below). The tribunal also considered that it could possibly damage the applicant's reputation in the trade if it became known that the respondents had withdrawn from him the right to work (*see* Exception (2) below).

EXCEPTIONS: (1) *Commission.* Where payment is made on a commission basis, there is usually an implied term to the effect that the employer will provide work to enable the employee to earn payment: *Turner* v. *Goldsmith* (1891).

(2) *Professional reputation.* Where an employee needs to be engaged in work in order to maintain or build a reputation, the employer will be bound to provide suitable work if the contract provides for payment to be made by way of salary. This rule

applies to journalists and actors. *See Clayton and Waller Ltd.* v. *Oliver* (1930).

13. Indemnity. The employee is entitled to be indemnified by his employer against expenses and liabilities incurred in the proper course of employment. However, where an employee incurs liability for an unlawful act he will be liable if he knew that the act was unlawful.

14. Insurance: statutory duties. The employer must pay his own and his employee's contributions under the Social Security Act 1975. The employer pays the contributions and is then entitled to recover the employee's contributions by deduction from pay. (*See* XI.)

The Employer's Liability (Compulsory Insurance) Act 1969 requires every employer carrying on business in Great Britain to insure against liability for bodily injury or disease sustained by his employees and arising out of, and in the course of, their employment in Great Britain in that business.

15. Safe system of work. The employer has a common law duty to make reasonable provision for the safety of his employees. Where an employer fails in his duty and, as a result, the employee is injured, the employer will have committed the tort of negligence. In *Wilson's and Clyde Coal Co. Ltd.* v. *English* (1938), a House of Lords case, this duty was explained by Lord Wright as: "a duty which rests on the employer and which is personal to the employer, to take reasonable care for the safety of his workmen, whether the employer be an individual, a firm, or a company, and whether or not the employer takes any share in the conduct of operations."

In the same speech it was said that the duty is threefold: the provision of (*a*) a competent staff, (*b*) adequate material, and (*c*) a proper system of work and effective supervision. These three aspects will now be considered separately.

(*a*) *The duty to provide a competent staff.* An employer should not employ (or continue to employ) a person at a particular task for which he is not qualified or sufficiently experienced where to do so would possibly endanger his fellow employees, e.g. to employ a colliery manager who has no knowledge of the dangers of carbon monoxide has been held to be a breach of this duty: *Black* v. *Fife Coal Co. Ltd.* (1912). There was also a breach of this duty where there was continued employment of a workman who habitually indulged in horseplay: *Hudson* v. *Ridge Manufacturing Co. Ltd.* (1957).

(*b*) *The duty to provide adequate material, premises and plant.* Where an employee is injured because of some defect in materials, equipment or plant in circumstances where the employer did not take reasonable care to make these things safe, the employee will have an action in negligence against the employer. The Employer's Liability (Defective Equipment) Act 1969 provides that where an employee suffers personal injury in consequence of a defect in equipment provided by his employer for the purposes of the employer's business, and the defect is due to the fault of a third party, the injury will be deemed to be also attributable to negligence on the part of the employer. Similarly the employer will be liable if injury is caused by some defect in his premises, provided it is shown that he did not take reasonable care. Where a factory was flooded and the subsiding waters left an oily film over the floors, the employer ordered sand and sawdust to be spread, but did not close the factory. It was held that there was no breach of the duty of care when an employee slipped and fell on an untreated part of the floor: *Latimer* v. *AEC* (1953).

(*c*) *The duty to provide a proper system of work and effective supervision.* A system of work is a practice which is permanent and continuous and not merely a method which is casual and emerging in the day's work. It may include the physical layout of the job, the sequence in which the work is carried out, the provision of warnings and notices, and the issue of special instructions. An employer's duty under this head is to take reasonable care for the safety of his employees. In order to discover whether reasonable care was or was not taken in any case, the court will consider all the relevant facts.

Clifford v. *Charles H. Challen & Son Ltd.* (1951): The work in which an employee was engaged involved sticking pieces of wool together with a synthetic glue. It was well known that this glue would cause dermatitis if allowed to dry on the skin. A government notice was displayed in the workshop warning of the danger and setting out the precautionary measures that were necessary, i.e. the use of a protective cream. The employer kept a stock of this cream in the store to which the men had access but none in the workshop, but the foreman did nothing to encourage or enforce the use of the cream. An employee contracted dermatitis through using the glue. HELD: the protective cream should have been provided in the workshop itself, and an effective system established to ensure the use of it. The employer was, therefore, in breach of his duty to the employee. However, the employee was guilty of contributory negligence, and the amount of damages awarded was a half of the full measure.

General Cleaning Contractors Ltd. v. *Christmas* (1953): An employee of the company was a window cleaner of considerable experience. The employer made safety belts available, but the employee did not use these while cleaning the windows of the Caledonian Club because there were no fittings to which they could be attached. In consequence, the employee fell and was injured when a sash fell on his hand. HELD: the employer should have provided wedges to prevent sashes from falling, and should have instructed the employee how to test for dangerously loose sashes. The employer was, therefore, in breach of his duty to provide a safe system of work.

NOTE: (1) The Health and Safety at Work Act 1974 restates the common law duties of employers in broad terms: *see* XII.

(2) If an employee is injured in an accident at work, or suffers an industrial disease arising out of his work, then he will be able to claim the relevant industrial injuries benefit from the Department of Health and Social Security (*see* XI).

(3) If an employee suffers injury as a result of a breach of statutory duty arising, for example, under the Factories Act 1961 (*see* XIII, 67), then this could give rise to a claim for damages.

16. References. An employer is not under a duty to provide his employee with a reference or testimonial unless there is a term in the contract of employment that this should be done. Thus where an employer refuses to give a reference or testimonial, the employee usually has no remedy. However, an employee has the right to receive a written statement of the reasons for his dismissal (*see* IX, **13**).

Where an employer does not give a reference or testimonial, he has a duty not to defame his employee. This arises from the tort of defamation.The test of whether a statement is defamatory is whether the words tend to lower the plaintiff in the estimation of right-thinking members of society generally. However, if the employer can prove that the statement complained of is true, or that it is fair comment, or that it is protected by qualified privilege, then the employer would have a defence to the action of defamation. Qualified privilege would arise where an employer gives a reference to another person who has a proper interest in the contents, e.g. a potential employer of the employee concerned. This means that the employer will not be in breach of his duty to the employee if the statement is not entirely true provided it was not made with malice. Malice will be proved where the employer did not believe that the statement was true, or where the employer made a false statement with ill-will, or where the employer published the statement to a person with no justifiable interest in it.

NOTE: The Rehabilitation of Offenders Act 1974 provides that a rehabilitated person must be treated for all purposes in law as a person who has not committed or been charged with the offence. Thus an employer is not under an obligation to disclose a spent conviction in a reference.

17. Discrimination. Employers are under a duty not to discriminate against potential or existing employees on the grounds of sex, marital status, colour, race, nationality or ethnic or national origins. This is based on the provisions of the Equal Pay Act 1970, Sex Dicrimination Act 1975, and Race Relations Act 1976. (For protection against other forms of discrimination, *see* **16, 49** and IX, **14**(*c*).)

18. Equal Pay Act 1970. The purpose of this statute is to eliminate discrimination between men and women with regard to pay and other terms of their contract of employment. The Act provides that every woman's contract of employment must include an equality clause, which is defined as:

(*a*) a provision by which any term of a woman's contract is automatically modified, if it is less favourable to the woman than a term of similar kind in the contract of a man employed on like work or on work rated as equivalent; and

(*b*) automatically including any term benefiting a man employed on the same work or on work rated as equivalent where such a term is not otherwise included in the woman's contract.

However, the equality clause does not apply if the employer proves that the difference between the contracts is genuinely due to a material difference other than one of sex.

Where any collective agreement contains any provisions applying specifically to men only or women only, the agreement may be referred by any party to it, or by the Secretary of State, to the Central Arbitration Committee (CAC) who must declare which amendments need to be made in the agreement so as to remove the discrimination.

NOTE: Although "woman" has been used above, the Act also applies to men who are treated less favourably than women who are doing the same or similar work.

Article 119 of the Treaty of Rome (European Economic

Community) provides that men and women should receive equal pay for equal work (see *Macarthy's Ltd.* v. *Smith* (1980) where, *inter alia*, the Court of Appeal had to reconcile the Equal Pay Act with the Treaty, and the case was referred to the European Court of Justice). Article 119 has been supplemented by directives which the United Kingdom must incorporate into its law. In *Commission of the European Communities* v. *United Kingdom* (1982) the European Court of Justice held that the Equal Pay Act 1970 denied the right to equal pay for work of equal value in circumstances where no formal job evaluation had been carried out, and so the Act did not comply with European Community law. The Act has now been amended by regulations in order to bring it into line with Community law.

There have been a considerable number of cases heard under the Equal Pay Act 1970. Generally the cases are concerned with whether there is any material difference between the work done by a woman employee and the work done by a male employee. (*See*, for example, *O'Brien* v. *Sim-Chem* (1980); *Noble* v. *David Gold & Son (Holdings)* (1980); and *Ministry of Defence* v. *Farthing* (1980).)

19. Sex Discrimination Act 1975. This act was passed to try to prevent discrimination against men and women on the grounds of sex and marriage. Discrimination means:

(*a*) treating a man or a woman less favourably than a woman or a man would be treated in the same circumstances because of his or her sex;

(*b*) treating a married person less favourably than a single person would be treated in the same circumstances, because of his or her marital status;

(*c*) treating a person less favourably than someone else would be treated in the same circumstances, because he or she has taken action, or been involved in any action, under the Sex Discrimination or Equal Pay Acts;

(*d*) applying to a person a requirement or condition which applies or would apply equally to a person of the opposite sex but:

(*i*) which is such that the proportion of people of the person's sex who can comply with it is considerably smaller than the proportion of the people of the opposite sex who can comply with it, and

(*ii*) which cannot be shown to be justifiable irrespective of the sex of the person to whom it is applied, and (*iii*) which is to that person's detriment because he or she cannot comply with it;

(*e*) applying to a person a requirement or condition as in (*d*) except that it discriminates on the basis not of sex but of marital status, as in (*b*).

Article 119 and relevant EEC directives (*see* **18**) can also affect provisions of the Sex Discrimination Act 1975. In *Garland* v. *British Rail Engineering* (1982) the House of Lords held, after referring the case to the European Court of Justice, that the Sex Discrimination Act should be interpreted so as to be consistent with EEC provisions. In *E.C. Commission* v. *United Kingdom* (1984) the European Court of Justice held that the Act was in breach of the relevant directive because it only applied to legally binding agreements, whereas the directive applied also to non-legally binding agreements.

As with the Equal Pay Act 1970, a considerable number of cases have arisen. Examples are *Price* v. *Civil Service Commission* (1977); *Ministry of Defence* v. *Jeremiah* (1980); *Noble* v. *David Gold & Son (Holdings)* (1980); *GLC* v. *Farrar* (1980); and *Skyrail Oceanic* v. *Coleman* (1980); *Hurley* v. *Mustoe* (1981); *Gill* v. *El Vino Co. Ltd.* (1982); *Home Office* v. *Holmes* (1984).

20. Race Relations Act 1976. This statute is the third legislative attempt to outlaw racial discrimination. The previous attempts were with the Race Relations Acts of 1965 and 1968. The 1976 Act extends the definition of discrimination and establishes a new institutional structure.

A person discriminates against another if:

(*a*) on racial grounds he treats that other less favourably than he treats or would treat other persons; or

(*b*) he applies to that other a requirement or condition which he applies or would apply equally to persons not of the same racial group as that other but:

(*i*) which is such that the proportion of persons of the same racial group as that other who can comply with it is considerably smaller than the proportion of persons not of that racial group who can comply with it; and

(*ii*) which he cannot show to be justifiable irrespective of the colour, race, nationality or ethnic or national origins of the person to whom it is applied; and

(*iii*) which is to the detriment of that other because he cannot comply with it;

(*c*) he treats that other less favourably than in those

circumstances he would treat other persons because that other has or intends to:

(*i*) bring proceedings under the Act; or
(*ii*) give evidence in connection with such proceedings; or
(*iii*) do anything else under the Act; or
(*iv*) allege that there has been a contravention of the Act.

NOTE: (1) "Racial grounds" means any of the following grounds: colour, race, nationality, or ethnic or national origins.

(2) "Racial group" means a group of persons defined by reference to colour, race, nationality or ethnic or national origins and references to a person's racial group refer to any racial group into which he falls.

(3) Segregating a person from other persons on racial grounds is treating him less favourably than they are treated.

There have been relatively few cases arising under this Act compared to the number brought under the Equal Pay Act 1970 and the Sex Discrimination Act 1975. Recent examples which could be considered are: *FTATU* v. *Modgill, Pel* v. *Modgill* (1980); *Kirby* v. *Manpower Services Commission* (1980); *Panesar* v. *Nestlé Co.* (1980); *Owen & Briggs* v. *James* (1981) and *Showboat Entertainment Centre* v. Owens (1984).

21. Discrimination in employment. The Sex Discrimination Act 1975 and the Race Relations Act 1976 contain very similar provisions which will be dealt with together. The Acts make it unlawful for a person to discriminate on the grounds of sex or marriage, or on racial grounds in:

(*a*) the arrangements he makes for the purpose of determining who shall be offered employment; or

(*b*) the terms in which he offers the individual employment; or

(*c*) refusing or deliberately omitting to offer the individual employment, or

(*d*) the way in which an employer affords the individual access to opportunities for promotion, or by refusing or deliberately omitting to afford the individual access to them; or

(*e*) dismissing or subjecting the individual to any other detriment. An employee who is dismissed in breach of these Acts does not have to satisfy the qualifying period of one year in order to bring an unfair dismissal claim (*see* IX, **9**).

EXCEPTIONS: Examples where it is not unlawful to discriminate are: (1) Employment in a private household, subject to certain qualifications. (2) Where being of one sex or belonging to a particular racial group is a genuine occupational qualification. (3) Where the employment is wholly or mainly outside Great Britain. (4) Discrimination on the grounds of sex or marriage, but not race, where an employer employs five or fewer employees. However, in *E.C.Commission* v. *United Kingdom* (1984), the European Court of Justice has held that provisions (1) and (4) are in breach of European Community law and so, presumably, will have to be revised.

The Commission for Racial Equality (*see* **25**) has issued a Code of Practice for the elimination of discrimination and the promotion of equality of opportunity in employment. It attempts to remedy the deficiencies and loopholes in the legislation. The Equal Opportunities Commission is also expected to issue a similar code dealing with sex discrimination.

22. Advertisements. It is unlawful to publish or cause to be published an advertisement which indicates an intention by a person to do any act which is unlawful under the provisions of the Acts, e.g. advertising "Vacancy for a Canadian waiter". However, "Chinese catering staff wanted" would not be unlawful if required for reasons of authenticity by a Chinese restaurant.

23. Application of the Acts. The Acts prohibit illegal discrimination in specified situations. Examples of these are as follows.

(*a*) Employers should not discriminate against employees and certain self-employed workers.

(*b*) Partners in a firm consisting of at least six partners should not discriminate against other partners.

(*c*) Organisations of workers or employers, and professional organisations should not discriminate against a person in the acceptance of members, the terms for members, the access to benefits, facilities or services for members, or the variation or deprivation of membership, or subject that person to any other detriment.

(*d*) Employment agencies should not discriminate in the provision of their services.

24. Enforcement provisions. There are two methods by which a complaint about discrimination may be investigated. These are as follows.

(*a*) Individual employees can bring complaints before an industrial tribunal within three months, where there has been discrimination in their employment. The tribunal may make an order declaring the rights of the parties in relation to the acts complained of, or require the respondent to pay damages up to a maximum of £6,240, or recommend that the respondent take such action as necessary to obviate or reduce the discrimination.

(*b*) A formal investigation may be carried out by the Equal Opportunities Commission or Commission for Racial Equality (*see* **25, 26**).

25. Equal Opportunities Commission and Commission for Racial Equality. The Equal Opportunities Commission was set up to monitor the working of the Equal Pay Act 1970 and the Sex Discrimination Act 1975. The Commission for Racial Equality replaces the Race Relations Board and the Community Relations Commission. It is closely modelled on the Equal Opportunities Commission, whose duties and powers are similar.

The Commissions are under a duty to:

(*a*) work towards the elimination of discrimination;

(*b*) promote equality of opportunity, and, in the case of the Commission for Racial Equality, promote good relations between persons of different racial groups generally; and

(*c*) keep under review the working of the Acts and when necessary draw up and submit proposals for amending them.

26. Other functions of the Commissions. The Commissions may also:

(*a*) undertake or assist research or education;

(*b*) conduct formal investigations for any purpose connected with the carrying out of their duties (*see*, for example, *R.* v. *Commission for Racial Equality ex p. Prestige Group* (1984));

(*c*) assist claimants where the case raises a question of principle, or where it is unduly complex, or where it is unreasonable to expect the claimant to deal with the case;

(*d*) issue non-discrimination notices if they find during an investigation that discrimination has taken or is taking place. (*See*, for example *R.* v. *Commission for Racial Equality ex p. Westminster City Council* (1984).) Within five years of a notice becoming final the Commissions may seek an injunction restraining an employer from continuing discriminatory practices.

DUTIES OF THE EMPLOYEE

27. Personal service. The employee's duty is to render personal service according to the terms of the contract. He may not delegate his duty without the consent of the employer.

28. Obedience. It is the duty of the employee to obey his employer's lawful orders.

(*a*) *Lawful orders*. Lawful orders are those orders given by the employer within the terms of the contract of employment and which are neither illegal nor contrary to public policy. Where an employer gives an order which is outside the scope of the contract, the employee is entitled to refuse to obey. In *Price* v. *Mouat* (1862) it was held that a sales representative who had been ordered to take part in the manufacturing process of his employer's goods was entitled to refuse.

(*b*) *Dismissal without notice*. Where an employee's refusal to obey a lawful order indicates an intention on his part to abandon the contract, the employer will be entitled to dismiss him without notice. Where the refusal to obey does not constitute abandonment of contract, the employer will not be entitled to dismiss the employee summarily: *Laws* v. *London Chronicle* (1959). (*See also UCATT* v. *Brain* (1981).)

(*c*) *Working to rule.* If an employee is working to rule then it is for him to show that he is ready and willing to perform his contract of employment and so be entitled to his wages: *Henthorn and Taylor* v. *Central Electricity Generating Board* (1980).

(*d*) *Duty to co-operate*. There does seem to be a duty to co-operate generally. In *Secretary of State for Employment* v. *ASLEF* (*No. 2*) (1972) three trade unions representing railway workers pressed for increases in pay. Offers of increases by the Railways Board were refused. The unions instructed their members to work to rule, and to ban overtime, rest-day and Sunday working. The instructions were obeyed causing much dislocation of services. Proceedings were taken under the Industrial Relations Act 1971. The Court of Appeal held, *inter alia*, that obedience to instructions to work to rule constituted breaches of contract. Lord Denning considered that an employee must not wilfully "obstruct the employer as he goes about his business". Buckley LJ stated that in his judgment there is an implied term to serve the employer faithfully within the requirements of the contract. "It does not mean that the employer could require a man to do anything which lay outside his obligations under the contract, such as to work excess hours of work or to work an unsafe system of work or anything of that kind, but it does mean that within the terms of the contract the employee must serve the employer faithfully with a view to promoting those commercial interests for which he is employed." Roskill LJ had no hesitation "in implying a term into the contract of service that each employee will not, in obeying his lawful instructions, seek to obey them in a wholly unreasonable way which has the effect of disrupting the system, the efficient running of which he is employed to ensure".

29. Reasonably skilled. The employee impliedly warrants that he is competent to do the job for which he is engaged unless he discloses his incompetence, or the employer is aware of his standard of competence: *see Harmer* v. *Cornelius* (1858).

30. Confidential information. The skills and abilities of the employee are his exclusive property to use as and where he wishes, subject to the terms of his contract of employment. Even the employer who has given an employee training, or the necessary experience to acquire and develop skills, has no special claim to the benefit of those skills. On the other hand, however, there are special circumstances where particular aspects of the employee's skill and knowledge may be said to belong to the employer. For example, where the employee possesses information connected with the employer's trade secrets or lists of customers, the employee may not use this information freely. The employee has a duty to respect his employer's confidential information (*see Faccenda Chicken* v. *Fowler* (1984)). There are three limitations imposed by the law on the employee and these are as follows.

(*a*) *Implied duty of fidelity*. This duty requires the employee to serve his employer faithfully. Thus, an employer may be protected from his employee (whether existing or former) disclosing trade secrets: *Printers & Finishers Ltd.* v. *Holloway (No. 2)* (1964). In addition, skilled men with access to their employer's secrets may not be able to work for a rival firm even in their spare time: *Hivac Ltd.* v. *Park Royal Scientific Instruments* (1946). This duty will be extended by the courts to meet the circumstances of a particular case. In *Sinclair* v. *Neighbour* (1967), for example, the manager of a betting shop took £15 from the till to pay for his own gambling, having left his wallet at home. He put an IOU into the till and replaced the money the next day. It was held that the employee's action was in breach of his contract of employment even though he had not been expressly forbidden to borrow from the till. The main point was that he knew that his employer would not approve.

(*b*) *Express term*. The contract between the employer and the employee may contain an express term restraining the employee from using trade secrets he acquired whilst employed by the employer for the benefit of subsequent employers. However, the restraint must be reasonable, seeking to protect the genuine trade interest of the employer.

Commercial Plastics v. *Vincent* (1964): The plaintiffs employed the defendant V in the production of PVC calendered sheeting which was made up into adhesive tape. V's contract forbade him seeking employment with any of the plaintiff's competitors in the PVC calendering field for one year after leaving their employment. V left the plaintiffs and wanted to take up employment with one of the plaintiff's competitors. The plaintiff applied for an injunction, but the Court of Appeal refused to grant the application because although V could remember material which could be protected by such a term in the contract, the particular term was excessive for the following reasons: (*i*) it was world-wide in scope and the plaintiffs did not require protection outside the United Kingdom: and (*ii*) the term extended to competitors in the whole PVC calendering field whereas protection with regard to V was only required for calendered sheeting for adhesive tape.

It seems that the courts are more likely to enforce a term restraining an employee from working for named rivals of his employer in a defined area than a blanket prohibition in such an area: *Littlewoods Organisation* v. *Harris* (1978) and *Greer* v. *Sketchley Ltd.* (1979). An employee cannot terminate the implied duty of confidence and good faith (*see* (*a*) above), or a duty imposed by an express term, by resignation: *Thomas Marshall (Exports) Ltd* v. *Guinle* (1978). Dismissal may be fair (*see* IX, **7–12**) where an employee's continued employment entails the risk of a leak of confidential information: *Skyrail Oceanic* v. *Coleman* (1980).

(*c*) *Duty to disclose certain information to the employer.* An employee is under a duty to disclose to his employer any information he acquires which affects his employer's interests.

Cranleigh Precision Engineering v. *Bryant* (1965): The defendant was the managing director of a company engaged in the manufacture of swimming pools. The defendant designed swimming pools for his employer and, during the course of this work, he had learnt of a foreign patent but had not passed this information to his employer. Instead, he set up a company of his own to exploit the foreign patent, advertising a swimming pool which incorporated certain design features of the pool manufactured by the employer. HELD: the employee was in breach of his duty of confidence in making use of the design features already used by the employer and also he was in breach of his duty of confidence in buying and exploiting the foreign patent without informing the employer. The court took the view that it was not relevant that the design features of the employer's pool were very simple and that the foreign patent was available to any member of the public who cared to look for it at the Patent Office. The defendant was in a special position in that he knew how best to use the design features involved, and where to buy suitable materials for the manufacture of pools of this type. These pieces of information were the trade secrets of the employer and the employee was not entitled to make use of them for his own purposes.

31. Patents, inventions and copyrights. An invention made by an employee will, as between him and his employer, be taken to belong to the employer if:

(*a*) it was made in the course of the normal duties of the employee or specifically assigned to him, and the circumstances in either case were such that an invention might reasonably be expected to result from the carrying out of his duties; or

(*b*) the invention was made in the course of the duties of the employee, and at the time of making the invention, because of the nature of his duties and particular responsibilities so arising he had a special obligation to further the interests of the employer's undertaking: Patents Act 1977, s.39.

However, if a patent has been granted for an invention and it is of outstanding value to the employer, the employee can be awarded compensation to be paid by the employer.

Any other invention made by an employee will as between him and his employer be taken for those purposes to belong to the employee. Any term in a contract which diminishes the employee's rights in his inventions is unenforceable: s.41.

Where a literary, dramatic or artistic work is made by the author in the course of his employment by the proprietor of a newspaper, magazine or like publication, the proprietor is entitled to the copyright unless otherwise provided: Copyright Act 1956, s.4.

32. Indemnity. Where a servant, in the normal course of his duties, causes injury or loss to a third person through want of care in the performance of his duties, the master will usually be vicariously liable. Where the third party succeeds against the master, the servant is under a duty to give an indemnity. In practice, the employee is seldom sued personally on the indemnity for he is seldom a substantial defendant. A prudent employer will insure against this kind of vicarious liability. *See Lister* v. *Romford Ice & Cold Storage Co. Ltd.* (1957).

RIGHTS OF EMPLOYEES

33. Legislative provisions. The Employment Protection Act 1975 established certain individual rights for employees which can be regarded as terms implied by statute into most contracts of employment. The Employment Protection (Consolidation) Act 1978 has consolidated most of the legislation on individual employment enacted since 1963, including the Contracts of Employment Acts 1963 and 1972, the Redundancy Payments Act 1965 and the relevant provisions of the Employment Protection Act 1975. The 1978 Act is concerned with the following matters.

(*a*) Particular terms of employment (*see* **10** and **11**).
(*b*) Rights arising in the course of employment (*see* **34–50**).
(*c*) Termination of employment (*see* **51** and IX).
(*d*) Resolution of disputes relating to employment (*see* X).

The Employment Act 1980 has amended certain of these provisions.

34. Guarantee payments. An employee who loses pay because of short-time working or lay-offs will be entitled to guarantee payments where a full day's work is lost. Usually the employee must have been continuously employed for not less than one month. The amount of the guarantee payment will be a normal day's pay, but limited to a maximum of £10 per day (from 1st February 1984). The amount is reviewed annually by the Secretary of State for Employment: 1978 Act, s. 148. Pay will be guaranteed for five days in any period of three months: 1978 Act, ss.12–18, as amended by 1980 Act, s.14.

Where there is no work because of a trade dispute involving other employees of the same or an associated employer, the employer will not be obliged to make guarantee payments. Payments made under a contract of employment are taken into account when assessing the maximum number of days when payment is due: *Cartwright* v. *G. Clancy* (1983).

NOTE: The Secretary of State can exclude employees from this scheme on the joint application of all parties to a collective agreement that provides guaranteed pay on terms which should include provision for referral to an independent arbitrator or adjudicator, or to an industrial tribunal where the employer has failed to pay an agreed guarantee payment. Twenty two exemption orders had been granted by 29th February 1984.

35. Medical suspension. An employee who has to be suspended from work under specified statutory regulations by his employer on medical grounds will be entitled to be paid his normal wage while he is suspended, up to a maximum of twenty-six weeks. This does not apply to ordinary absence as a result of sickness: 1978 Act, ss. 19–22.

NOTE: If an employee is dismissed from work on these medical grounds, he can bring a claim for unfair dismissal, where applicable, so long as he was employed for a minimum period of four weeks, not one year which is the normal qualifying period for such a claim.

36. Statutory sick pay. The Social Security and Housing Benefits Act 1982 and consequent regulations radically altered the administration of sick pay for employees. Under the Social Security Act 1975 sickness benefit was paid to sick employees and other suitably qualified persons, by the Department of Health and Social Security (*see* XI, **13**). An employer is now initially under a statutory duty to pay sick pay to his employees. The employer recovers the amount of any sick pay paid to employees by withholding that amount from any primary or secondary Class 1 social security contributions that he is bound to pay (*see* XI, **3**). There is no provision to recompense the employer for any costs incurred in administering this scheme. Sickness benefit (*see* XI, **13**) will still be paid to non-employees and the unemployed who are suitably qualified, as well as to employees who have exhausted their right to statutory sick pay.

37. Entitlement to statutory sick pay. An employee who is ill is entitled to receive sick pay from his employer. A day of incapacity for work through illness occurs where an employee is incapable of doing his usual work by reason of some specific disease or bodily or mental disablement. Statutory sick pay is not payable for the first three days of an illness. Where an employee is ill twice within a two-week period then that is treated as one illness, so the employee will receive sick pay for the first three days of the second illness (compare sickness benefit). The maximum sick pay that can be paid in any one tax year is normally eight weeks. After that an employee who satisfies the relevant conditions (*see* XI, **13**) can claim sickness benefit. Sick pay is only paid for the days on which the employee is normally required to be available for work. Regulations deal with the situation where an employee is dismissed in order to avoid payment of sick pay, and govern the manner and time within which notice of the illness must be given to the employer. Failure to give the required notice can result in a loss of sick pay.

A sickness certificate from a doctor is only required from the eighth day of illness. Prior to that day self-certification by the employee is required. An employer can require an employee claiming sick pay to provide information so that the employer can decide whether the employee is entitled to sick pay and, if so, for how long. An employee absent from work because of illness can ask the employer for a written statement which states first, for which days the employer considers himself to be liable to pay sick pay, and secondly the amount of the sick pay. The employer must give reasons why on any other days he is not liable to pay sick pay.

Contravention of the requirements concerning time limits for payments, documentation to the Secretary of State, the maintenance of records and the furnishing of information, is a criminal offence making the offender liable to a fine.

38. Disentitlement. The following employees will not be entitled to receive sick pay.

(*a*) Men and women over state retirement age.
(*b*) Employees who have done no work under their contract of employment.
(*c*) Employees on strike.
(*d*) Women on maternity leave.
(*e*) Employees in legal custody.
(*f*) Employees travelling outside the EEC.
(*g*) Temporary employees engaged for three months or less.
(*h*) Employees who are sick within fifty-seven days of claiming certain social security benefits including sickness benefit and maternity allowance.

39. Rate of sick pay. The rate of pay is earnings-related and from 6th April 1984 is as follows:

(*a*) £42.25 a week in a case where the employee's normal weekly earnings are not less than £68;
(*b*) £35.45 a week where the earnings are less than £68 but not less than £50.50; or
(*c*) £28.55 a week in any other case.

The amount of pay payable by the employer is calculated on a daily basis, being the weekly rate (e.g. £42.25) divided by the number of days in the normal working week (e.g. five which would give a daily rate of £8.45 from the fourth day of illness).

40. Determination of disputes. This is governed by the Act and by regulations.

(*a*) The Secretary of State will resolve questions relating to the employer's obligation or otherwise, to pay sick pay. Questions of law may be referred to the High Court, either on an application by the Secretary of State, or on appeal by an aggrieved person.

(*b*) A social security appeal tribunal will decide certain questions laid down in regulations or referred to it by an adjudication officer.

(*c*) An adjudication officer can decide all other questions and should make his decision, so far as it is practicable, within fourteen days.

41. Appeals. Appeal within twenty-eight days lies as of right from the decision of the adjudication officer to the social security appeal tribunal, unless the sole ground of the insurance officer's decision is a determination by the Secretary of State (*see* **40** (*a*)). In that case an appeal can be made only with the permission of the social security appeal tribunal. An appeal can be made within three months from the social security appeal tribunal to a Social Security Commissioner (*see* XI, **38**).

42. Review of decisions. The Secretary of State may review his decisions if there was a mistake as to, or ignorance of, a material fact. An adjudication officer or a social security appeal tribunal (on a reference from an adjudication officer) may review any other decision on the same ground and on the following additional grounds:

(*a*) any relevant change of circumstances; or

(*b*) where the decision was based on a determination by the Secretary of State which has now been revised.

An adjudication officer can review his own or another's decision if it was based on a mistake of law.

43. Maternity provisions. These apply to any woman who has either:

(*a*) been in continuous employment for two years with the same employer working sixteen hours or more a week until eleven weeks before the expected date of birth, or (*b*) been in continuous employment for five years with the same employer working eight hours or more a week until eleven weeks before the expected date of birth.

The expectant mother will be entitled to have time off for ante-natal care (*see* **44**), to receive maternity pay (*see* **45**), to return to work (*see* **46**), and not to be dismissed (see **47**); 1978 Act, ss. 33-48, 56, 60, as amended by 1980 Act, ss. 11-13.

NOTE: (1) A female employee who has made sufficient social security contributions at the full rate will also be entitled to eighteen weeks' maternity allowance commencing eleven weeks before the expected date of birth, if she gives up work at that time. She will also be entitled to a maternity grant either on the basis of her full-rate contributions, or where she has paid the married woman's rate on the basis of her husband's contributions.

(2) Employees often have express terms in their contract of employment relating to maternity pay and leave. An employee who has a right both under the Act and under her contract of employment to return to work, may not exercise the two rights separately, but may in returning to work take advantage of whichever right is, in any particular respect, the more favourable. (But *see Bovey* v. *Board of Governors of the Hospital for Sick Children* (1978) and *ILEA* v. *Nash* (1979) for differing approaches.)

44. Time off for ante-natal care. An employee who is pregnant and who has on the advice of a registered medical practitioner, midwife or health visitor, made an appointment to receive ante-natal care, has the right not to be unreasonably refused *paid* time off during her working hours to enable her to keep the appointment. The employee can be required by her employer for second and subsequent visits to produce a certificate from one of the above-mentioned medical personnel stating that she is pregnant and an appointment card showing that the appointment has been made. If an employer fails either to let the employee have time off or to pay her for the time off, she can complain to an industrial tribunal.

45. Maternity pay. An employee who is away from work because she is having a baby is entitled to receive pay for the first six weeks of her absence, provided that she has informed her employer, in writing if he so requests at least twenty-one days before her absence begins (or as soon thereafter as is reasonably practicable) that her absence is because of pregnancy or confinement. The employer contributes nine-tenths of her normal pay less the amount of the flat-rate social security maternity allowance.

A central Maternity Pay Fund has been established. Employers will normally be able to claim a refund of any maternity pay they have paid from this fund. All employers will contribute to the fund through the employers' social security contributions.

The Government has published a discussion document on all forms of maternity benefits, but it seems that no changes will be made in the near future to the present system whereby both the employer and the state pay benefits which depend upon length of employment or satisfactory contribution records.

46. Return to work. An employee who has been away from work to have a baby is entitled to return to her job at any time up to twenty-nine weeks after her baby is born. The 1980 Act has imposed more stringent conditions as regards the notice which must be given to employers, and has in effect excluded the right to return in certain cases (*see* **48**). The requirements as to notice are mandatory: *Lavery* v. *Plessey Telecommunications* (1982). Failure to comply with the provisions leads to a forfeiture of the employee's right to be treated as dismissed from the date of the employer's refusal to permit her to return to work. This reduces the period of employment and affects the employee's rights to redundancy and unfair dismissal compensation. Three notifications are now required, as follows.

(*a*) The employee must notify her employer *in writing* at least twenty-one days before her absence begins or as soon as is reasonably practicable:

(*i*) that she is or will be absent from work wholly or partly because of pregnancy, or the birth;

(*ii*) that she intends to return to work with her employer; and

(*iii*) the expected week of birth or if it has occurred the date of the birth.

(*b*) An employer can then request, in writing, not earlier than forty-nine days after the beginning of the expected week of the birth (or the date of the birth), that the employee gives him written confirmation that she intends to return to work. The employee will not be entitled to return to work unless she gives that confirmation within fourteen days of receiving the request or as soon as is reasonably practicable. The request by the employer must be accompanied by a written statement explaining the effect of failing to give such confirmation.

(*c*) The employee must then give written notice to her employer at least twenty-one days before the day on which she proposes to start work, that she wishes to return.

The period of twenty-nine weeks can be extended by a further four weeks if she is too ill to work and if she produces a medical certificate to this effect. Her employer must give her back her old job or a suitable alternative job, but he may postpone her return to work by four weeks after the date notified by the employee for her return, provided that he notifies her before the date and specifies the reasons for the postponement. An employee whose employer has refused to re-employ her can obtain an order for re-employment or compensation from an industrial tribunal (*see McFadden* v. *Greater Glasgow Passenger Transport Executive* (1977) where the applicant was not given her old job back when she returned from maternity leave, but a supernumerary post). If she has been made redundant during her absence she will be entitled to redundancy pay.

47. Unfair dismissal. If an employee is dismissed because of her pregnancy (or for any reason connected with it) the dismissal will be unfair. She can apply for a reinstatement or re-engagement order, or compensation from an industrial tribunal: 1978 Act, s.60.

However, the dismissal will not be considered unfair if at the date of the termination of her employment:

(*a*) she is unable to do the work because of her pregnancy; or

(*b*) she cannot continue to do her job without contravening a legislative provision, e.g. because of lead or radioactive material in a factory.

Even if the dismissal is fair she must be offered a suitable alternative job if one is available. If this is not possible she can still claim maternity pay and re-employment or compensation.

Where an employer engages another employee as a temporary replacement for the employee who is absent as a result of her pregnancy or confinement, the employer can dismiss the temporary replacement fairly to make it possible to give work to the returning mother, so long as the temporary replacement was thus informed on his or her engagement, and the employer acted reasonably in dismissing the replacement: 1978 Act, s.61.

48. Not allowed to return to work. Where an employee is entitled to return to work, but is prevented from doing so because the employer has dismissed her, she will be treated as having been employed until the notified day of return after the birth, and dismissed from that date. The employee may then bring a claim for unfair dismissal or a redundancy payment if she satisfies the relevant conditions (*see* IX).

However, an employee who, although entitled to, is not allowed to return to work will not be regarded as dismissed in the following circumstances.

(*a*) When:

(*i*) her employer employed five or less employees immediately before her absence began; and

(*ii*) it is not reasonably practicable for the employer to permit her to return to her original job or a suitable alternative which is not substantially less favourable.

(*b*) When it is not reasonably practicable for a reason other than redundancy for the employer to permit her to return to her original job, and her employer offers her a suitable alternative which is not substantially less favourable, which she accepts, or unreasonably refuses.

If an employee brings a claim for unfair dismissal in the circumstances described in (*a*) and (*b*), it is for the employer to show that he satisfied the requirements of these provisions: 1978 Act, s.56, as amended by 1980 Act, s.12.

49. Trade union membership and activities. Every employee has the right not to have action short of dismissal taken against him, as an individual, by his employer for the purpose of:

(*a*) preventing him or deterring him from being, or seeking to become, a member of an independent trade union, or taking part in its activities at any appropriate time, or penalising him for doing so (*see Carlson* v. *Post Office* (1981)); or

(*b*) compelling him to become a member of a trade union; or

(*c*) enforcing a requirement that if he is not a member of a trade union then he must make certain alternative payments: 1978 Act, ss. 23–26 as amended by the 1980 Act, s.15 and the 1982 Act, s.10.

NOTE: Where a closed shop exists then the action under (*b*) will not be unlawful unless:

(1) the employee genuinely objects on grounds of conscience or other deeply held personal conviction; or

(2) the employee had not been a union member prior to and after the introduction of the closed shop; or

(3) the closed shop agreement has not been approved through a ballot held within the previous five years;

(4) the closed shop agreement has come into effect after 8th September 1980 having been approved by at least 80 per cent of the relevant employees, but the particular employee has not since the ballot been a member of a specified trade union.

An industrial tribunal can, on the application of the employee, order the employer to pay him compensation. If the employer or the employee claims that the employer was induced to take the action because a trade union or other person threatened or took industrial action, then that third party can be made a party to the tribunal proceedings at the request of either the employer or the employee at any time before the hearing of the complaint begins. After that time the third party may be joined at the tribunal's discretion. If the claim is well-founded the third party can be required to pay a contribution to the employer in respect of that contribution. (*See also* X, **37**.)

50. Time off work. Employees will be entitled to time off work for the following purposes.

(*a*) *Trade union duties.* An official of a recognised independent trade union is entitled to reasonable *paid* time off to carry out his official duties connected with industrial relations, where they concern his employer, and for approved training connected with those duties: 1978 Act, s. 27 (but *see Marley Tile Co.* v. *Shaw* (1980) and *Sood* v. *GEC Elliott Process Automation* (1980)).

(*b*) *Trade union activities.* Employees who are members of recognised independent trade unions are entitled to reasonable time off in working hours to take part in that union's activities (other than industrial action): 1978 Act, s.28. The Advisory, Conciliation and Arbitration Service has drawn up a Code of Practice which provides guidance on the circumstances in which time off for trade union activities may be allowed, and what constitutes reasonable time off. (*See Rasool* v. *Hepworth Pipe Co.* (*No. 2*) (1980); and *White* v. *Pressed Steel Fisher* (1980) which was concerned with time off for a union safety representative (*see* XII, **5**) to attend a health and safety course at a technical college.)

(*c*) *Public duties.* An employee is entitled to reasonable time off to carry out specified public duties, e.g. as a Justice of the Peace, or a member of a local authority: 1978 Act, s.29. *See Emmerson* v. *Commissioners of Inland Revenue* (1977) where it was held by an industrial tribunal that the respondents had failed to allow the applicant reasonable time off for the performance of his duties as leader of the opposition of Portsmouth City Council.

(*d*) *Looking for work.* An employee who has been employed

continuously for at least two years and who is given notice of dismissal by reason of redundancy, is entitled to reasonable *paid* time off to look for work or to arrange training for a new job: 1978 Act, s.31. However, the employer will not be liable to pay more than two-fifths of a week's pay.

(*e*) Ante natal care (*See* **43**.)

51. Insolvency. An employee has the following rights on the insolvency of his employer.

(*a*) Application to the Secretary of State for Employment: 1978 Act, s.122. An employee whose employer becomes insolvent will be able to apply to the Secretary of State for the payment of the following debts.

(*i*) Any arrears of pay in respect of one or more (but not more than eight) weeks.

(*ii*) Any payment of wages for a statutory minimum period of notice under s.49 of the 1978 Act which will be reduced by any money which the employee earns or could reasonably be expected to have earned during that period: *Secretary of State for Employment* v. *Jobling* (1980).

(*iii*) Any amount of holiday pay, up to a maximum of six weeks, accrued during the previous twelve months.

(*iv*) Any basic award of compensation for unfair dismissal.

(*v*) Any reasonable sum by way of reimbursement of a premium paid by an apprentice or an articled clerk.

NOTE: The employee will receive payment up to a maximum of £145 a week. This amount is reviewed annually by the Secretary of State: 1978 Act, s.148.

(*b*) Priority of certain debts: 1978 Act, s.121. The Act also provides that certain debts will be treated as wages and have priority on the insolvency of an employer. These are any amount owed by an employer to an employee in respect of:

(*i*) a guarantee payment (*see* **34**);

(*ii*) payment during suspension on medical grounds (*see* **35**);

(*iii*) time off for trade union duties (*see* **50**(*a*)) and for looking for work (*see* **50**(*d*)); and

(*iv*) payments under a protective award where there has been lack of consultation preceding dismissal for redundancy (*see* IX **36**(*e*)).

PROGRESS TEST 8

1. How does the law distinguish between a contract of service and a contract for services? **(1–4)**

2. When is an employer liable for the torts of his employees? **(6, 7)**

3. What are the sources of the terms of a contract of employment? **(8)**

4. When can an employer deduct money from an employee's wages? **(9)**

5. What information must be given to an employee (*a*) within thirteen weeks of the start of his employment, and (*b*) when he is paid? **(10, 11)**

6. Is an employer bound to provide an employee with work? **(12)**

7. What do you understand by the employer's duty at common law to provide a safe system of work for his employees? **(15)**

8. Against what forms of discrimination by his employer is an employee protected? **(17, 49)**

9. How is it ensured that men and women receive the same pay for the same work? **(18)**

10. When will the employer be found to have discriminated against an employee on the grounds of (*a*) sex, and (*b*) race? **(19–21)**

11. How can an employee formally complain about sex or race discrimination? **(24)**

12. Is an employee under a duty to obey his employer? **(28)**

13. What obligations are there on an employee not to use or disclose his skill or knowledge? **(30, 31)**

14. When is an employee entitled to a guarantee payment? **(34)**

15. If an employee is sick is he entitled to be paid his normal wages? **(35, 36)**

16. When can a pregnant woman claim maternity pay? **(43)**

17. What conditions must an employee satisfy in order to return to work after having a baby? **(46)**

18. Can a woman be fairly dismissed (*a*) because of her pregnancy, or (*b*) on her return to work after the birth? **(47–48)**

19. When can an employee claim (*a*) paid time off from work, and (*b*) unpaid time off from work? **(50)**

20. What debts owed by an employer to an employee (*a*) will be paid on application to the Secretary of State, and (*b*) will have priority on the insolvency of the employer? **(51)**

CHAPTER IX

Termination of the Contract of Employment

COMMON LAW AND STATUTE LAW

1. General. The rights and obligations under a contract of employment may be brought to an end in the same way as in the case of any other kind of contract. Thus, a contract may be terminated by the following.

(*a*) Performance.
(*b*) Agreement.
(*c*) Breach.
(*d*) Frustration.
(*e*) Lapse of time
(*f*) Operation of law.

However, statute law has radically altered the common law in relation to contracts of employment.

2. Common law. Until the Industrial Relations Act 1971, which was repealed in 1974, the employee's remedy for wrongful dismissal rested upon the basis of a breach of contract which would be heard in the common law courts. The right of dismissal at common law was based on two propositions:

(*a*) an implied term existed allowing either party to terminate the contract by reasonable notice; and
(*b*) breach of a fundamental term of the contract by either party would be deemed to be a repudiation by that party of the contract.

This will rarely form the basis of a claim now, because of the unfair dismissal provisions (*see* **4**, note (2) 7). But *see Burdett-Coutts* v. *Herts C.C.* (1984).

3. Notice. The Employment Protection (Consolidation) Act 1978 lays down the following *minimum* periods of notice.

(*a*) An employee continuously employed for one month is entitled to one week's notice.

(*b*) An employee with two years' service or more but less than twelve years of continuous employment is entitled to one week's notice for each year of continuous employment.

(*c*) An employee with twelve years or more of continuous employment is entitled to not less than twelve weeks' notice of termination.

(*d*) An employee with one month or more continuous employment is required to give not less than one week's notice of termination of employment: s.49.

The parties may provide for a longer period of notice, but not for a shorter period. The right to receive the specified period of notice may be waived, or payment in lieu of the notice due may be accepted.

The employee has certain rights during the period of notice, for example wages if sick, whether the required notice was given or not: 1978 Act, ss.51, 52.

If no minimum period of notice is specified, but there is an implication that it is longer than the period allowed for under the Act, then the period of notice is that which is reasonable in the circumstances of the particular case. The statutory period of notice might also be affected by provisions in the contract of employment relating to, for example, disciplinary procedures. In *Gunton* v. *Richmond upon Thames London Borough Council* (1980), the Court of Appeal held, *inter alia*, that a letter of dismissal giving an employee one month's notice as required by his contract of employment amounted to wrongful dismissal because the contractual disciplinary procedure had not been followed.

4. Termination without notice. At common law a fundamental breach of the contract of employment will be construed as a repudiation of that contract by that party. Summary dismissal of the employee or summary departure on the part of the employee will bring the contract to an end. This holds true whether or not the dismissal or departure is in breach of contract. Where there is a breach the remedy available to the innocent party is damages for wrongful dismissal. This is not synonymous with a claim for unfair dismissal (*see* 7): *Fox Brothers (Clothes) (in Liquidation)* v. *Bryant* (1979).

Where summary dismissal or summary departure is in breach of contract, there has been an abandonment of the contract which gives the other party the right to elect to treat the contract as at an end. Where, however, the employer is justified in dismissing his employee without notice, no breach of contract is involved.

Wilson v. *Racher* (1974): The plaintiff had been engaged as head gardener by the defendant for approximately six weeks when he stopped work early outside one Friday afternoon because of the rain, and he cleaned tools for the rest of the afternoon. The following Sunday he passed by the defendant and his family in the garden. The defendant showered the plaintiff with questions, was aggressive and accused the gardener of stopping work early on the previous Friday. The plaintiff tried to explain but the defendant continued with trivial complaints, calling the plaintiff back when he tried to depart. Finally the gardener resorted to the use of obscene language and the defendant summarily dismissed him. The plaintiff brought an action for wrongful dismissal. The Court of Appeal held that the plaintiff's use of obscene language on a solitary occasion did not justify summary dismissal and accordingly he had been wrongfully dismissed. The test for this case was whether the plaintiff's conduct was insulting and insubordinate to such a degree as to be incompatible with the continuance of the relation of employer and employee. (Cf. *Pepper* v. Webb (1969).)

NOTE: (1) If an action for unfair dismissal is brought, the employer will have to show that the dismissal was fair and reasonable in all the circumstances.

(2) An employee is only likely to bring an action for wrongful dismissal if he cannot bring a claim for unfair dismissal, because, for example, he falls within one of the exceptions (*see* **9**), or where he could recover more compensation by way of damages because there is no upper limit to the amount the court can award, whereas there is a limit to the amount an industrial tribunal can award for unfair dismissal (*see* **20–22**). Only the highly paid are likely to find it worth while to bring an action for wrongful dismissal because of the chance of greater compensation.

5. Remedies. The remedies for breach of contract of employment are generally damages at common law, and in appropriate circumstances an injunction in equity (but *see* X, **39**). The case would be heard in the county court or High Court, not by an industrial tribunal.

(*a*) *Damages.* In an action for wrongful dismissal, damages are awarded to compensate the employee for wages due to the date of the wrongful repudiation, plus the amount of wages which would have been earned during the period of notice which should have been given to terminate the contract. (*see* also XI, **48**).

Where an employer seeks damages for breach of contract by an employee, e.g. absenteeism, he can claim as damages moneys wasted by the breach provided that such a loss was in the contemplation of the parties at the time of making the contract: *Anglia Television* v. *Reed* (1972).

(*b*) *Injunction.* In certain circumstances an injunction may be awarded by the court to restrain the breach of a negative term, usually where the employee promises not to work for another employer during a specified period: *see*, for example, VIII, **30**(*b*). In *Hill* v. *C. A. Parsons Ltd.* (1972) the Court of Appeal issued an injunction against an employer who purported to terminate an employee's employment with the totally inadequate notice of one month instead of six months. (Damages were not an adequate remedy.)

6. Statutory provisions. The relevant statutory provisions which will be considered in the rest of this chapter in relation to the termination of a contract of employment are:

(*a*) the Employment Protection (Consolidation) Act 1978; and
(*b*) the Employment Act 1980; and
(*c*) the Employment Act 1982.

UNFAIR DISMISSAL

7. Employee's statutory right. The right of an employee to bring a claim where he is unfairly dismissed was introduced by the Industrial Relations Act 1971. The relevant provisions are now found in the Employment Protection (Consolidation) Act 1978, Part V, as amended by the Employment Acts 1980 and 1982.

The importance of this concept cannot be over-emphasised. It has in practice superseded the common law action for wrongful dismissal and provides a much more effective remedy from the employee's point of view.

An employee who is able to show that he was dismissed and that the dismissal was unfair will be able to claim re-employment or compensation from his employer. This is quite independent of the common law action for wrongful dismissal.

The employee who claims that he has been unfairly dismissed must make a complaint to an industrial tribunal within three months of the effective date of termination of his contract of employment. The tribunal may hear the complaint within such further period as it considers reasonable where it is satisfied that it was not reasonably practicable for the complaint to be presented before the end of this period. What is meant by reasonably practicable has given rise to much judicial debate; *see*, for example, *Palmer* v. *Southend-on-Sea Borough Council* (1984). The employee is known as the applicant, the employer as the respondent. An appeal will lie from the decision of the industrial tribunal on a point of law to the Employment Appeal Tribunal.

8. The action for unfair dismissal. There are two stages in an action for unfair dismissal, as follows.

(*a*) The industrial tribunal will satisfy itself that the employee has been dismissed within the meaning of the Act and that he has neither been excluded from the provisions of the Act nor presented his complaint more than three months after his effective date of termination, or within such further period as the tribunal considers reasonable where it was not reasonably practicable for the complaint to be presented within the period of three months (*see* **7**).

(*b*) The tribunal then has to consider whether in the circumstances the employer acted reasonably or unreasonably in dismissing the employee: 1978 Act, s.57, as amended by 1980 Act, s.6.

9. Meaning of "employee". An employee is defined as an individual who has entered into or works under, or where the employment has ceased, has worked under, a contract of employment. A contract of employment is a contract of service or of apprenticeship, whether it is oral, implied or in writing: 1978 Act, s.153.

EXCEPTIONS: The unfair dismissal provisions do not apply to the following.

(1) Anyone who is not an employee, e.g. an independent contractor or a freelance agent.

(2) Part-time employees who normally work less than sixteen hours a week for their employer, unless they normally work for eight hours or more a week but less than sixteen, and they have done so for five years. (*See Lake* v. *Essex County Council* (1979) and *Bullock* v. *Merseyside County Council* (1979).)

(3) Employees who have not completed one year's continuous employment with their employer at the time of their effective date of termination (*see Ford* v. *Warwickshire County Council* (1983)). However, if the employer has not employed more than twenty employees during the employee's continuous employment then the qualifying period is increased to two years. (But *see* **14** and VIII, **35**.)

(4) Employees who before the effective date of termination

of their employment reached the age of retirement, which is regarded as being the normal retiring age for relevant employees, but if there is no such norm, then age 65 for a man and 60 for a women: *Nothman* v. *Barnet London Borough Council* (1979) HL (*see also Waite* v. *G.C.H.Q.* (1983)).

(5) Fixed-term contracts of one year or more, where the dismissal consists only of the expiry of the term without its being renewed and the employee has previously agreed to exclude any right to bring a claim for unfair dismissal: 1978 Act, s.142, as amended by 1980 Act, s.8. (*See also* **10**(*b*); *Dixon* v. *British Broadcasting Corporation* (1979) and *Wiltshire County Council* v. *NATFHE* (1980).)

(6) Any employment where the employer is the husband or wife of the employee.

(7) Any employment as a registered dock worker.

(8) Any employment as a master or member of the crew of a fishing vessel where the remuneration is by a share in the profits or gross earnings of the vessel.

(9) Any employment where under the contract of employment the employee ordinarily works outside Great Britain.

(10) Employment as a member of the police service and armed forces.

(11) Employees covered by a dismissal procedures agreement which has been exempted from the unfair dismissal provisions by an order made by the Secretary of State for Employment.

10. Meaning of dismissal. The statutory definition is wider than that under the common law and means:

(*a*) the termination of an employee's contract of employment by his employer with or without notice, or

(*b*) where under that contract he is employed for a fixed term, the expiry of that term without it being renewed under the same contract, or

(*c*) the termination of the contract of employment by the employee, with or without notice, in circumstances such that he is entitled to terminate it without notice by reason of the employer's conduct: 1978 Act, s.55.

It is for the employee to show that he has been dismissed. There is no dismissal where the employee wishes to leave unless he has no choice, as for example, in *Kendrick* v. *Aerduct Productions* (1974). This can amount to constructive dismissal. In *Western Excavating (EEC)* v. *Sharp* (1978) the Court of Appeal considered that the correct test in deciding whether an employee has been constructively dismissed is whether or not the employer has been guilty of conduct which constitutes a significant breach going to the root of the contract of employment which shows that the employer no longer intends to be bound by one of its essential terms. Then the employee is entitled to leave without notice, or to give notice, but the conduct in either case must be sufficiently serious to entitle him to leave at once. The employee must make up his mind soon after this conduct occurs, because if he does not then he will be considered to have affirmed the contract and will have lost the right to treat himself as discharged. However, constructive dismissal is not automatically unfair dismissal: *Industrial Rubber Products* v. *Gillon* (1977).

11. Reason for dismissal. The Employment Protection (Consolidation) Act 1978, ss.57–59 (as amended by the Employment Act 1980, ss.6 and 7 and the Employment Act 1982, s.3) sets out guidelines for establishing whether the dismissal was fair or unfair. The employer must show what was the reason, or, if more than one, the principal reason for the dismissal, and that the reason either:

(*a*) related to the capability or qualifications of the employee for performing work of the kind which he was employed to do, or

(*b*) related to the conduct of the employee, or

(*c*) was that the employee was redundant, or

(*d*) was that the employee could not continue to work in the position which he held without a contravention of a duty or restriction imposed by an enactment, or

(*e*) was some other substantial reason of a kind such as to justify the dismissal of the employee.

(*See Hollister* v. *National Farmers' Union* (1978), and *Rasool* v. *Hepworth Pipe Co. (No. 2)* (1980).)

In determining whether the employer had sufficient reason to dismiss the employee, no account should be taken of any pressure, such as threatening to take or taking industrial action, which was put on the employer: s.63 (but *see also* **24**).

12. Fair or unfair dismissal? Even where the employer has fulfilled these requirements special provisions apply where an employee has been dismissed for trade union membership or non-membership and activities (*see also* X, **26**). This is particulary relevant where there is a closed shop (*see also* **14**(*b*)).

(*a*) Dismissal of an employee will be regarded as having been *unfair* if the reason for it was that the employee:

(*i*) was, or proposed to become, a member of an independent trade union,

(*ii*) had taken, or proposed to take part, in the activities of an independent trade union at an appropriate time, or

(*iii*) was not a member of any trade union and had refused or proposed to refuse to become a member, or if a member refused to remain one: 1978 Act. s.58(1) as substituted by the 1982 Act s.3 (*see Maund* v. *Penwith District Council* (1984); *Therm-a-Stor Ltd.* v. *Atkins* (1983).)

(*b*) Dismissal of an employee by an employer will be regarded as *fair* if:

(*i*) it is the practice, in accordance with a union membership agreement, for employees, who are of the same class as the dismissed employee, to belong to a specified independent trade union, and

(*ii*) the principal reason for the dismissal was that the employee was not and would not be a member of a specified union; 1978 Act s.58(3) as substituted by the 1982 Act, s.3.

(*c*) The dismissal of an employee as described in (*b*) (*i*) and (*ii*) will be *unfair* if:

(*i*) the employee genuinely objects on grounds of conscience or other deeply held personal conviction to being a member of a trade union; or

(*ii*) the employee had been an employee of the employer before the closed shop agreement (union membership agreement *see* X, **4** and **22**) came into force, and he has not joined any trade union in accordance with the agreement; or

(*iii*) a closed shop agreement came into force after 14th August 1980 in accordance with the provisions of the 1978 Act, s.58A (*see* X, **22**) and the employee was entitled to vote in the ballot and has not at any time since the ballot been a member of a specified trade union; or

(*iv*) a closed shop agreement is in force and there either has not been a ballot in the five years preceding the dismissal or any such ballot has not obtained a sufficient majority of employees in favour of the closed shop (*see* X, **23**); or

(*v*) there is in force a declaration made on a complaint under the Employment Act 1980 s.4 (*see* X, **18**) that the employee has been unreasonably excluded or expelled from the trade union, or alternatively such proceedings are pending; or

(*vi*) the employee has professional obligations embodied in a written code, and is expelled from the union for failing to take part in industrial action which would be in breach of that code, or refused to join the union lest he is required to take part in such action.

(*d*) Dismissal of an employee will be regarded as having been *unfair* if the reason for it was that the employee was made redundant (unlike other employees who held similar positions) either:

(*i*) for an unfair trade union reason (*see (a*), (*b*) and (*c*)),

or

(*ii*) in contravention, without special reasons, of a customary arrangement or agreed procedure relating to redundancy.

Generally, however, subject to the above provisions of the Acts, the determination of whether the dismissal was fair or unfair is based on the question whether in the circumstances (including the size and administrative reasources of the employer's undertaking) the employer acted reasonably or unreasonably in treating the reason given as sufficient ground for dismissing the employee. The industrial tribunal must answer this question in accordance with equity and the substantial merits of the case: 1978 Act, s.57, as amended by 1980 Act, s.6. The approach which should be adopted by an industrial tribunal was discussed by Donaldson LJ in *UCATT* v. *Brain* (1981) CA. Where dismissal is based on a belief of an employee's dishonesty the employer must establish: (*i*) the fact of his belief of misconduct; (*ii*) reasonable grounds to sustain the belief; and (*iii*) that he had carried out as much investigation as was reasonable in the circumstances: *British Home Stores* v. *Burchell (Note)* (1980). The employer must also in such a case give the employee a proper chance to refute the allegations: *W. Weddell & Co.* v. *Tepper* (1980).

It is doubtful whether there can be an unfair dismissal in the case of a properly conducted entry into liquidation: *Fox Brothers (Clothes) (in Liquidation)* v. *Bryant* (1979); though of course there might well be grounds for a redundancy claim.

13. Written statement. Employees who have been continuously employed for six months have the right to receive from their employer, on request, a written statement of the reasons for their dismissal or non-renewal of a fixed-term contract. If the employer refuses, or fails to provide such a statement, the employee may complain to an industrial tribunal which may require the employer to pay the employee compensation equivalent to two weeks' pay if it decides that the complaint was well-founded: 1978 Act, s.53.

14. Additional provisions. There are additional provisions which apply to certain special types of dismissal.

(*a*) Unfair selection for redundancy will amount to unfair dismissal in certain circumstances (*see* **12**(*d*)).

(*b*) Dismissal for an unfair trade union reason (*see* **12**(*a*), (*b*) and (*c*)) will be unfair dismissal even if the employee falls into some of the classes of employees who are not normally protected by these provisions, e.g. employees who have not been continuously employed for one year.

(*c*) In certain circumstances dismissal because of a spent conviction, or failure to disclose a spent conviction or any circumstances connected with it will be unfair: Rehabilitation of Offenders Act 1974.

(*d*) Dismissal on grounds of pregnancy will normally be unfair, as will dismissal where an employee who is so entitled, is not permitted to return to work within twenty-nine weeks after the birth (*see* VIII, **47**).

(*e*) Dismissal during an industrial dispute: where at the date of dismissal the employer was conducting or instituting a lockout or the employee was taking part in a strike or other industrial action, the industrial tribunal will only determine whether the employee was fairly or unfairly dismissed if it is proved that:

(*i*) one or more relevant employees of the same employer have not been dismissed, or

(*ii*) any such employee has within three months of his dismissal been offered re-engagement and that the complainant has not been offered re-engagement: 1978 Act s.62 as amended by the 1982 Act s.9. The complainant may only claim for unfair dismissal within six months of his own dismissal.

(*f*) An employee who is dismissed because he would otherwise have been suspended for medical reasons can complain to an industrial tribunal of unfair dismissal if he had been continuously employed for four weeks (*see* VIII, **35**).

(*g*) An employee who is dismissed in breach of the Sex Discrimination Act 1975 or the Race Relations Act 1976 does not have to satisfy the qualifying period of one year in order to bring an action for unfair dismissal (*see also* VIII, **21**).

(*h*) Where one company or firm takes over or merges with another business any takeover dismissals will be automatically unfair, except as a result of economic, technical or organisational changes (*see also* **33**).

15. Remedies. The Employment Protection (Consolidation) Act 1978 provides for several methods of settling disputes arising from an allegation of unfair dismissal. There is the possibility of:

(*a*) conciliation before the case is heard by an industrial tribunal;

(*b*) interim relief in certain circumstances, which prevents a dismissal coming into force before the complaint has been fully considered and decided upon; and
(*c*) reinstatement or re-engagement; or
(*d*) compensation.

16. Conciliation. The conciliation officer receives a copy of the form used when making an application to an industrial tribunal for unfair dismissal, and he will try to promote a settlement if he is asked to do so by the employee and employer concerned, or on his own initiative if he considers that he could act with a reasonable prospect of success: 1978 Act, s.134.

The conciliation officer will normally act after a complaint had been referred to him by an industrial tribunal, but his services will be available at the request of either or both the parties before such a complaint has been made.

17. Interim relief. This is available to an employee who complains that he was dismissed for unfair trade union reasons (*see* **12**(*a*), (*b*) and (*c*)). Such an employee has the right to apply to the tribunal for an order for him to be temporarily reinstated or re-engaged or for his contract of employment to be continued until his complaint of unfair dismissal has been finally settled by agreement or decided at a tribunal hearing. Applications must be made not later than seven days after the date of dismissal and must be supported by a certificate signed by an authorised official of the employee's union. If appropriate, notice of the application should be given to a trade union which is to be joined as a party to the proceedings as soon as is reasonably practicable. If the tribunal thinks it likely that at a full hearing of the complaint it will find both that the dismissal was unfair, and that the main reason for the dismissal was an unfair trade union reason then it must grant the employee's application for interim relief: Employment Protection (Consolidation) Act, 1978, s.77 as amended by the Employment Act 1982, s.8.

18. Reinstatement and re-engagement. The Employment Protection (Consolidation) Act, 1978, s.69 gives these additional powers to industrial tribunals.

(*a*) *Reinstatement* means restoring the employee to the job from which he was dismissed as though the dismissal had never happened.
(*b*) *Re-engagement* normally means that the employee will work in a different job either with his previous employer, or where there has been a change of employer since his dismissal, with his previous employer's successor or with an associated company.

The tribunal asks the employee if he wishes to be reinstated or re-engaged, and considers whether to make such an order. In deciding whether to make the order the tribunal will consider whether it is practicable and just for the employee to be reinstated or re-engaged. Where the tribunal makes such an order it will set out the terms under which the employee is to be reinstated or re-engaged. The tribunal can also order the employer to recompense the employee for any loss suffered as a result of the dismissal, such as arrears of pay. In practice these new remedies are not often used by industrial tribunals.

19. Failure to comply with a re-employment order. If the tribunal finds that the employee has been reinstated or re-engaged, but that the terms of the order have not been fully complied with, it must order the employer to pay the employee compensation for the loss caused to the employee as a result of the employer's failure to comply with the order up to a maximum of £7,000.

If the employee has not been reinstated or re-engaged, the tribunal will make an award of compensation for the unfair dismissal and unless the employer convinces the tribunal that is was not feasible for him to comply with its order, it will make a special additional award of compensation against the employer of not less than thirteen nor more than twenty six weeks' pay.

However, if the dismissal was for an unfair trade union reason (*see* **12**(*a*), (*b*) and (*c*)) then a special award (*see* **23**) may be made; if it involved unlawful discrimination (*see* VII, **21**) then an award may be made of not less than twenty-six nor more than fifty-two weeks' pay: 1978 Act, ss. 71 and 75. These amounts are reviewed annually: 1978 Act, s.148. One week's pay for 1984 may not exceed £145.

20. Compensation. Where an employee has made it clear that he does not wish to return to work for his previous employer, or where the tribunal considers that it would not be practicable or just, the tribunal will provide the alternative remedy of an award of compensation, which usually consists of a basic award (*see* **21**) and a compensatory award (*see* **22**): 1978 Act, s.72, and a special award (*see* **23**) in certain circumstances: 1982 Act, s.5.

21. Basic award. This is calculated in a similar way to an employee's entitlement to redundancy payments (*see* **39**). The amount is calculated by reference to the period during which he has been continuously employed before the effective date of termination of his contract of employment. Thus he will receive the following.

(*a*) One-and-a-half weeks' pay for each year of employment in which the employee was aged 41 or above.

(*b*) One week's pay for each year of employment not falling within (*a*) which consists wholly of years in which the employee was not below the age of 22 (i.e. age 22–40).

(*c*) Half a week's pay for each such year of employment not falling within (*a*) or (*b*): 1978 Act, s.73, as amended by 1980 Act, s.9.

However, no more than twenty years of employment can be taken into account, and the amount of one week's pay for calculating a basic award shall not exceed £145. This amount is reviewed annually by the Secretary of State: 1978 Act, s.148. Thus the maximum basic award is currently £4,350. Where the dismissal is for an unfair trade union reason (*see* **12**(*a*), (*b*) and (*c*)) then the amount of the basic award cannot be less than £2,000. Where a person is dismissed by reason of redundancy but is not entitled to a redundancy payment then the basic award will be two weeks' pay.

NOTE: (1) the amount of the award can be reduced where (*a*) the employee's conduct makes it just and equitable to do so; (*b*) the employee received a payment in respect of redundancy; (*c*) compensation in respect of the same matter was also awarded under the Sex Discrimination Act 1975 or the Race Relations Act 1967 – the total compensation awarded should not exceed £7,000; (*d*) the employee has unreasonably refused an offer of reinstatement; (*e*) the employee is within twelve months of the normal retiring age.

(2) An industrial tribunal should not reduce an award because of an employee's refusal either to pay money to some source other than the union in lieu of union dues or to belong to or resign from a particular trade union. This applies to both basic and special awards (*see* **23**).

22. Compensatory award. This is an award of whatever amount of compensation the tribunal considers just and equitable in the circumstances of the employee's case, subject to a maximum of £7,000 for the actual loss which he has suffered as a result of his dismissal insofar as the employer can be held responsible for that loss, other than loss of entitlement to redundancy payment: 1978 Act, s.74. The amount can be reviewed by the Secretary of State: 1978 Act, s.75. However, the employee is under a duty to mitigate his loss.

It is the duty of industrial tribunals themselves when hearing complaints of unfair dismissal to raise the five different categories of compensatory awards, namely:

(*a*) immediate loss of wages;
(*b*) manner of dismissal;
(*c*) future loss of wages;
(*d*) loss of protection in respect of unfair dismissal by reason of redundancy;
(*e*) loss of pension rights: *Tidman* v. *Aveling Marshall Ltd.* (1977).

The maximum compensation currently available in ordinary claims will be:

Basic award	£4,350
Compensatory award	£7,000
	£11,350

However, where the employer has failed to comply with a re-employment order or where a special award is made then the maximum amount of compensation is higher (*see* **19** and **23**).

23. Special award. This award was introduced by the Employment Act 1982 s.5, and is to be paid where the dismissal is for an unfair trade union reason (see **12** (*a*), (*b*) and (*c*)) and the employee asks the tribunal to order his re-employment (*see* **18**). If an order is not made, the amount of the special award will be either:

(*a*) one week's pay x 104; or
(*b*) £10,000,

whichever is the greater, but the amount may not exceed £20,000.

If an order is made but the employer satisfies the tribunal that it was not practicable to comply with the re-employment order then the amount of the special award is increased to either:

(*a*) one week's pay $\times$156; or
(*b*) £15,000,

whichever is the greater amount.

The maximum amount of one week's pay is currently £145. This amount is reviewed annually: 1978 Act, s.148.

The special award can be reduced in certain circumstances; for example, on account of any conduct by the complainant, or where the employee has unreasonably prevented compliance or refused to comply with a re-employment order (*see also* **21**).

24. Contributions. In certain circumstances the employer will be able to obtain a contribution from a third party towards the compensation which he has to pay his employee: 1980 Act, s.10. This right to a contribution arises in the following circumstances.

(*a*) Where an industrial tribunal is hearing a case of unfair dismissal and the employer claims that he was pressurised to dismiss the employee by threats of or actual industrial action, because the employee was not a member of a trade union. The third party, e.g. a trade union, putting the pressure on the employer, should be joined as a party to the proceedings. If this request is made after the beginning of the hearing, then the tribunal has a discretion to refuse the request. If the claim is well-founded then the third party can be required to contribute towards any compensation paid by the employer to the employee.

(*b*) Where an employee is dismissed because he is not a member of a suitable trade union and the employer could only provide work with a particular contractor who required under the contract that the work should be done by employees who were members of a trade union(s), this requirement being confirmed by the contractor in respect of the particular employee, then the contractor can be made a party to the tribunal proceedings and can be required to indemnify the employer for the full amount of the compensation paid.

(*c*) If the contractor in (*b*) was under pressure similar to that described in (*a*), then the third party may also be joined to the proceedings and if the contractor's claim is well-founded, the tribunal may order the third party to make a contribution towards the contractor's liability to indemnify the employer under (*b*).

This right to contribution is most likely to arise where an employer has had to dismiss an employee because of a closed shop agreement (*see* X, **22**).

However, the 1982 Act s.12 makes void union only (or non-union only) requirements in contracts for the supply of goods or services. Refusal to enter into a contract on the ground that an employer uses non-union (or union) labour is illegal, and any contravention would be a breach of statutory duty. There are similar provisions dealing with union recognition requirements as terms of a contract: s.13. Trade union immunity under TULRA 1974 s.13 (*see* X, **35**) does not apply to tortious acts intended to bring about breaches of ss.12 and 13: s.14. The immunity is also removed where any person induces another to interfere with the performance of, or to break, a contract of employment because of the use or non-use of union labour, by a supplier who is not the employer. The supplier, but not the employer, could sue the employee.

REDUNDANCY

25. Statutory provisions. The Employment Protection (Consolidation) Act 1978 consolidated the existing law relating to redundancy which was found in the Redundancy Payments Act 1965 as considerably amended by the Employment Protection Act 1975. The effect of the legislation is to make provision for a system of compensation in the event of the loss of jobs through redundancy. Redundant employees become entitled to lump-sum payments based on length of service before dismissal as a result of redundancy. Other factors, such as the job prospects of a redundant employee, are not taken into account when calculating the redundancy payment in each case, nor is an employee's right to a redundancy payment affected by the fact that he may find employment with another employer immediately after being made redundant.

26. Definition of redundancy. Section 81(2) of the 1978 Act states that an employee is to be regarded as having been made redundant if he is dismissed because:

(*a*) the employer has ceased, or intends to cease, to carry on the business, or

(*b*) the employer has ceased, or intends to cease, to carry on the business in the place at which employees were contracted to work, or

(*c*) the requirements of the business for employees to carry out work of a particular kind have ceased or diminished or are expected to cease or diminish (*see Higgs & Hill* v. *Singh* (1977)).

NOTE: "Cease" and "diminish" apply to both permanent and temporary cessations and diminishments in business.

27. Meaning of "employee". An employee for the purposes of the 1978 Act is defined as an individual who has entered into, or works under (or where the employment has ceased, worked under) a contract of employment: 1978 Act, s.153 (*see* VIII, **5**).

However, in order to qualify for a redundancy payment the employee must have had at least two years' continuous employment with his employer. Service up to and including the week which began before the employee attained the age of 18 does not count.

EXCEPTIONS: Certain employees will not qualify for redundancy payments. Examples are: (1) An employee who works less than sixteen hours a week, or less than eight hours a week after five years' service. (2) An employee whose reckonable service ends on or after the age of retirement. (3) A registered dock worker. (4) A share fisherman who is paid solely by a share of the catch. (5) An employee employed by his/her spouse. (6) A Crown servant. (7) An employee dismissed for misconduct (other than for taking part in an industrial dispute) after having been dismissed for redundancy: 1978 Act, ss.82 and 92. (8) Where an exemption order has been issued because of an agreement between employers and trade unions making alternative provision.

28. Dismissal and redundancy. An employee is taken to have been dismissed by his employer if:

(*a*) the contract under which he is employed by the employer is terminated by the employer, whether it is so terminated by notice or without notice; or

(*b*) under that contract he is employed for a fixed term, and that term expires without being renewed under the same contract; or

(*c*) the employee terminates that contract, with or without notice, in such circumstances that he is entitled to terminate it without notice by reason of the employer's conduct: 1978 Act, s.83.

The Act provides that an employee who has been dismissed by his employer will, unless the contrary is proved, be presumed to have been dismissed by reason of redundancy: 1978 Act, s.91. Thus the onus is upon the employer to prove, on the balance of probabilities, that the reason for the dismissal was not redundancy. However, the dismissal must be wholly or mainly due to redundancy before there can be any entitlement to a redundancy payment: *see Lesney Products & Co. Ltd.* v. *Nolan* (1977) below.

An employee is not entitled to a redundancy payment where the employer, being entitled to terminate the contract of employment without notice by reason of the employee's conduct, terminates it either without notice, with short notice, or allows him to work out his normal notice despite his conduct in which case the employer must make the position clear by giving a written statement to the employee to the effect that his conduct has been such as to justify summary dismissal: 1978 Act, s.82.

However, it seems that if the employee was initially dismissed for redundancy but then dismissed for striking, he is still entitled to a redundancy payment: 1978 Act, s.92. (*see* also *Simmons* v. *Hoover Ltd.* (1976)).

29. Additional provisions. Additional provisions apply in the following circumstances.

(*a*) Where the employer gives notice to the employee, who then gives notice to terminate the contract an an earlier date, e.g. where he has found another job: 1978 Act, s.85.

(*b*) Where an employee is entitled to return in accordance with s.47 (*see* VIII, **46**).

(*c*) Where there are lay-offs and short-time working: 1978 Act, ss.87, 88, 89.

30. Example cases.

Marriot v. *Oxford and District Co-operative Society Ltd. (No 2)* (1970): M had worked for some years an an employee of the Oxford and District Co-operative Society. He was then told that there was insufficient work for him and that he could be demoted from foreman to supervisor at a reduced wage. M protested and tried unsuccessfully to find work elsewhere. He received a letter from his employer telling him that his wages would be reduced by £1 per week. Again M protested and, several weeks later, he left to take another job. On the question whether he had been dismissed by his employer within the meaning of s.3 of the Redundancy Payments Act, it was held that the employer's letter amounted to a termination of the employee's contract of employment unless and until the new terms proposed were accepted by him; since the employee had vigorously protested against the terms of the letter, it was clear that he had not accepted those terms, despite his continuing to work for several weeks after receiving the letter; the contract had been terminated within the meaning of the Act. The employee was entitled to redundancy payment. (*See* also *Land* v. *West Yorkshire Metropolitan County Council* (1981).)

O'Brien v. *Associated Fire Alarms Ltd.* (1969): The employer was a company with a branch office at Liverpool. The company had a business which extended into most parts of the United Kingdom, and the Liverpool office controlled an area stretching from mid-Wales to Cumberland. Three of the employees who worked in the area controlled by the Liverpool office and who had their homes in Liverpool and were able to return home each day were requested by the company to work in Cumberland. The employees refused to do this because it would mean their being able to return to their homes only at the weekends. The company thereupon dismissed the employees, who then claimed redundancy payments. The company contended that there was an implied term in their contracts of employment, namely that they should work anywhere in the area controlled from the Liverpool office, and that there had been a breach of this implied term. HELD: the employer has not shown that there was an implied term that the employees could be sent anywhere in the area controlled by the Liverpool office and, accordingly, the employees were presumed to have been dismissed by reason of redundancy.

North Riding Garages Ltd. v. *Butterwick* (1967): An employee had been employed in a garage for thirty years, during which time he rose to the position of workshop manager in charge of the repairs workshop. He had given good service until the business was taken over by a new employer, who introduced new methods to which the employee found it difficult to adapt. Some months later, the new employer dismissed the employee by giving due notice. The employer then appointed another workshop manager. When the employee applied for a redundancy payment, the employer claimed that he was dismissed on the grounds of incompetence and not by reason of redundancy. On the question whether the employee was dismissed by reason of redundancy, HELD: the employee was not entitled to a redundancy payment because the overall requirements of the employer's business was unchanged. It was not relevant that the duties of the new workshop manager were not identical with the employee's duties before dismissal. *Per* Widgery J: "The very fact of dismissal shows that the employee's services are no longer required by his employer and that he may, in a popular sense, be said to have become redundant; but if the dismissal was attributable to age, physical disability or inability to meet his employer's standards, he was not dismissed on account of redundancy within the meaning of the Act. For the purpose of the Act an employee who remains in the same kind of work is expected to adapt himself to new methods and techniques, and cannot complain if his employer insists on higher standards of efficiency than those previously required; but if new methods alter the nature of the work required to be done, it may follow that no requirement remains for employees to do work of the particular kind which has been superseded and that they are truly redundant. Thus, if a motor manufacturer decides to use plastics instead of wood in the bodywork of his cars and dismisses his woodworkers, they may well be entitled to redundancy payments on the footing that their dismissal was attributable to a cessation of the requirements of the business for employees to carry out work of a particular kind, namely, woodworking."

Hindle v. *Percival Boats* (1969): An employee, a highly skilled craftsman in woodworking, who had been employed most of his life in boat-building, was dismissed because he was "too good and too slow". For several years before his dismissal, the employer's business was in difficulties because of the decline in the work on wooden boats due to the emergence of fibreglass as a boat-building material. For this reason the employer's business suffered some diminution. On the question whether the employee was entitled to a redundancy payment, it was held that there was no entitlement to redundancy payment because the dismissal was not attributable to any diminution of the employer's business but to the fact that he did not come up to the standards required by the employer. *Per* Sachs LJ: "The onus placed on the employer is simply to show (using the standard test of balance of probabilities applicable where the facts are largely within the knowledge of a party against whom a claim is made) that the dismissal of the employee was not attributable to redundancy; once the tribunal is satisfied that the ground put forward by the employer is genuine and is one to which the dismissal is mainly attributable the onus is discharged; and it ceases to be in point that the ground was unwise or based on a mistaken view of the facts."

Johnson v. *Nottinghamshire Combined Police Authority* (1974): For over twenty years two women clerks had worked a five-day week from 9.30 a.m. to 5 p.m. or 5.30 p.m. at a police station. They were dismissed when they declined for domestic reasons to change to an alternating shift system, 8 a.m. to 3 p.m. and 1 p.m. to 8 p.m. and a six-day week, introduced by the police authority to achieve greater efficiency in police work. They were replaced by two women clerks doing the same work and working the same number of hours but on the shift system. They claimed redundancy payments on the ground that their dismissals were mainly attributable to redundancy in that the changes in the hours of work was sufficient to effect a change in the kind of work which they had been employed to do. The Court of Appeal held that the change in the hours of working, without any change in the tasks to be performed or in the total number of hours worked, did not effect a change in the particular kind of work for which the applicants had been required, such as to make redundancy the reason for their dismissal. The employers had shown that the reason for their dismissal was to bring about greater efficiency not to reduce their work force.

Lesney Products & Co. Ltd. v. *Nolan* (1977): The appellant company suffered a falling off in sales which led to a reorganisation in the way the work was done. A night-shift was eliminated altogether, and the employees given redundancy payments. On the day-shift, work was reorganised so that in place of a shift 8 a.m. to 5 p.m. for four days a week and 8 a.m. to 2.30 p.m. on Fridays, with extensive overtime working, two day-shifts were introduced. All employees on the old day-shift were offered work on the new double day-shifts. Those who refused, including the respondent employees, were dismissed. The employees claimed redundancy payments. The Court of Appeal held that the appellant company's reorganisation was done in the interests of efficiency and was not due to a diminution in the employer's requirements for employees to carry out work of a particular kind.

NOTE: The employees could still claim unfair dismissal on other grounds.

31. Offer of re-employment. If an employee has been given notice because of redundancy, and he accepts an offer of further employment, either on the same terms or on different terms, or in a different place, made before the date of the expiry of the notice given to him, and starting not later than four weeks after the end of the current contract of employment, he is not entitled to a redundancy payment and the employment is regarded as continuous: 1978 Act, ss.82 and 84.

If the employee refuses the offer which is made on the *same terms* as his existing employment, he is not entitled to a payment unless he has reasonable grounds for refusing. Where the offer is one of *alternative* employment on different terms or in a different place, then the job should be suitable in relation to the employee. If the employee unreasonably refuses an offer of continued employment in suitable alternative work there is no entitlement to a redundancy payment.

Taylor v. *Kent County Council* (1969): A boys' school was amalgamated with another school, and as a result of this reorganisation a headmaster's employment was terminated, prima facie, on the ground of redundancy. The local authority (the employer in this case) offered the headmaster alternative employment in a mobile pool of teachers serving for short periods in various schools where there was a shortage of staff. The alternative employment offered would require the former headmaster to serve under the authority of the headmaster of each school to which he would be sent. The alternative offer provided for the payment of the same salary as previously paid.

The headmaster refused the offer. On the question whether the local authority had made an offer of alternative suitable employment which had unreasonably been refused it was held that "suitable employment" means employment which is substantially equivalent to the employment which had ceased; the offer of a postion in a mobile pool of teachers to a headmaster with the appellant's qualifications, experience and status, and necessitating his moving house, was not suitable; nor could it be made so merely by guaranteeing the same salary. The headmaster was entitled to a redundancy payment. (Applied in *Hindes* v. *Supersine* (1979).)

The employee, however, is allowed a trial period of four weeks from the beginning of the new job in which to decide whether or not it is suitable. In *Turvey* v. *C. W. Cheyney* (1979) the Employment Appeal Tribunal considered that employees having started alternative jobs were entitled to a reasonable period to decide whether to accept the new contracts, and only then did the four-week trial period commence. Both the employer and employee can terminate the new contract. Entitlement to redundancy payment will arise if the usual conditions were satisfied at the date of the termination of the old job, but the employer can withhold a payment on the grounds that the employee had, in effect, unreasonably ended a suitable job. The onus is on the employer to prove his case.

32. Offer of work with an associated employer. In general where an employee is made redundant with one employer, but is offered employment with an associated employer, the two employers are effectively regarded as one and the same, and the conditions for the offer of renewed or alternative employment apply. The two periods of employment will be regarded as continuous and this fact should be included in the written statement of the terms of employment issued by the employer to the employee: 1978 Act, ss.82 and 84.

33. Offer of work with a new owner of the business. If an employee accepts an offer of work with the new owner and continues with him beyond the expiry of any trial period, his service is regarded as continuing from the old to the new owner, and as in **32** this should be confirmed in the written statement of the terms of employment: 1978 Act, s.94. Where a company or a firm takeover or merge with another business then the company or firm must honour the employees' contracts of employment, collective bargains and trade union recognition agreements. Takeover dismissals are automatically unfair. Recognised trade unions must be consulted in anticipation of such transfers: Transfer of Undertakings (Protection of Employment) Regulations 1981.

34. Death. Where an employer (i.e. a sole proprietor) dies then in the case of a claim for redundancy payment, the death counts as dismissal: 1978 Act, s.93. The deceased employer's personal representative is liable to pay any redundancy payments, but he can offer re-employment within eight weeks of the death of the employer: 1978 Act, Sched. 16, Part III.

Where an employee dies, after receiving notice of the termination of his employment, before the expiry of the notice, then the date of the expiry of the notice for the purpose of redundancy is taken to be the date of death: 1978 Act, Sched. 16, Part IV.

35. Procedure for handling redundancies. The Employment Protection Act 1975 introduced provisions for notification and consultation where redundancies are proposed. The Act gave trade unions and individual employees specific rights and it gave employers specific duties (*see* **36, 37**).

However, there is no legal requirement as to the method of selecting employees for redundancy. The most common practice is on a last-in-first-out basis.

36. Consultations with trade unions. The Employment Protection Act 1975 lays down the following provisions. (*See* also **33**.)

(*a*) *Consultation.* Employers are required to consult appropriate trade unions about proposed redundancies. An employer, who proposes to dismiss any employee as redundant and who recognises an independent trade union for the group or category of employees to which the redundant employee belongs, must consult a representative of that trade union about the dismissal before it takes place, whether or not the employee is a member of that union. The consultation with the union should begin at the earliest opportunity regardless of the number of employees, but the Act lays down a specified minimum period of consultation before the first dismissal takes place, as follows.

(*i*) If 10–99 employees may be dismissed as redundant at one establishment over a period of thirty days or less, then at least thirty days must be allowed for consultation.

(*ii*) If 100 or more employees may be dismissed as redundant at one establishment over a period of ninety days or less, then at least ninety days must be allowed for consultation: s.99.

(*b*) *Notification.* Employers are under a duty to notify the Secretary of State in writing where they propose redundancies described in (*a*). In the case of (*a*)(*i*) notification should take place at least thirty days before the first of the dismissals takes effect, and in the case of (*a*)(*ii*) at least ninety days. Where the notice relates to employees of any description in respect of which an independent trade union is recognised by the employer, he must give a copy of the notice to representatives of that union: s.100. Penalties for non-compliance are either a reduction in rebate for any redundancy payments made to those employees, or possible criminal proceedings.

(*c*) *Disclosure of information.* Employers are required to disclose in writing to trade union representatives certain information about the proposed redundancies. The employer must tell the union:

(*i*) the reasons for his proposals;

(*ii*) the numbers and descriptions of employees whom it is proposed to dismiss as redundant;

(*iii*) the total number of employees of any such description employed by the employer at the establishment in question;

(*iv*) the proposed method of selecting the employees who may be dismissed; and

(*v*) the proposed method of carrying out the dismissals, with regard to any agreed procedure, including the period over which the dismissals are to take effect.

(*d*) *Complaint to tribunal.* An appropriate trade union may complain to an industrial tribunal that an employer has not met the requirements to consult about proposed redundancies, as in *Amalgamated Society of Boilermakers, Shipwrights, Blacksmiths and Structural Workers* v. *George Wimpey M. E. & C.* (1977). The employer may raise the defence that there were special circumstances which prevented him from complying fully and that he took all possible steps to comply with them as far as he could. The defence is also available for failing to disclose information. Where there is de facto recognition of a union by an employer the requirements as to consultation must be complied with, even where the employer genuinely believed, albeit unreasonably, that he had not recognised the union. This did not amount to a special circumstance: *Joshua Wilson & Bros.* v. *USDAW* (1978). Insolvency does not amount to a special circumstance: *Clarks of Hove* v. *Bakers' Union* (1978). Nor does ignorance of the statutory requirement to consult: *UCATT* v. *H. Rooke & Son* (1978).

(*e*) *Tribunal declaration and award.* Where the tribunal finds a union's complaint justified it will make a declaration to that effect.

This is an indication to the employer to postpone dismissal notices, where necessary, to enable consultation to take place. The tribunal can also make a protective award to safeguard the employee's remuneration. A protective award will require the employer to pay specified employees their normal week's pay for a specified period, the protected period, which depends upon the number of days of consultation due (thirty or ninety days under (*a*)(*i*) and (*ii*) above, or twenty-eight days in all other cases) and the number of those days lost. The purpose of a protective award is to compensate the employee and to penalise the employer. It is not necessary to show that the employee has suffered financial loss.

NOTE: The Secretary of State may make an order modifying the requirements of the Act if he is satisfied that there is a collective agreement which makes satisfactory alternative arrangements for handling redundancies.

37. Employees. The Employment Protection Act 1975 provides as follows.

(*a*) An employee covered by a protective award (*see* **36**(*e*)) has the right to be paid his normal week's pay by his employer for the protected period, whether he is working for him or not, provided that he is entitled to payment under his contract of employment or under his statutory rights during a period of notice. For this purpose the whole remaining part of his employment is treated as if it were a statutory period of notice.

(*b*) An offer of renewed or new employment can be made to the employee by the employer during the protected period. If the employee refuses the offer without good reason he will lose his right to payment for the rest of the protected period.

38. Claims for redundancy payments. An employee must make a written claim for a redundancy payment to the employer within six months of the date of termination of his employment. If termination occurs during a trial period of employment on different terms, the date from which the six months start to run is the date of termination of the latest contract. Where a complaint of unfair dismissal has been presented by the employee to an industrial tribunal, a written claim to the employer for redundancy payment is not necessary: 1978 Act, s.101.

NOTE: An employer may waive his right to refuse payment where the employee has not commenced his claim within the six-month period, but if the employer declines to pay the employee, the latter may apply within a further period of six months to an industrial tribunal, who may award a payment if it appears to be just and equitable to do so.

39. Calculation of payment. The rules governing the calculation of a redundancy payment to be made in any case are set out in Sched. 4, paras. 13 and 14 of the 1978 Act. There are three basic factors involved in the computation:

(*a*) a week's pay;
(*b*) the period of continuous employment;
(*c*) age.

40. A week's pay. The gross weekly pay is calculated on the normal working hours of the employee based on his contract of employment. Where the amount of work done varies from week to week, the average number of weekly hours is calculated from the average of the hours worked and remuneration received during the previous twelve weeks. Special provision is made for time-workers, piece-workers, employees with variable bonuses or commission, shift or rota workers and employees with no normal working hours.

A week's pay is taken into account up to a maximum of £145 a week. This sum is reviewed annually by the Secretary of State for Employment: 1978 Act, s.148.

Overtime will only be counted for the purposes of redundancy payments if a fixed amount of overtime had been made obligatory on both employer and employee and made a term of the contract: *Tarmac Roadstone Holdings Ltd.* v. *Peacock* (1973).

41. The period of continuous employment. The employee must have had at least two years' continuous and reckonable employment since the age of 18. The number of complete years of continuous employment is reckoned backwards from the date of the expiry of the due statutory notice. Complete years of service up to a maximum of twenty will count for payments as follows.

(*a*) One-and-a-half weeks' pay for each year of employment which consisted wholly of weeks in which the employee was aged 41 or above.

(*b*) One week's pay for each year of employment which consisted wholly of weeks in which the employee was aged 22 to 40 years (inclusive).

(*c*) Half a week's pay for each year of employment which consisted wholly of weeks in which the employee was aged 18 to 21 years (inclusive).

Thus the maximum payment at present would be £4,350.

42. Weeks which count towards continuous employment.

(*a*) Any week counts in which an employee is employed for at least sixteen hours.

(*b*) If the employee had been employed under a contract involving sixteen hours or more a week, but is then employed under a contract involving between eight and sixteen hours a week, then those weeks (up to a maximum of twenty-six) can count towards the period of continuous employment.

(*c*) If the employee has been employed for five years or more under a contract with his employer which normally involves employment for at least eight hours a week then those weeks will count.

(*d*) a week may also count in some circumstances even if the contract of employment has ended for a spell (e.g. because of sickness) but the employee was re-engaged within twenty-six weeks of the end of his previous contract, or where the employee has taken maternity leave and has returned to work in accordance with the provisions of the Employment Protection (Consolidation) Act 1978.

(*e*) Strikes do not break continuity of employment, but the period of the strike does *not* count towards continuous employment.

43. The Redundancy Fund. This is now governed by ss. 103–109 of the 1978 Act and Redundancy Fund Act 1981.

(*a*) *Contributions*. The Fund is maintained by part of the social security contributions (*see* XI) paid by employers for each employed earner. Contributions by employees are earnings related and the current allocation is 0.2 per cent of the amount of earnings in respect of which those contributions were paid.

(*b*) *Rebates*. When an employer makes a redundancy payment, he may claim a rebate from the Fund of 41 per cent of the cost. Rebate on a redundancy payment for which the employer is liable should be claimed within six months of the date the payment was made to the employee. The employer does not have an automatic right to a rebate: *see*, for example, *Secretary of State for Employment* v. *Globe Elastic Thread Co.* (1979). The Secretary of State has discretion whether to pay a rebate where the employee was not strictly entitled to the redundancy payment: 1978 Act, ss.104, 105. The method of calculating the rebate is found in Sched. 6 of the 1978 Act.

(*c*) *Direct payments*. Where an employee fails to receive a redundancy payment from his employer, the Secretary of State may make a payment direct to the employee: 1978 Act, s.106.

PROGRESS TEST 9

1. What is the basis of the common law action for wrongful dismissal? Why would an employee rarely bring such an action now? When might he bring such an action? **(2, 4, 7, 9)**

2. What does the law state to be the minimum periods of notice which an employer can give to an employee? **(3)**

3. What remedies are available in the common law action for wrongful dismissal? **(5)**

4. What are the stages in an action for unfair dismissal? **(8)**

5. Who can bring an action for unfair dismissal? Must all employees have been employed for a minimum of one year? **(9, 14)**

6. What is meant by dismissal? **(10)**

7. How is the question whether a dismissal is fair or unfair generally determined? **(12)**

8. Can an employee be fairly dismissed because of trade union membership or activities? **(12, 14)**

9. Can an employee be fairly dismissed for refusing to become a member of a trade union? **(12)**

10. Does an employee have the right to know why he was dismissed? **(13)**

11. What additional rights does an employee have if he is dismissed because of trade union membership or activities? **(17)**

12. Describe what remedies are available where an industrial tribunal is satisfied that an employee has been unfairly dismissed. **(18, 20)**

13. What can the tribunal do if an employer fails to comply with a re-employment order? **(19)**

14. If the tribunal does not make a re-employment order, what alternative remedy is available? How is it calculated? **(20–23)**

15. In what circumstances will (*a*) an employer, and (*b*) a contractor be entitled to obtain a contribution from a third party towards the compensation paid by the employer to the employee? **(24)**

16. What is meant by redundancy? **(26)**

17. When is an employee entitled to a redundancy payment? **(27, 28)**

18. Will an offer of re-employment affect an employee's right to a redundancy payment? **(31–33)**

19. When an employer proposes to make employees redundant, what procedures, if any, must he follow? **(35, 36)**

20. What protection is offered to employees while the redundancy procedures are taking place? **(37)**

21. When and how must an employee make a claim for a redundancy payment? **(38)**

22. How is the amount of the redundancy payment calculated? **(39–42)**

CHAPTER X

Industrial Relations

CHANGES IN LEGISLATION

1. Introduction. The Industrial Relations Act 1971 introduced some important innovations in the field of industrial relations. Its stated purpose was to promote good industrial relations. However, the Act proved to be unpopular and in certain respects difficult to enforce. It was repealed by the Trade Union and Labour Relations Act 1974, although some of its less controversial provisions were maintained, e.g. those relating to unfair dismissal.

2. Current legislation. The Trade Union and Labour Relations Act 1974 (TULRA) has, as far as it relates to industrial relations, been subsequently amended by the Trade Union and Labour Relations (Amendment) Act 1976, the Employment Protection Act 1975, the Employment Act 1980 and the Employment Act 1982. Further changes will be made when the Trade Union Bill (1984) becomes law.

3. General effect of these Acts. The main purposes of this legislation with regard to industrial relations are to:

(*a*) provide for the status and regulation of trade unions and employers' associations, including definitions of "trade union", "independent trade union" and "employers' association";

(*b*) state the legal immunities against actions in tort for certain acts undertaken in contemplation of a trade dispute, and provide a definition of "trade dispute";

(*c*) provide for payments out of public funds towards trade unions' expenditure in respect of secret ballots; and

(*d*) provide certain legal machinery and practical guidance for the promotion of good industrial relations.

4. Terminology. The terminology of industrial relations is defined in the Trade Union and Labour Relations Act 1974, as follows.

(*a*) "Trade union" means an organisation which consists wholly or mainly of workers of one or more descriptions and is an organisation whose principal purposes include the regulation of relations between workers of that description or those descriptions and employers or employers' associations.

(*b*) "*Independent trade union*" means a trade union which:

(*i*) is not under the domination or control of an employer or a group of employers or of one or more employers' associations,

(*ii*) is not liable to interference by an employer or any such group or association (arising out of the provision of financial or material support or by any other means whatsoever) tending towards such control, and

(*iii*) the Certification Officer has determined is independent and has accordingly issued a certificate.

(*c*) "*Official*", in relation to a trade union, means any person who is an officer of the union (or its sections or branches), or who is elected or appointed as a representative of union members, according to the rules of the union.

(*d*) "*Employers' association*" means an organisation consisting wholly or mainly of employers or individual proprietors, whose principal purposes include the regulation of relations between employers and workers or trade unions.

(*e*) "*Collective agreement*" means any agreement or arrangement made by or on behalf of one or more trade unions and one or more employers or employers' associations, and which relates to any of the matters which may be the subject of a "trade dispute". Examples would be terms and conditions, recruitment and terminations, discipline, work allocation, union membership, facilities for union officials, negotiation and consultation machinery and recognition.

(*f*) "*Union membership agreement*" means an agreement or arrangement which:

(*i*) is made by or exists between one or more independent trade unions and one or more employers or employers' associations, and

(*ii*) relates to employees of an identifiable class, and

(*iii*) has the effect in practice of requiring the employees for the time being of the class to which it relates (whether or not there is a condition to that effect in their contract of employment) to be or become a member of the union or one of the unions which is or are parties to the agreement or arrangement or of another specified independent trade union.

This is more commonly known as a closed shop agreement.

(*g*) "*Trade dispute*" means a dispute between workers and their employer which relates wholly or mainly to one or more of the following:

(*i*) terms and conditions of employment, or the physical conditions in which any workers are required to work;

(*ii*) engagement or non-engagement, or termination or suspension of employment or the duties of employment, of one or more workers;

(*iii*) allocation of work or the duties of employment as between workers or groups of workers;

(*iv*) matters of discipline;

(*v*) the membership or non-membership of a trade union on the part of a worker;

(*vi*) facilities for officials of trade unions; and

(*vii*) machinery for negotiation or consultation, and other procedures, relating to any of the foregoing matters, including the recognition by employers or employers' assocations of the right of a trade union to represent workers in any such negotiation or consultation or in the carrying out of such procedures (*see* **35** for cases).

NOTE: The 1982 Act s.18 narrowed the definition of "trade dispute" in two ways. First it no longer covers a dispute between employers and workers, nor between workers and workers. Secondly the dispute must now not merely be "connected with" but must "relate wholly or mainly" to the specified circumstances.

(*h*) "*Worker*" means an individual who works or normally works or seeks to work:

(*i*) under a contract of employment; or

(*ii*) under any other contract whereby he undertakes to do or perform personally any work or services for another party to the contract who is not a professional client of his; or

(*iii*) in certain government employments which do not fall within (*i*) or (*ii*).

NOTE: (1) "Worker" in relation to a dispute with an employer (*see* (*g*) above) means (*a*) a worker employed by that employer; or (*b*) an ex-employee the termination of whose employment was one factor giving rise to the dispute, or was in connection with the dispute.

(2) "Worker" is wider in scope than "employee" (*see* VIII, **5**).

CODES OF PRACTICE

5. Purpose of Codes of Practice. The legislation on industrial relations is being supplemented by Codes of Practice. These are aimed at promoting the improvement of industrial relations, and are prepared and issued by the Advisory, Conciliation and Arbitration Service (ACAS). The Code of Industrial Relations Practice, which was drawn up under the Industrial Relations Act 1971, is preserved during its progressive replacement by Codes issued by ACAS. The Employment Act 1980, s.3, also provides for the issue of Codes of Practice by the Secretary of State for Employment.

6. Code of Industrial Relations Practice. The Code contains the following two main themes.

(*a*) The vital role of collective bargaining carried out in a reasonable and constructive manner between employers and strong representative trade unions.
(*b*) The importance of good human relations between employers and employees in every establishment based on trust and confidence.

The scheme of the Code is as follows.

(*a*) *Responsibilities:* management, trade unions, employers' associations and the individual employee.
(*b*) *Employment policies:* planning and the use of manpower, recruitment and selection, training, payment systems, status and security of employees, and working conditions.
(*c*) *Communication and consultation.*
(*d*) *Collective bargaining:* bargaining units, recognition of trade unions, collective agreements and disclosure of information.
(*e*) *Employee representation:* functions, appointment and qualifications, status, co-ordination, facilities and training.
(*f*) *Grievance and dispute procedures:* individual grievance procedures and collective disputes and procedures.
(*g*) *Disciplinary procedures.* (But also *see* **7**(*a*).)

7. ACAS Codes of Practice. ACAS has so far drawn up three Codes of Practice which have come into effect. These Codes supersede similar provisions under the Code of Industrial Relations Practice.

(*a*) *Code of Practice 1: Disciplinary practice and procedures in employment.* This document gives practical guidance on how to draw up disciplinary rules and procedures and how to operate them effectively. It includes, for example, a list of essential features of disciplinary procedures, such as that they should be in writing, and ensures that, except for gross misconduct, no employees are dismissed for the first breach of discipline. These provisions supersede paras. 130–133 of the Code of Industrial Relations Practice.

(*b*) *Code of Practice 2: Disclosure of information to trade unions for collective bargaining purposes.* Section 17 of the Employment Protection Act 1975 places a general duty on an employer to disclose at all stages of collective bargaining information requested by representatives of independent trade unions. The information which employers may have a duty to disclose, is information which it would be in accordance with good industrial relations practice to disclose. In determining what would be in accordance with good industrial relations practice, regard is to be had to any relevant provisions of the Code, e.g. pay and benefits, conditions of service, manpower, performance and financial position. These provisions supersede paras. 96-98 of the Code of Industrial Relations Practice.

(*c*) *Code of Practice 3: Time off for trade union activities.* The Code gives practical guidance on the time off to be permitted by an employer:

(*i*) to a trade union official in accordance with s.27 of the Employment Protection (Consolidation) Act 1978; and

(*ii*) to a trade union member in accordance with s.28 of the same Act. (*See* VIII, **50**.)

These provisions supersede paras. 116-118 of the Code of Industrial Relations Practice.

Failure to observe any provision of a Code of Practice does not render anyone liable to any proceedings, but the Code may be used as *evidence* in proceedings before an industrial tribunal, the Employment Appeal Tribunal and the Central Arbitration Committee, and if relevant will be taken into account in reaching a decision.

8. Government Codes of Practice. The Secretary of State for Employment may issue Codes of Practice, following consultation with ACAS, containing such practical guidance as he thinks fit for the purpose of promoting the improvement of industrial relations. Failure to observe the provisions of such a code will not amount to a breach of the law, but like the ACAS Codes of Practice, it may be used as evidence in proceedings and can be taken into account by the body reaching a decision.

The Secretary of State has so far issued the following two Codes of Practice.

(*a*) *Code of Practice on Picketing.* This explains the law on picketing and sets out rules on good practice which are aimed to help avoid the conflict and disorder to which picketing has sometimes given rise. The Code also examines the role of the police; the number of pickets; the organisation of picketing; the problems relating to essential supplies and services; and secondary picketing (*see* **36, 42**).

(*b*) *Code of Practice on Closed Shop Agreements and Arrangements* (1983). This replaces the 1980 Code. The new Code aims to provide practical guidance on questions which arise out of the formulation and operation of closed shop agreements. The legal provisions on the closed shop are outlined. The Code gives practical guidance on the introduction of closed shops, union treatment of members and applicants, and on the closed shop and freedom of the press. The general approach is that any agreement or practice on union membership should:

(*i*) protect basic individual rights;
(*ii*) enjoy the overwhelming support of those affected; and
(*iii*) be flexibly and tolerantly applied (*see* also **22–24**).

THE INSTITUTIONS

9. The settlement of individual industrial disputes. This has largely been removed from the ordinary court system. The legislation is aimed at providing a system of conciliation, but if that fails the dispute can be referred to an industrial tribunal, and on appeal to the Employment Appeal Tribunal.

10. Conciliation and arbitration. There are two bodies which are now concerned with these matters, although their functions existed in various forms prior to the Trade Union and Labour Relations Act 1974.

(*a*) First, there is the Advisory, Conciliation and Arbitration Service (ACAS) which was set up on a statutory basis by the Employment Protection Act 1975. It provides assistance for the settlement of disputes, whether between employer and employee, or between employer and trade union (*see* **11**).

(*b*) Secondly, there is the Central Arbitration Committee (CAC) which has jurisdiction to settle certain specified disputes (*see* **12**).

11. Advisory, Conciliation and Arbitration Service. This service is headed by a chairman and a council of nine members, all of whom are appointed by the Secretary of State for Employment. One-third of the council members are nominated by the TUC and one-third by the CBI. There are eight regional offices which provide conciliation and arbitration assistance in their area. The functions of ACAS include the following.

(*a*) A general duty of promoting the improvement of industrial relations and in particular of encouraging the extension of collective bargaining. In addition, the development and, where necessary, the reform of collective bargaining machinery.

(*b*) Providing advice on any matter concerned with industrial relations or employment policies.

(*c*) Inquiring into any question relating to industrial relations generally, or to industrial relations in any particular industry or particular undertaking. In addition, publishing the findings of that inquiry if it appears that publication is desirable for the improvement of industrial relations.

(*d*) Providing assistance to the parties to a trade dispute, by way of conciliation, or other means, with a view to bringing about a settlement.

(*e*) Referring matters in a trade dispute, at the request of one or more parties, and with the consent of all parties to the dispute, to arbitration by one or more persons appointed by the Service or to the Central Arbitration Committee.

(*f*) Providing the conciliation stage before a complaint of failure to supply information for the purpose of collective bargaining goes to arbitration by the CAC.

(*g*) Issuing Codes of Practice containing practical guidance.

12. Central Arbitration Committee (CAC). This Committee replaced the Industrial Arbitration Board in 1975 under the provisions of the Employment Protection Act. It consists of a chairman, deputy chairman and members appointed by the Secretary of State for Employment from persons nominated by ACAS as experienced in industrial relations. Under its original jurisdiction it may deal with matters arising out of a trade dispute if both parties agree. Voluntary procedure agreements can specify the Committee as the final stage of bargaining machinery. The Committee can arbitrate in certain specific situations, including the following.

(*a*) A claim by a trade union or an employers' association that an employer is observing terms and conditions of employment which are less favourable than the recognised negotiated terms and conditions for the trade or industry, or that the terms and conditions of employment are less favourable than the general level in the same trade or industry in the district.

(*b*) References alleging disregard of the Fair Wages Resolution which imposed on contractors of the government and certain other public authorities the obligation to observe agreed or established standards of terms and conditions of employment.

(*c*) References alleging disregard of similar standards imposed by statute on certain specific industries, e.g. civil aviation.

(*d*) Reference by a trade union in writing for arbitration about a recognition issue.

(*e*) Reference by a trade union alleging that an employer failed to supply certain information to bargaining representatives of recognised trade unions.

13. Industrial tribunals. These are independent judicial bodies, each with a legally qualified chairman and two other members.

(*a*) The chairman is appointed by the Lord Chancellor. The other two members are approved by the Secretary of State for Employment, after consultation with bodies representing employees and employers.

(*b*) The tribunals sit in most parts of the country and have permanent offices in the larger centres of population. Applications are dealt with in the office which is considered to be most convenient for all the parties concerned.

(*c*) The tribunals hear complaints both from individual employees, e.g. on unfair dismissal, and from trade unions, e.g. on whether an employer has complied with the requirements to consult recognised trade unions about proposed redundancies.

(*d*) It is important that an application is made within the prescribed time limit as failure to do so may deprive the applicant of any right to have the case heard.

NOTE: The decision of an industrial tribunal does *not* create a legal precedent which is binding on other tribunals.

14. Employment Appeal Tribunal (EAT). This tribunal was established by the Employment Protection Act 1975. It consists of judges nominated from among the judges of the High Court, the Court of Appeal and the Court of Session (of Scotland). When hearing claims, each judge will be assisted by lay members (usually two or four) who have special knowledge or experience of industrial relations, and who represent both the employers' and the employees' points of view. The tribunal has a central office in

London, but can sit anywhere in Great Britain. The jurisdiction is limited to hearing appeals on:

(*a*) questions of law from industrial tribunals; and

(*b*) questions of fact or law arising from proceedings before, or a decision of, the Certification Officer with regard to the listing of trade unions and employers' associations.

An appeal to the EAT must be brought within forty-two days of an industrial tribunal's decision.

In *Wells* v. *Derwent Plastics Ltd.* (1978) Mr Justice Bristow, in the Employment Appeal Tribunal, considered that judges' observations on the application of statutes to particular facts were only guidelines intended to help in the particular case under consideration. Failure to follow these observations would not amount to an error of law as they were not binding legal rules. However, any industrial tribunal which did not give such observations serious consideration might arrive at the wrong answer.

TRADE UNIONS

15. Registration of trade unions. This was first introduced in 1871, and is now governed by the Trade Union and Labour Relations Act 1974. A distinction is drawn between independent trade unions and others (*see* **4**). Independent trade unions can be registered with the Certification Officer (*see* **16**). It is an administrative procedure which requires the payment of a fee, together with a copy of the rules of the organisation, a list of its officers, the address of its head or main office, and the name under which it shall be known. This list of trade unions and employers' associations is maintained by the Certification Officer, an official of ACAS.

16. Certification Officer. Section 7 of the Employment Protection Act 1975 transferred the functions of the Registrar of Friendly Societies to this official of ACAS. The functions of the Certification Officer are as follows.

(*a*) To maintain a list of trade unions and a list of employers' associations.

(*b*) To make inquiries as he thinks fit, and to take account of any relevant information in order to certify that a trade union already on the list of trade unions is an independent trade union.

The certificate is conclusive evidence of the independence of the union, and refusal or cancellation of a certificate is conclusive evidence that the trade union is not independent. In the case of both a refusal to grant, and a withdrawal, the trade union may appeal to the Employment Appeal Tribunal.

(*c*) To keep available for public inspection copies of the annual returns of listed organisations, who are also required to submit audited accounts.

(*d*) Where two or more unions propose to amalgamate:

(*i*) to approve an agreed Instrument of Amalgamation,

(*ii*) to approve the notice in writing sent to every member of the union, informing them of the proposals, before the ballot on acceptance of the proposals takes place,

(*iii*) to hear complaints from members of any union involved in the ballot, and

(*iv*) to register the merger.

(*e*) To contribute towards the cost of secret ballots (*see* **19**).

An appeal on a point of law lies from any decision of the Certification Officer to the Employment Appeal Tribunal.

17. Legal status of trade unions. Theoretically trade unions are unincorporated associations, although like partnerships (*see* II) special rules apply to them which virtually make this statement meaningless in practice. However, it does mean that trade unions, unlike, for example, a limited company, do not have a legal personality separate from that of their members. The status of a trade union is governed by TULRA 1974, s. 2. which provides that a trade union is not a body corporate, but:

(*a*) it is capable of making contracts;

(*b*) all property belonging to the trade union is vested in trustees in trust for the union;

(*c*) it is capable of suing and being sued in its own name;

(*d*) proceedings for any offence alleged to have been committed by it or on its behalf may be brought against it in its own name;

(*e*) any judgment, order or award made in proceedings against the trade union is enforceable against the trade union's property as if it were a body corporate.

NOTE: The purposes of any trade union, insofar as they relate to the regulation of relations between employers and employer's associations and workers will not by reason only that they are in restraint of trade be unlawful so as:

(1) to make any member of the trade union liable to criminal proceedings for conspiracy or otherwise; or

(2) to make any agreement or trust void or voidable; or

(3) to make any trade union rule unlawful or unenforceable.

For a recent discussion on the legal status of a trade union *see Electrical, Electronic, Telecommunication and Plumbing Union* v. *Times Newspapers Ltd.* (1980).

18. Trade unions and their members. The relationship between a trade union and its members is contractual and the terms of the contract will usually be found in the rules of the union. These rules are mostly concerned with the admission, disciplinary and election procedures of the union. The common law has added little to these rules, so the individual member is usually bound by the terms of a contract which has been drawn up and enforced by the other party to the contract, the trade union. The Trade Union Bill 1984 purports to make trade unions democratically accountable to their members, chiefly through the use of secret ballots (*see* **19**).

(*a*) *Discipline.* With regard to disciplinary procedures the common law rules of natural justice are sometimes of assistance to dissatisfied members. These rules require that:

(*i*) no one should be a judge in his own cause; and

(*ii*) the other party to a dispute should be given a hearing.

If a trade union disciplinary body reaches a decision in breach of these rules then a court can quash the decision. It also seems likely that the courts would be prepared to intervene where a union rule was wholly unreasonable.

(*b*) *Termination of membership.* TULRA 1974, s.7, provides that in every contract of membership of a trade union there will be an implied term conferring a right on the member, on giving reasonable notice and complying with any reasonable conditions, to terminate his membership.

(*c*) *Closed shops.* The Employment Act 1980, ss.4 and 5 provide that every person who is, or is seeking to be, employed in a job where a closed shop agreement exists, has the right:

(*i*) not to have an application for membership of an appropriate trade union unreasonably refused; and

(*ii*) not to be unreasonably expelled from an appropriate trade union.

An employee may make a complaint to an industrial tribunal:

(1) if these two rights are not observed; or

(2) where no decision is made on the application within a reasonable time; or

(3) where according to the union rules he ceases to be a

member on the happening of a specified event—this will be regarded as expulsion.

(For other provisions relating to closed shop agreements, *see* **22–26**.)

19. Secret ballots. The use of secret ballots was encouraged by the Employment Act 1980. The Trade Union Bill 1984 imposes a duty on trade unions to hold elections in certain circumstances. The Employment Act 1980 provides that:

(*a*) The Certification Officer (*see* **16**) may make payments towards expenditure incurred by independent trade unions in respect of certain secret ballots: s.1. The secret ballot should be for one or more of the following purposes:

(*i*) obtaining a decision or ascertaining the views of members of a trade union as to the calling or ending of a strike or other industrial action;

(*ii*) carrying out an election provided for by the rules of a trade union;

(*iii*) electing a worker who is a member of a trade union to be a representative of other members also employed by his employer;

(*iv*) amending the rules of a trade union;

(*v*) approving an amalgamation with or a transfer of functions to another trade union (*see* **16**(*d*)).

The Secretary of State may by order specify that payment may be made towards the cost of secret ballots for purposes other than those listed above.

(*b*) An employer must, so far as is reasonably practicable, comply with a request by an independent trade union to use his premises for a relevant ballot under (*a*), so that his workers who are members of the union have a convenient opportunity of voting: s.2. This provision does not apply unless the union is recognised by the employer for the purpose of collective bargaining (*see* **21**), and the number of workers employed by the employer is twenty-one or more.

(*c*) Closed shop agreements must be approved by secret ballot in certain circumstances (*see* **23, 25** and **26**).

The Trade Union Bill 1984 provides that trade union members will have the right:

(*d*) to elect the governing body of their trade union by secret ballot;

(*e*) to be consulted in a secret ballot before being called out on strike. Failure to hold a ballot will result in loss of the immunity granted under TULRA s.13 (*see* **35**);

(*f*) to vote at least once every ten years on whether their union should continue to fund political activities. Failure to hold the ballot or failure to obtain majority support would make unlawful any expenditure on political objects.

NOTE: Secret ballots are also required in certain circumstances by the Factories Act 1961 (*see* XIII, **57**).

COLLECTIVE AGREEMENTS

20. Enforceability. The Trade Union and Labour Relations Act 1974 provides that any collective agreement made before 1st December 1971 and after 16th September 1974 must be conclusively presumed not to have been intended by the parties to be a legally enforceable contract unless the agreement:

(*a*) is in writing, and
(*b*) contains a provision which (however expressed) states that the parties intend that the agreement shall be a legally enforceable contract.

Any such agreement which satisfies the conditions in (*a*) and (*b*) will be conclusively presumed to have been intended by the parties to be a legally enforceable contract: s.18.

(For the definition of a collective agreement *see* **4**(*e*).)

21. Collective bargaining. One purpose of the Employment Protection Act 1975 was to encourage the extension of collective bargaining between trade unions and employers. Two provisions were introduced whereby trade unions could apply for: (*i*) disclosure of information by employers for collective bargaining purposes (*see* **7**(*b*)); and (*ii*) recognition for the purposes of collective bargaining. Where an employer refused to recognise the trade union for the purpose of collective bargaining, the union could refer the dispute to ACAS as happened in *Grunwick Processing Laboratories Ltd.* v. *Advisory, Conciliation and Arbitration Service* (1978).

This second provision of the 1975 Act has been repealed by the Employment Act 1980, which means that the law is no longer directly involved in deciding whether an employer has recognised a particular trade union. However, there are certain rights which are granted only to recognised trade unions (*see* IX, **33**, **36**).

NOTE: Recognition in relation to a trade union means the recognition of the union by an employer, or two or more associated employers, to any extent, for the purpose of collective bargaining: 1975 Act, s.126(1), substituted by the 1980 Act, Sched. 1.

In practice a large number of contracts of employment are the result of collective bargaining, rather than negotiation between the individual employee and employer. The resolution of disputes is often to be found in voluntary procedures. These collective agreements are usually negotiated at a local rather than at national or industry level, which tends to result in informality and flexibility. However, there are various ways in which the law recognises and supports the existence of collective bargaining.

(*a*) First, there are various institutions such as wages councils (*see* VIII, **9**(*c*)), the CAC (*see* **12**) and ACAS (*see* **11**).

(*b*) Secondly, various statutory rights can be waived where a suitable alternative agreement has been reached between trade unions and employers (*see*, for example, VIII, **34**, note; IX, **9**, exception (11); IX, **27**, exception (8)).

(*c*) Finally, the provisions relating to closed shop agreements also affect the position of trade unions as negotiators on behalf of their members.

22. Closed shop agreements. The Trade Union and Labour Relations Act 1974 made such agreements lawful again, calling them "union membership agreements" (*see* **4**(*f*)). The Act defined a closed shop agreement for the first time. There is no need for a formal written agreement, and the class of employees covered need not be all employees in a particular grade.

The Employment Act 1980 provided that to be lawful closed shop agreements had to be approved by secret ballot. The detailed provisions have been amended by the Employment Act 1982 s.3.

(*a*) For closed shop agreements which came into force on or before 14th August 1980 the agreement will be approved if at least 80 per cent of those entitled to vote or at least 85 per cent of those who actually voted, voted in favour of the agreement.

(*b*) For closed shop agreements which came into effect after that date then at least 80 per cent of those entitled to vote must have voted in favour of the agreement.

(*c*) Dismissal of a non-union member is automatically unfair unless the closed shop agreement has been approved by a ballot within the preceding five years. However, where a ballot is held subsequent to the introduction of the closed shop agreement and *both* less than 80 per cent of those entitled to vote and less than 85 per cent of those actually voting, voted in favour of the closed shop, then it is not an approved agreement.

23. Employment Act 1980. This Act introduced the following provisions.

(*a*) Closed shop agreements have to be approved by secret ballot (*see* **22**).

(*b*) Employees have the right not to be unreasonably excluded or expelled from a trade union (*see* **18**).

(*c*) New grounds are laid down for an employee to rely on in claims for (*i*) action short of dismissal, or (*ii*) unfair dismissal where the employee is not a member of a trade union and there is a closed shop agreement (*see* **25, 26**).

(*d*) Acts done for the purpose of compelling workers to become members of particular trade unions will not in certain circumstances benefit from the immunity provided by TULRA, s.13 (*see* **37**).

(*e*) There is a right to a contribution to the compensation paid to an employee dismissed because of trade union pressure (*see* IX, **24**).

24. Code of Practice. The Code of Practice on Closed Shop Agreements and Arrangements (*see* **8**) provides practical guidance on questions which arise out of the formulation and operation of closed shop agreements. The general approach is that any closed shop agreement or practice should protect basic individual rights, enjoy the overwhelming support of those employees affected, and be flexibly and tolerantly applied. Guidelines are given regarding:

(*a*) the legal rights of individuals;

(*b*) other protection for non-union employees: union labour only requirements;

(*c*) the matters which should be examined before a closed shop agreement is considered;

(*d*) the scope and the content of agreements;

(*e*) review of closed shop agreements and secret ballots;

(*f*) the operation of new or existing arrangements;

(*g*) union rules and procedures relating to applications for, and membership of, the trade union, and relating to refusal to take part in industrial action;

(*h*) the closed shop and the freedom of the press.

25. Action short of dismissal where there is a closed shop agreement. Section 23 of the 1978 Act as amended by the 1982 Act s.10 (*see* VIII, **49**) provides that every employee has the right not to have action short of dismissal taken against him by his employer:

(*a*) as a means of pressurising him with regard to trade union activities or membership; or

(*b*) for the purpose of enforcing a requirement that if he is not a member of a trade union then he must make payments, for example to a charity, in place of union dues.

The 1980 Act, s.15 and the 1982 Act, s.10, have limited this provision where there is a closed shop agreement. In that situation:

(*a*) only specified trade unions have the right to use the employer's premises for taking part in union activities at an appropriate time; but

(*b*) the right described in (*a*) will apply only if the closed shop agreement has been approved by the requisite number of employees through a ballot held during the preceding five years (*see* **22**).

(*c*) An employee who is not a member of a specified trade union can have action taken against him to compel him to become a member of a trade union unless:

(*i*) he genuinely objects on grounds of conscience or other deeply held personal conviction to being a member of a trade union; or

(*ii*) he has been employed by his employer since before the introduction of the closed shop and has at no time been a member of the trade union in accordance with the agreement.

26. Dismissal where there is a closed shop agreement. Dismissal by an employer will be *fair* if there is a union membership agreement which has been approved in a secret ballot held during the preceding five years (*see* **22** and IX, **49**) and the reason for the dismissal was that the employee was not a member and refused to become a member of a specified union, or threatens to resign from the union. However, the dismissal will be *unfair* where:

(*a*) the employee genuinely objects on ground of conscience or other deeply held personal conviction to being a member of a trade union; or

(*b*) the employee has been employed by the employer since before the introduction of the closed shop and has at no time been a member of the trade union in accordance with the agreement; or

(*c*) the closed shop agreement had not been approved by a large enough majority during the preceding five years (*see* **22**); or

(*d*) the employee had been unreasonably excluded or expelled from the trade union (*see* **18**); or

(*e*) the employee holds qualifications relevant to his employment, which make him subject to a written code of conduct (e.g. professions) which requires individuals not to take part in any form of industrial action, or not to be a member of a trade union.

TRADE DISPUTES

27. Introduction. The basis of the law that controls industrial action is to be found in the law of tort, although criminal law is occasionally used, particularly against pickets.

28. Civil law. The law of tort provides, for the purposes of industrial law, three main headings of liability:

(*a*) interference with an existing contract;
(*b*) intimidation;
(*c*) consipiracy.

29. Interference with an existing contract. A commits this tort if without lawful justification he intentionally interferes with a contract between B and C either:

(*a*) by persuading B to break his contract with C; or
(*b*) by some other act which prevents B from performing his contract.

Lumley v. *Gye* (1853): The plaintiff, who was the proprietor of a theatre, made a contract with a Miss Wagner for the performance by her for a period of three months at his theatre. The defendant induced Miss Wagner to break her contract with the plaintiff, so that she refused to sing or perform at the theatre during the agreed period. It was held that an action lay not just where a servant had been enticed from his master's employment but could be extended to any wrongful interference with any contract of personal service.

30. The essential feature of the tort. There are four elements which must be proved, as follows.

(*a*) A's conduct must have brought about the breach of contract between B and C.
(*b*) C must have suffered damage as a result of the breach of contract.
(*c*) A must have known, or should have been aware, that his actions would result in a breach of the contract.
(*d*) The breach of contract arose either by:
(*i*) direct persuasion applied by A to B to break the contract with C: *Lumley* v. *Gye* (1853); or by
(*ii*) direct intervention by A which results in B breaking his contract with C: *GWK Ltd.* v. *Dunlop Rubber Co. Ltd.* (1926); or by
(*iii*) indirect intervention by A through a third party D,

which results in B breaking his contract with C: *J. T. Stratford and Son Ltd.* v. *Lindley* (1965).

NOTE: (1) It is no longer essential that a breach of contract occurs: *Torquay Hotel Co. Ltd.* v *Cousins* (1969).

(2) Where (*d*)(*ii*) and (*iii*) are relied upon it is likely that the use of unlawful means by A is required.

(3) The defence of justification is available to A.

31. Intimidation. This tort arises where A threatens B that he will do an unlawful act with the intention of making B act (or refrain from acting) either:

(*a*) to his own detriment; or
(*b*) to the detriment of C.

Rookes v. *Barnard* (1964): The plaintiff was a skilled draughtsman employed by BOAC. He left his union even though the union had an informal "100 per cent union membership" agreement with BOAC. Three union officials indicated to BOAC that labour would be withdrawn if the plaintiff was not removed from the design office within three days. BOAC eventually dismissed the plaintiff. A collective agreement stated that there would be no strike or lockout, and this clause was incorporated into each individual contract of employment with BOAC. The threat of withdrawal of labour was, in consequence, a threat to break their contracts, and this amounted to an unlawful act, for the purposes of the tort of intimidation, which was detrimental to the plaintiff.

32. Conspiracy. The tort of conspiracy overlaps to a certain extent with the previous torts where two or more persons combine to injure a third party by unlawful means and damage actually results. "Unlawful means" include a tort and a crime, and probably a breach of contract. However, the tort of conspiracy also includes situations where two or more persons combine "to act in a certain way, resulting in deliberate damage to others... even though the same thing if done by a single individual without any element of combination, would not expose him to liability": *Crofter Hand-Woven Harris Tweed Co. Ltd* v. *Veitch* (1942).

33. The essential features of the tort. There are three elements which must be proved, as follows.

(*a*) The object or purpose of the combination must be to cause damage to the plaintiff.

(*b*) There must be joint action between two or more persons.
(*c*) There must be a particular act causing damage.

34. Trade union immunity. It is essential to consider these three torts in the light of the immunity that trade unions have from civil liability. The present law is found in the Trade Union and Labour Relations Act 1974. This immunity has been restricted by the Employment Act 1982 and will be affected by the provisions of the Trade Union Bill 1984.

35. Immunity for actions done in contemplation or furtherance of a trade dispute. (For the definition of a trade dispute *see* **4**(*g*).)

(*a*) An act done by a person in contemplation or furtherance of a trade dispute will not be actionable in tort on the ground only:

(*i*) that it induces another person to break a contract or interferes or induces any other person to interfere with its performance; or

(*ii*) that it consists in his threatening that a contract (whether one to which he is a party or not) will be broken or its performance interfered with, or that he will induce another person to break a contract or to interfere with its performance.

(*b*) An agreement or combination by two or more persons to do or procure the doing of any act in contemplation or furtherance of a trade dispute will not be actionable in tort if the act is one which, if done without any such agreement or combination, would not be actionable in tort: Trade Union and Labour Relations Act 1974, s.13 as amended.

The 1982 Act, s.19, has amended the 1974 Act with the aim of making it possible to sue an individual for the tort of interference with trade and business (otherwise known as intimidation), even where the action is in contemplation or furtherance of a trade dispute. There have been doubts as to the existence of such a tort, but Lord Diplock, in *Merkur Island Shipping* v. *Laughton* (1983), considered that this tort requires an unlawful act but that it need not involve procuring another person to break or interfere with the performance of a subsisting contract.

The cases have chiefly turned on whether there is a "trade dispute" and in particular whether the dispute relates to the "terms and conditions of employment". The case of *Universe Tankships Inc. of Monrovia* v. *International Transport Federation* (1982) involved a consideration of the pre-1982 Act definition of "trade dispute". The House of Lords was split 3 to 2 on whether, on the facts of the case, there was such a dispute, which indicates the difficulty involved in applying the legislation to particular cases.

Mercury v. *Scott-Garner* (1983): The United Kingdom government granted a licence to the plaintiffs to set up a telecommunications system which would be connected to the system operated by British Telecommunications, a state-owned public corporation which up till that time had a monopoly. The defendant union, the vast majority of whose members were employed by BT, waged a campaign against the licensing of competitors and the privatisation of BT, in order to protect the jobs and job opportunities of its members. This culminated in a refusal by the union and its members to connect the plaintiff to the BT system, and the blacking of the plaintiff's shareholders and BT services at the plaintiff's premises. There was also a threat of industrial action against the plaintiff's customers. The Court of Appeal held, *inter alia*, that there was no trade dispute between BT and its employees because the dispute did not relate wholly or mainly to the loss of jobs and job opportunities, but was part of a wider campaign opposing the privatisation of BT and so there was no immunity from action for the defendants. The court had to look at the predominant purpose in the dispute. The court considered that since the 1982 Act a trade dispute must "not only be between workers and their employer, but must relate wholly or mainly to matters which are specific to that employment." Thus there could be no trade dispute between employer A and his workers relating to the pay and conditions of workers employed by employer B. Sir John Donaldson MR considered that the court should not consider the reason why the parties are in dispute about a certain matter.

In *BBC* v. *Hearn* (1977) Lord Denning MR considered what was meant by "the terms and conditions of employment". He thought that the phrase included "not only the contractual terms and conditions, but those terms which are understood and applied by the parties in practice, or habitually, or by common consent, without ever being incorporated into the contract." This interpretation has been approved by the House of Lords in subsequent cases.

NOTE: The Employment Act 1980, ss.17 and 18, have further amended TULRA 1974, s.13, making special provision for secondary action (*see* **36**) and acts to compel trade union membership (*see* **37**). The Employment Act 1982, s.14, removes the immunity from persons who commit torts (in particular interference with an existing contract) aimed at ensuring the inclusion in contracts of terms requiring the use of union (or non-union labour) or negotiation with or recognition of a trade union (*see* IX, **24**).

36. Secondary action. The provisions of TULRA 1974, s.13(1)(*a*) and (*b*) (*see* **35**(*a*)) now protect certain forms of secondary action (as occurred against the Press Association and Express Newspapers in *Express Newspapers Ltd.* v. *McShane* (1980)) which result in the breach of a contract of employment: 1980 Act, s.17. Basically the 1980 Act restricts trade union immunity to action, sympathy strikes or "blacking" specifically aimed at supplies of goods or services going to or from the company in dispute. Lord Diplock in *Merkur Island Shipping* v. *Laughton* (1983) (*see* below) criticised the complexity of the law in this area as follows: "The statutory provisions ... are drafted in a manner ... which ... can ... only be characterised as most regrettably lacking in the requisite degree of clarity."

Secondary action which will benefit from the provisions of s.13 arises:

(*a*) where a person:

(*i*) induces another to break a contract of employment or interferes or induces another to interfere with its performance, or

(*ii*) threatens that a contract of employment under which he or another is employed will be broken or its performance interfered with, or that he will induce another to break a contract of employment or to interfere with its performance; and *either*

(*b*) (*i*) the purpose of the secondary action was directly to prevent or disrupt the supply during the dispute of goods or services *between an employer who is a party to the dispute and the employer under the contract of employment to which the secondary action relates*, and

(*ii*) the secondary action was likely to achieve that purpose; *or*

(*c*) (*i*) the purpose of the secondary action was directly to prevent or disrupt the supply during the dispute of goods or services *between any person and an associated employer* of an employer who is a party to the dispute, and

(*ii*) the goods or services are *in substitution* for goods or services which but for the dispute would have fallen to be supplied to or by the employer who is a party to the dispute, and

(*iii*) the secondary action was likely to achieve the purpose described in (*i*); *or*

(*d*) the secondary action was done in the course of peaceful picketing (*see* **42**):

(*i*) by a worker employed or last employed by a party to the dispute, or (*ii*) by a person who is a trade union official, at or near the place of work of a member of that union whom he is accompanying and whom he represents.

All other forms of secondary action will not come within the protection afforded by TULRA 1974, s.13(1), e.g. interference with a commercial contract.

EXAMPLE: (1) There is a trade dispute between employer A and union B. In order to further its cause B asks its members who work for employer C not to let the goods which are normally supplied to A, reach A. If C's employees agree to B's request there is a breach of their contract of employment with C. Can B be sued for interfering with the contract?

ANSWER: Union B are inducing their members to break their contracts of employment with C (*see* (*a*)(*i*) above). The purpose of the action by C's employees is to prevent goods reaching A. This amounts to interference with a commercial contract between A and C. However, there is a trade dispute between B and A so the proposed action by C's employees falls within (*b*)(*i*) above which means that B will have immunity from civil liability so long as it can show that the action by C's employees is likely to prevent or disrupt the supply of goods and services to A during the dispute (*see* (*b*)(*ii*)). Note that C's employees will be protected from civil liability if they threaten to breach their contract of employment (*see* (*a*)(*i*)). If they strike then they are breaking their contracts of employment, which would give C the right to terminate their contracts of employment subject to a claim for unfair or possibly wrongful dismissal (*see* IX, in particular **14**(*e*)).

(2) There is a trade dispute between employer W and union X. In order to further its cause union X asks its members who work for employer Y to disrupt the supply of goods which Z normally obtains from W, but is now obtaining from Y because of the trade dispute. Z is an associated employer of W. Can union X be sued for interfering with the contract of employment between employer Z and his employees?

ANSWER: The purpose of Y's employees breaking their contract of employment (*see* (*a*)(*i*) above) is to disrupt the supply of goods to Z. This amounts to interference with a commercial contract between Y and Z. However, as Z is an associated employer of W, and a party to the dispute (*see* (*c*)(*i*)), and as Z would usually obtain those goods from W (*see* (*c*)(*ii*)) then X will be protected from civil liability. If Z was not an associated employer of W then X would not be protected from civil liability for interfering with the contract between Z and Y, but X would still be protected by s.13 (*see* **35**) for civil liability arising from inducing Y's employees to breach their contract of employment.

Merkur Island Shipping v. *Laughton* (1983). The plaintiff shipowners (M) chartered a ship to X who sub-chartered it to Y. The crew of the ship were paid less than the union rates. The union (L) persuaded tugmen employed by a tug company, to refuse to help move the ship, so that it was unable to leave the port. M brought an action against L seeking damages in tort for, inter alia, unlawful interference with their charter contract with X. The House of Lords suggested that in order to decide whether the blacking of the ship by the union with the assistance of the tugmen, was lawful, involved a three-stage approach.

(1) Had the plaintiff (M) established that the blacking was unlawful, in that a tort had been committed? If yes, then

(2) Was the liability for the tort removed as against individual defendants (L) by TULRA 1974, s.13? If yes, then

(3) Was liability restored by s.17 of the Employment Act 1980? The House of Lords HELD that the blacking was secondary action by the union which was not protected by TULRA 1974, s.13, as the immunity given there was withdrawn by s.17(1) of the 1980 Act. The contract concerned was the charter. The employers who were parties to the trade dispute were the shipowners (M). The charter was a contract for the supply of services, to which the shipowners and the charterers alone were parties. The shipowners were not parties to any subsisting contract with the tugowners. The tugowners were the employers under the contract of employment to which the secondary action related. So the requirements of sub-s. (3)(*a*) (*see* (*b*) (*i*) above) were not satisfied.

In *Dimbleby & Sons Ltd.* v. *National Union of Journalists* (1984), a newspaper publisher used a printing company which was an associated company (i.e. a different legal person) of a company with which his journalists' union was in dispute. The House of Lords HELD that the journalists' refusal to work for their employer, the publisher, was unlawful secondary action because, *inter alia*, their breach of contract resulted in commercial contracts made by the publisher with the printers and with advertisers being broken.

37. Acts to compel trade union membership. The provisions of TULRA 1974, s.13(1)(*a*) and (*b*) (*see* **35**(*a*)) will not provide immunity where a person induces or threatens to induce an employee to break his contract of employment with the intention of compelling workers, employed by a different employer or at a different place, to join a particular union or unions: 1980 Act, s.18.

EXAMPLE: D, an official of trade union G, instructs members employed at E. Co. not to supply essential goods to F. Co. because G wants certain employees of F. Co. to join the union.

38. Immunity of trade unions to actions in tort. The Employment Act 1982, s.15, removed the immunity of trade unions and employers' associations from liability for torts relating to trade disputes, which was found in TULRA 1974, s.14. These organisations are now treated as if they were individuals and so have certain immunities under TULRA 1974, s.13 (*see* **35**). Unless the union is so protected, it, and therefore its funds, will be liable for any of the three torts described above (*see* **28–33**), if the tort was authorised or endorsed by a "responsible person". This term includes employed and other officials, certain committees, and any other person so empowered. The principal executive committee, the president and the general secretary may each repudiate an authorised or endorsed action. However, the repudiation must be made as soon as is reasonably practicable and, the "responsible person" notified in writing and without delay. Furthermore, the repudiation must be consistent with later behaviour.

39. Limits on the courts' powers.

(*a*) No court may compel any employee to do any work or attend at any place for the doing of any work by way of:

(*i*) an order for specific performance; or
(*ii*) an injunction: TULRA 1974, s.16.

(*b*) Where an application for an *ex parte* injunction is made to the court (i.e. in the absence of the defendant or his representative) in respect of acts connected with a trade dispute, it cannot be granted unless all steps reasonable in the circumstances have been taken to ensure that the defendant has been notified of the application, and is given an opportunity of being heard. In addition, the court must consider, in deciding whether to grant the application, the likelihood of the defendant being able to establish at the trial of the action the defence that the action was done in contemplation or furtherance of a trade dispute, or that it was peaceful picketing: s.17.

(*c*) Limits have been placed on the amount of damages in tort which can be awarded against a trade union: 1982 Act, s.16. No financial limit is placed on awards (in tort) in personal injury or property cases. In other tort cases, unless the trade union has immunity under TULRA 1974, s.13, the financial limit will depend on the number of members belonging to the union. The limit is as follows:

(*i*) up to £10,000 if the union has less than 5,000 members;

(*ii*) up to £50,000 if the union has 5,000 or more but less than 25,000 members;

(*iii*) up to £125,000 if the union has 25,000 or more but less than 100,000 members;

(*iv*) up to £250,000 if the union has 100,000 or more members.

The Secretary of State may vary these sums.

(*d*) No award of damages, costs or expenses against a trade union, an employers' association, or their trustees, officials or members, will be recoverable by enforcement against any protected property: 1982 Act, s.17. Protected property includes the political fund and the provident benefits fund of the union as well as the personal property of the trustees, officials and members. The political fund is a fund set aside to achieve political objectives, and is not used to finance industrial action. The provident benefit fund is a fund set aside solely to provide provident benefits, which include payments to members who are sick or incapacitated by personal injury, or out of work, or elderly, and payment to dependants.

40. Criminal law. The criminal law provides, for the purposes of industrial law, two main headings of liability:

(*a*) criminal intimidation;
(*b*) picketing.

41. Criminal intimidation. Section 7 of the Consipiracy and Protection of Property Act 1875 provides that every person who, with a view to compel any other person to abstain from doing or to do any act which such other person has a legal right to do, or abstain from doing, wrongfully and without legal authority:

(*a*) uses violence to or intimidates such other person or his wife or children, or injures his property; or

(*b*) persistently follows such other person about from place to place; or

(*c*) hides any tools, clothes or other property owned or used by such other person, or deprives him, or hinders him in the use, thereof; or (*d*) watches or besets the house or other place where such other person resides or works or carries on business, or happens to be, or the approach to such house or place; or

(*e*) follows such other person with two or more other persons in a disorderly manner in or through any street or road, will on conviction be guilty of a criminal offence.

42. Peaceful picketing. The Employment Act 1980, s.16, substituted a new s.15 (which has been amended by the 1982 Act) for the original s.15 found in TULRA 1974, which governs peaceful picketing. The new s.15 provides a limited immunity for peaceful picketing, but it is also aimed at limiting the immunity from civil liability available to sympathetic pickets (*see* **35** and **36**(*d*)). The idea is to prevent mass picketing and flying pickets who come long distances in order to picket on behalf of strikers or others not employed by the pickets' company or companies.

It is lawful for a person in contemplation or furtherance of a trade dispute to attend:

(*a*) at or near his own place of work; or

(*b*) if he is an official of a trade union, at or near the place of work of a member of that union whom he is accompanying and whom he represents,

for the purpose *only* of peacefully obtaining or communicating information, or peacefully persuading any person to work or abstain from working. A former employee, the termination of whose contract of employment was partly the cause of, or connected with the trade dispute, will come within this provision. However, a lawful picket is still subject to the criminal law and can be charged with, for example, obstruction.

The immunity provided by TULRA 1974,s.13 (*see* **35**) will only apply to picketing which is done in the course of lawful attendance as defined in s.15. In other words, pickets from another workplace will only be protected from civil liability if they interfere with a contract of employment. If they interfere with a commercial contract, e.g. prevent supplies getting through the picket line, they will only be protected from civil liability if their behaviour comes within the definition of secondary action (*see* **36**).

43. Code of Practice. The Secretary of State for Employment issued in December 1980 a Code of Practice on Picketing (*see* **8**). The Code of Practice suggests, *inter alia*, that:

(*a*) the number of pickets at an entrance to a workplace should not exceed six, and frequently a smaller number will be appropriate;

(*b*) the picket organiser should ensure that employees from other places of work do not join the picket line and that any offers of support on the picket line from outsiders are refused;

(*c*) disciplinary action should not be taken or threatened by a union against a member on the ground that he has crossed a picket line which it had not authorised or which was not at the member's place of work (*see* **18**).

PROGRESS TEST 10

1. What are the main purposes of the current industrial relations legislation? **(3)**
2. How is the legislation on industrial relations supplemented? Give examples. **(5–7)**
3. Describe the procedure followed in settling a dispute between an employer and an employee, using the machinery provided by legislation. **(9–14)**
4. Describe the role of (*a*) ACAS; (*b*) the CAC. **(11, 12)**
5. What are the functions of the Certification Officer? **(15, 16)**
6. Describe the legal position of a trade union. **(17, 38)**
7. To what extent does the law regulate the relationship between a trade union and its individual members? **(18)**
8. When and why would a trade union hold a secret ballot? **(19)**
9. To what extent does the law acknowledge the existence of collective agreements and collective bargaining? **(20, 21)**
10. Where there is a closed shop agreement, what rights, if any, does an employee have if he does not wish to be a member of a specified trade union? **(25, 26)**
11. What areas of civil law can be used to control trade disputes? **(27–33)**
12. When will trade unions be immune from liability for actions in tort? **(35, 38)**
13. Summarise in not more than a hundred words the definitions of (*a*) trade dispute and (*b*) secondary picketing. **(35, 36)**
14. M. Co.'s employees are on strike in support of a trade dispute between N. Co. and its employees. M. Co.'s employees have mounted a picket line at their own place of work in the course of their strike. Can M. Co.'s employees picket the supply of all goods and services to their employer, M.Co.? **(36, 42)**
15. Who is a lawful picket? What is a lawful picket entitled to do when peacefully picketing? **(42)**

CHAPTER XI

Social Security

SCOPE OF THE SCHEME

1. Origins of the scheme. The Beveridge Report 1942 (*Report on Social Insurance and Allied Services*) advocated the setting up of a national scheme to insure individuals against a number of contingencies, some of which might result in the interruption, reduction or termination of earning capacity, while others made additional demands upon the individual or family income. Beveridge recommended the inclusion in the scheme of industrial injury and disablement as insurable risks along with the other main causes of loss of earning capacity—unemployment, sickness and old age. The aim of the scheme was to provide benefits in return for contributions and to provide freedom from want for insured persons by providing against interruption and loss of earning power.

2. Current legislation. The Social Security Act 1975 forms the basis of the present scheme, and the relevant law is to be found in the Social Security Acts 1975–1980. Two recent statutes, the Social Security Act 1980 and the Social Security (No. 2) Act 1980, indicate a shift in social policy by the Government. Prior to these provisions the Secretary of State for Social Services was under a duty to uprate certain benefits, including unemployment, sickness and industrial injuries benefits, in line with increases in earnings and prices. However, the Social Security Act 1980 provided that future uprating need only be in line with increases in prices. The Social Security (No. 2) Act provided for the abolition of earnings-related supplement in 1982, and redefined "period of interruption of employment" (*see* **9, 13**).

The Social Security and Housing Benefits Act 1982 radically altered the administration of sickness benefit and the provision of industrial injuries benefits. Employees who are sick are now entitled to statutory sick pay for the first eight weeks of illness (*see* VIII, **37**). Industrial injury benefit is abolished. It is replaced by sickness benefit and statutory sick pay. Two other industrial injuries benefits remain. The adjudication of social security claims has been altered by the Health and Social Services and Social Security Adjudications Act 1983.

Section references are to the 1975 Act, unless otherwise stated.

NOTE: It should be added that there is a third arm to the social security system. In addition to the contributory schemes outlined in this chapter there is a non-contributory system of benefits known as supplementary benefits. A claimant for supplementary benefit must show that he is not in full-time employment, and that his income, whether from state benefits or from his own resources, is below a certain prescribed limit. It follows that a person who is claiming sickness, unemployment or industrial injuries benefit may also claim supplementary benefit if the total of those benefits does not amount to the sum prescribed as necessary for his requirements. In calculating his requirements, factors such as the number of dependants are taken into account.

3. Population classes. In order to take into account different needs, the population is divided into seven population classes, five main classes of working age, and two others below and above working age. Housewives, that is married women of working age, are a class to whom special provisions apply, since they are entitled to certain benefits by virtue of their husbands' contributions. The four other categories of insured persons who are required to make contributions are as follows.

(*a*) Class 1 earnings-related contributions are paid by:

(*i*) employed earners—the primary contributors; and

(*ii*) employers and other persons paying earnings—the secondary contributors.

(Employed earners who are also self-employed will have to pay both Class 1 and Class 2 contributions.)

(*b*) Class 2 flat-rate contributions of £4.60 in 1984/5 are payable weekly by self-employed earners.

(*c*) Class 3 contributions are payable voluntarily by earners and others who are non-employed because, for example, their income is inherited, but they wish to ensure entitlement to benefit.

(*d*) Class 4 contributions are payable in respect of the profits or gains of a trade, profession or vocation, or in respect of equivalent earnings. These are payable by the self-employed in addition to their Class 2 contributions and for the tax year 1984/5 amount to 6.3 per cent of any profits or gains between £3,950 and £13,000 in that year.

The Secretary of State for Social Services has extensive powers to make regulations under the Social Security Act 1975 with regard to the categorisation of earners.

4. Class 1 contributions. These will be paid where in any tax week earnings are paid to or for the benefit of an earner in respect of any one employment of his, being employed earner's employment, and:

(*a*) he is over school-leaving age; and
(*b*) the amount paid is equal to or exceeds the current lower earnings limit.

NOTE: (1) The lower earnings limit for the tax year beginning April 1984 is £34 a week and the upper earnings limit for that tax year is £250 a week.
(2) Women who were already married at 5th April 1977 had until 11th May 1977 to elect to pay reduced-rate Class 1 contributions, but if a woman married after that date she *must* pay the full-rate contributions.

5. Class 1 exemptions. No primary contributions will be payable in respect of an employed earner who:

(*a*) is over pensionable age and has retired from regular employment;
(*b*) is over pensionable age, but has not retired from regular employment, and who did not satisfy the contribution conditions for a full pension when he reached retirement age;
(*c*) is a woman over pensionable age who was married when she attained that age and has not retired from regular employment, but who
(*i*) does not have a satisfactory earnings record following marriage to receive a full pension, and
(*ii*) married the man to whom she is married on reaching her retirement age before she attained the age of 55;
(*d*) is an employed earner earning below the lower earnings limit for Class 1 contributions; or
(*e*) is under the age of 16.

NOTE: Exemptions (*a*), (*b*) and (*e*) also apply for Class 2 contributions. In addition self-employed earners can apply for exemption where their income from self-employment is less than £1,850 in the 1984/5 tax year.

6. Insurable risks. The Social Security Act 1975 provides for the following contributory benefits to be payable.

(*a*) Unemployment benefit.
(*b*) Sickness benefit.
(*c*) Invalidity benefit.
(*d*) Maternity benefit.
(*e*) Widow's benefit.
(*f*) Retirement pensions.
(*g*) Child's special allowance.
(*h*) Death grant.

In addition, the Act provides for the following non-contributory benefits to be payable.

(*i*) Attendance allowance.
(*j*) Invalidity pension (this will be replaced by severe disablement allowance under the Health and Social Security Bill 1984).
(*k*) Invalid care allowance.
(*l*) Guardian's allowance.
(*m*) Certain retirement pensions for those over 80 years of age.
(*n*) Age addition to retirement pension.

Unemployment benefit, sickness benefit, industrial accident and diseases benefit are social security benefits of concern to employed persons, and the provisions concerning these will be discussed below.

CONDITIONS FOR UNEMPLOYMENT AND SICKNESS BENEFIT

7. General qualifications for benefit. An employee claiming benefit must fulfil a number of conditions. He must be a person who:

(*a*) satisfies the contribution conditions, and
(*b*) shows that he is unemployed or sick within the meaning of the Act.

A person will not be entitled to unemployment benefit for the first three days of any period of interruption of employment. From April 1984 the rate of benefit for a man under 65 and a woman under 60 is £27.05 a week.

The Social Security and Housing Benefits Act 1982 (*see* VIII, **37**), makes employers responsible for paying statutory sick pay to their employees for the first eight weeks of illness. If the illness extends beyond that time, or where someone is unemployed, non-employed or self-employed, then sickness benefit is payable. From April 1984 the rate of sickness benefit is £25.95 a week.

8. Contributions. The contribution conditions for unemployment or sickness benefit are as follows.

(*a*) The claimant must have paid a minimum contribution before he qualifies for benefit. The minimum contribution is at least twenty-five times the amount of contribution payable on the weekly lower earnings limit paid in any one tax year since 6th April 1975.

(*b*) For the standard rate of benefit the claimant must have paid or been credited in the relevant tax year with contributions equivalent to the Class 1 contributions paid in fifty weeks by someone at the weekly lower earnings limit. A reduced rate of benefit may be payable if the total of the contributions paid and credited is equivalent to contributions on earnings of less than fifty but not less than twenty-five times the weekly lower earnings limit. Generally a minimum of thirteen paid contributions is required.

The relevant tax year is the year which ended on 5th April before the benefit year in which the claim is made.

A benefit year starts on the first Sunday in January of each year.

Therefore if X claims unemployment or sickness benefit on 16th January 1982 the relevant tax year for deciding whether he has satisfied the contribution conditions is 6th April 1980 to 5th April 1981.

NOTE: (1) Class 1 contributions are necessary in order to claim unemployment benefit. Class 1 or 2 contributions are necessary in order to claim sickness benefit. Thus the self-employed earner will only be able to claim sickness benefit, and will not be entitled to unemployment benefit. Married women who have elected to pay the reduced rate of Class 1 contributions will be unable to claim either of these benefits.

(2) Where an employed earner is sick as a result of an accident at work (*see* **18–23**), or a prescribed industrial disease (*see* **32**), then he is entitled to receive sickness benefit, even if the contribution conditions are not satisfied.

(3) For unemployment benefit, additional contribution conditions are imposed on students, and on seasonal workers in their off-season.

(4) Earners claiming unemployment or sickness benefit can also claim increases of benefit for a wife, or one other dependent adult, and for children.

(5) It is possible to satisfy the contribution conditions by working in a member state of the European Economic Community, other than the UK.

UNEMPLOYMENT BENEFIT

9. When benefit is payable. A qualified claimant will be treated as unemployed if he is available to be employed in employed earner's employment, and he will be entitled to unemployment benefit in respect of any day of unemployment which forms part of a period of interruption of employment. If an employed earner is unemployed for two days, whether consecutive or not, within a period of six consecutive days these will be treated as a period of interruption of employment, and any two such periods not separated by more than eight weeks will be treated as one period of interruption of employment, although the usual rule (*see* 7) is that a claimant will not be entitled to benefit for the first three days of unemployment.

In certain cases where an employed earner is suspended from his employment by his employer he may be treated as unemployed from the seventh day of the suspension, if the Secretary of State so orders.

10. Duration of unemployment benefit. A qualified claimant is entitled to receive unemployment benefit for a maximum of 312 days excluding Sundays. He will not be entitled to any further unemployment benefit until he has requalified for such benefit. A person who has exhausted his right to unemployment benefit requalifies for it when:

(*a*) he has been in employment as an employed earner for thirteen weeks since the last day for which he was entitled to that benefit, and

(*b*) in each of those weeks he has worked in such employment for sixteen hours or more.

11. Disqualification from unemployment benefit. A claimant may be disqualified from claiming unemployment benefit in the following circumstances.

(*a*) A person who has lost his employment as an employed earner by reason of a stoppage of work, which was due to a trade dispute at his place of employment, will be disqualified from receiving unemployment benefit so long as the stoppage continues.

(*b*) A person will be disqualified from receiving unemployment benefit for a period not exceeding six weeks if:

(*i*) he has left his employment through his misconduct, or has voluntarily left such employment without just cause;

(*ii*) after a situation in any suitable employment has been properly notified to him as vacant or about to become vacant, he has without good cause refused or failed to apply for that situation, or refused to accept that situation when offered to him;

(*iii*) he has neglected to avail himself of a reasonable opportunity of suitable employment;

(*iv*) he has without good cause refused or failed to carry out reasonable official recommendations given to him with a view to assisting him to find suitable employment; or

(*v*) he has without good cause refused or failed to avail himself of a reasonable opportunity of receiving approved training for the purpose of becoming or keeping fit for entry into, or return to, regular employment.

(*c*) Detention or imprisonment in legal custody.

(*d*) A man aged 60 and over who receives an occupational pension of £35 or more will not be entitled to receive unemployment benefit: Social Security (No. 2) Act 1980, s.5.

The Secretary of State has the power to make regulations imposing additional conditions if it appears necessary to do so for the purpose of preventing inequalities or injustice to the general body of employed earners or earners generally.

EXCEPTION: The disqualification from unemployment benefit under (*a*) will not apply: (1) where during the stoppage of work a person has become bona fide employed elsewhere in the occupation which he usually follows or has become regularly employed in some other occupation, or (2) where the employed earner proves that he is not participating in or directly interested in the trade dispute which caused the stoppage of work. ("Directly interested" has been broadly interpreted. It has been applied to a dispute where the earner's working conditions, for example his afternoon tea-break, would be affected.)

NOTE: The dependants of the disqualified person may claim supplementary benefit, which is a benefit awarded on a non-contributory basis for people who are not in full-time employment and whose other income is not enough to meet their requirements.

12. Terminology. The Social Security Act 1975 defines the following expressions.

(*a*) "*Trade dispute*" means any dispute between employers and employees or between employees and employees, which is connected with the employment or non-employment, or the conditions of employment of any persons, whether employed in the employment of the employer with whom the dispute arises or not. (Compare X, **4**(*g*).) (*See Presho* v. *Insurance Officer* (1984).)

(*b*) "*Place of employment*" means the factory, workshop, farm or other premises at which a person was employed. However, where separate branches of work which are commonly carried on as separate businesses in separate premises or at separate places are in any case carried on in separate departments on the same premises or at the same place, each of those departments will be deemed to be a separate factory or workshop or farm or separate premises or a separate place.

(*c*) "*Suitable employment*" is defined in terms of what is considered unsuitable employment. Employment will not be deemed to be suitable if it is either:

(*i*) employment in a situation vacant in consequence of a stoppage of work due to a trade dispute; or

(*ii*) employment in his usual occupation in the district where he was ordinarily employed at a rate of remuneration lower, or on conditions less favourable than those he might reasonably have expected to obtain, having regard to those which he habitually obtained in his usual occupation in that district, or would have obtained had he continued to be so employed; or

(*iii*) employment in his usual occupation in any other district at a rate of remuneration lower, or on conditions less favourable, than those generally observed in that district.

However, after a reasonable lapse of time as unemployed, employment will not be deemed to be unsuitable by reason only that it is employment of a kind other than employment in his usual occupation, provided that the remuneration and the conditions of service are not less favourable than those generally observed in the district.

SICKNESS BENEFIT

13. When is benefit payable. A qualified claimant will be treated as sick if he is incapable of work by reason of some specific disease (including prescribed industrial diseases) or bodily or mental disablement (including industrial injuries). The claimant will be entitled to sickness benefit in respect of any day of incapacity for work which forms part of a period of interruption of employment.

If a claimant suffers four or more consecutive days of sickness that will be treated as a period of interruption of employment (*see* **7**). Any two such periods not separated by more than eight weeks will be treated as one period of interruption of employment, which means that the claimant will be able to receive sickness benefit for all the second period of interruption of employment, whereas usually the claimant will not receive sickness benefit for the first three days of an illness.

14. Duration of sickness benefit. A qualified claimant is entitled to sickness benefit for 168 days excluding Sundays, but then he will cease to be entitled to sickness benefit for the rest of that period of interruption of employment. However, he may then be entitled to an invalidity pension or industrial disablement benefit.

15. Disqualification from sickness benefit. A person may be disqualified from receiving sickness benefit for a period not exceeding six weeks if:

(*a*) he has become incapable of work through his own misconduct; or

(*b*) he fails without good cause to attend for, or submit himself to, such medical or other examinations as may be required in accordance with the regulations, or to observe any prescribed rules of behaviour; or

(*c*) he is detained or imprisoned in legal custody.

The Secretary of State has the power to make regulations imposing additional conditions if it appears necessary to do so for the purpose of preventing inequalities or injustice to the general body of employed earners, or earners generally.

INDUSTRIAL ACCIDENTS AND DISEASES

16. Employment covered by the scheme. The industrial injuries scheme provides cash payments where an employed earner suffers:

(*a*) personal injury caused by an accident arising out of and in the course of his employment, being employed earner's employment s.50; or

(*b*) any prescribed disease or personal injury, not covered by (*a*), being a disease or injury due to the nature of that employment: Social Security Act 1975, s.76.

17. Terminology. The Social Security Act 1975 provides the following definitions.

(*a*) "*Employed earner*" means a person who is gainfully

employed in Great Britain either under a contract of service or in an office with emoluments chargeable to income tax under Schedule E.

(*b*) "*Employed earner's employment*" means any employment by virtue of which a person is, for the purposes of industrial injuries benefit, an employed earner.

NOTE: (1) The Act does not in general insure self-employed earners who work under a contract for services (*see* VIII, **3**).

(2) The Act states that regulations may provide for special classes of individuals to be treated as employed earners in respect of industrial injuries benefit and its administration, or for a prescribed person to be treated as the earner's employer.

INDUSTRIAL INJURY

18. Personal injury. A personal injury can consist of either physical or mental injury to the claimant. Mental shock caused by the accident is covered by the scheme. However, the phrase refers to the physical damage and mental attributes, of the claimant himself, and it is not a personal injury within the meaning of the scheme when damage is caused to personal property, such as clothing. Nor is damage to an artificial addition to the body, such as an artificial limb, false teeth, or a hearing aid, included, even though the damage may result in loss of working capacity.

19. Accident. The injury must have been caused by an accident. There is no definition of the word "accident" in the statute, but there have been judicial interpretations of the word which are of some assistance. The courts have defined the word "in the popular and ordinary sense of the word as denoting an unlooked-for mishap or an untoward event which is not expected or defined": *Fenton* v. *Thorley & Co. Ltd* (1903). "The word accident is not a technical legal term with a clearly defined meaning. Speaking generally, but with reference to legal liabilities, an accident means any unintended and unexpected occurrence which produces hurt or loss" (ibid). These definitions give rise to the following rules.

(*a*) An injury must not arise out of a deliberate act of the claimant which caused injury to himself. Cases of suicide would seem to be outside the definition, but in certain cases it has been held that self-inflicted injury leading to death entitles beneficiaries of the dead person to claim benefit. The rule seems to be that if, as a result of an accident, or of shock resulting from an accident, a condition of nervous derangement leads to a person committing suicide, the applicant can get compensation.

(*b*) The wilful act of another person may result in an accident as far as the claimant is concerned.

(*c*) There must have been a specific event for there to have been an accident. Incapacity resulting from exposure to a process is not incapacity resulting from an accident. However, an event will be regarded as an accident even though the effect is to produce a disease.

20. Accidents covered by the scheme. An accident arising in the course of an employed earner's employment will be deemed, in the absence of evidence to the contrary, to have arisen out of that employment: s.50.

The following kinds of accident will be deemed to have arisen out of and in the course of the employed earner's employment.

(*a*) *Earner acting in breach of regulations.* Where the employed earner was at the time of the accident acting:

(*i*) in contravention of regulations applicable to his employment, or

(*ii*) in contravention of orders given by the employer, or

(*iii*) without instructions from his employer, if the accident would have arisen anyway or the act was done for the purpose of and in connection with the employer's trade or business: s.51.

(*b*) *Earner travelling in employer's transport.* Where the accident occurred while the employed earner was travelling with permission from his employer, in a vehicle to or from his place of work if:

(*i*) it would have arisen if the employed earner was under an obligation to his employer to travel by that vehicle, and

(*ii*) the vehicle is being operated by or on behalf of the employer and is not a public transport service: s.53.

(*c*) *Accidents happening while meeting an emergency.* Where an accident happens to an employed earner in or about any premises at which he is employed for the purposes of his employer's trade or business, if it happens, while he is taking steps in an actual or supposed emergency at those premises to protect persons and property from injury and serious damage: s.54.

(*d*) *Accidents caused by another's misconduct.* Where an accident arises:

(*i*) in the course of employment; and

(*ii*) the accident is caused either by another person's misconduct, skylarking or negligence, or by steps taken in consequence of such misconduct, etc., or by the behaviour or presence of an animal, or by the employed earner being struck by any object or by lightning; and

(*iii*) the employed earner did not directly or indirectly induce or contribute to the happening of the accident by his conduct: s.55.

NOTE: In (*a*), (*b*) and (*c*) the accident is deemed to have arisen in the course of employment, but in (*d*) it must be shown to have so occurred.

To arise out of the claimant's employment, the accident must have occurred while he was carrying out some task which he was employed to do, or which was reasonably incidental to it.

21. In the course of employment. To come within this part of the definition, an accident must normally occur during the contractual hours of work, i.e. during the period after the daily commencement of work and before its termination. If a person suffers an accident during the time when he is working, there is a general presumption that the accident arose out of the employment: s.50 (*see* **20**). The burden of proof then rests upon the adjudication officer (*see* **45**) to show that the injury was in fact caused in some manner not connected with the employment. The presumption is rebuttable as is shown by the phrase "in the absence of evidence to the contrary" in s.50. Should the presumption in s.50 be refuted by evidence to the contrary, "it is then for the applicant to prove that the accident did arise not only in the course of but also out of his employment"; *R.* v. *National Insurance (Industrial Injuries) Commissioner, ex p. Richardson* (1958). *See* also *R.* v. *National Insurance Commissioner, ex p. Michael* (1977) where a policeman was injured in a police football match, in which he was expected but not compelled to play. The Court of Appeal held that he was not entitled to industrial injury benefit. (*See* also VIII, **7**.)

22. Commencement and termination of work. In general, the course of employment coincides with the contractual hours of work, but there are exceptions to this rule as follows.

(*a*) *Travelling to work* (*see* **20**(*b*)).

(*b*) *Travelling as part of employment.* It seems that, in general, a claimant will be entitled to benefit for an accident occurring on the highway only if he was under a contractual duty and was, with the express or implied permission of his employers, travelling there at the time of the accident.

(*c*) *Accidents before and after working hours.* An employed earner will be covered by the scheme if he arrives at work at a reasonable time before working hours, in order, for example, to change his clothing or to collect tools. Similarly, should a person remain at the workplace for a reasonable period after the end of the contractual hours of work, an accident occurring during that period may give rise to a successful claim for benefit.

23. Interruption in working hours. An accident which occurs during an interruption of work may still be in the course of employment if the circumstances are reasonably incidental to work being done. For instance, an employee may take a break to eat a meal, to have a smoke or to have a cup of tea. Whether a claim will succeed seems to depend primarily upon whether it can be found that the employer consents expressly or by implication to the break.

R. v. *Industrial Injuries Commissioners, ex p. AEU* (1966): C was employed in a factory. Employees were entitled to a tea-break of ten minutes in the morning. A buzzer sounded at the end of the tea-break. Smoking was not permitted in the workshops, but was allowed in a small smoking booth which was close to a passage-way. When C reached the booth it was full. He squatted in the passage outside the booth, waiting to go in and smoke. He had overstayed the tea-break by five minutes when he was injured by a fork-lift truck. HELD: the test whether an employee was acting in the course of his employment was whether he was doing something incidental to his contract of service, although he might be under no duty to do it. C had taken himself out of the course of his employment in this case.

24. Express declaration. Where it is determined that the relevant accident was or was not an industrial accident, an express declaration of that fact must be made and a person is entitled to have this question determined, whether he is a claimant or not, although a declaration may be refused if it is unlikely that it will be necessary to determine the question for the purposes of any claim for benefit. Such a declaration will be conclusive for the purpose of any claim for industrial injuries benefit in respect of that accident: s.107.

INDUSTRIAL INJURY BENEFITS

25. Qualification for benefit. An employee claiming industrial injury benefits must fulfil certain conditions. He must be an employed earner in an employed earner's employment (*see* **17**). This means that he will make weekly contributions into the scheme since it is based on the insurance principle. However, there are no contribution conditions to be fulfilled before benefit can be paid in relation to this part of the scheme, unlike the situation which applies where unemployment or sickness benefit is claimed (*see* **8**). Industrial injury benefits can be paid from the first day of employment in an employed earner's employment. The conditions for the receipt of benefit are the same for a claim arising as a result of an industrial disease.

NOTE: (1) A person who has not attained school-leaving age will not be entitled to injury benefit, except as may be provided by regulations.

(2) A person will be disqualified from receiving any benefit for any period during which he: (*a*) is absent from Great Britain, or (*b*) is undergoing imprisonment or detention in legal custody, except where regulations otherwise provide.

(3) Regulations may provide for the suspension of payment of benefit to a person during any period in which he is undergoing medical or other treatment as an in-patient in a hospital or similar institution.

26. Industrial injuries benefits. The Social Security and Housing Benefits Act 1982 abolished industrial injury benefit, which was paid weekly for up to a maximum of twenty-six weeks where an employed earner was incapable of work as a result of an industrial accident. The employee will now be able to claim statutory sick pay and sickness benefit (*see* **7, 8, 13** above). There are now two types of industrial injuries benefit payable for personal injury as a result of industrial accident:

(*a*) industrial disablement benefit;
(*b*) industrial death benefit.

From November 1984 the following rates of benefit apply. A person over 18 claiming disablement benefit will receive £11.12 a week for a 20 per cent disablement and £55.60 a week for a 100 per cent disablement. Where a gratuity is paid this would amount to £369 for 1 per cent disablement, and £3,690 for 19 per cent disablement. A widow claiming the death benefit will receive £47.65 a week for the first twenty-six weeks and then either £36.40 a week or £10.22 a week depending on whether she is entitled to the higher or lower permanent rate.

27. Disablement benefit. An employed earner will be entitled to disablement benefit if he suffers as the result of the relevant accident from loss of physical or mental facility such that the assessed extent of the resulting disablement amounts to not less than one per cent. References to loss of physical faculty include disfigurement, whether or not accompanied by any actual loss of faculty. Disablement benefit cannot be paid until fifteen weeks after the accident: s.57, as amended by the 1982 Act, s.39.

The accident must have been an industrial accident. However, an employed earner can claim disablement benefit even if he has not stayed off work, so long as he has suffered some disablement as a result of the accident. An adjudicating medical practitioner assesses the loss of faculty and the degree and duration of the resulting disablement.

28. Method of assessment of disablement. The extent of disablement is assessed by taking into account, among other things:

(*a*) the disabilities to which the claimant may be expected to be subject, as compared with a person of the same age and sex, whose physical and mental condition is normal;

(*b*) the age, sex, physical and marital condition of the claimant; and

(*c*) the disabilities resulting from such loss of faculty.

The assessments for certain clearly defined injuries are laid down in a scale, e.g. loss of both hands, the scale assessment is 100 per cent, loss of one hand 60 per cent, loss of an index finger 14 per cent.

The period to be taken into account by an assessment of the extent of a claimant's disablement will be the period (beginning not earlier than fifteen weeks after the accident, and limited by reference either to the claimant's life or to a definite date) during which the claimaint has suffered, and may be expected to continue to suffer, from the relevant loss of faculty. The assessment should state the degree of disablement in the form of a percentage.

NOTE: Disablement benefit can be claimed in certain circumstances, after the right to sickness benefit has expired.

29. Disablement gratuity and disablement pension. Where the extent of disablement is less than 20 per cent, disablement benefit will be in the form of a disablement gratuity, which is a fixed amount payable usually in a lump sum, but in certain cases it is payable in instalments. Where the extent of disablement is 20 per cent or more, disablement benefit will be a disablement pension on a weekly basis (*see* **26**).

30. Supplements to the disablement pension. The Social Security Act 1975 provides for an increase in the weekly disablement pension in the following circumstances.

(*a*) *Unemployability supplement.* This is payable where as a result of the relevant loss of faculty the beneficiary is incapable, and is likely to remain so permanently, of work providing earnings of £780 or more a year.

(*b*) *Special hardship allowance.* This is payable where as a result of the relevant loss of faculty the beneficiary has a current disablement assessment of less than 100 per cent and:

(*i*) is incapable, and is likely to remain so permanently, of following his regular occupation; and

(*ii*) is incapable of following employment of an equivalent standard which is suitable in his case; or

(*iii*) if as the result of the relevant loss of faculty the beneficiary is, and has at all times since fifteen weeks after the accident been, incapable of following that occupation or any such employment.

(*c*) *Constant attendance allowance.* Where a disablement pension is payable in respect of an assessment of 100 per cent, if as the result of the relevant loss of faculty the beneficiary requires constant attendance the weekly rate of the pension will be increased by reference to the extent and nature of the attendance required by the beneficiary. It can be further increased for exceptionally severe disablement.

(*d*) *Hospital treatment allowance.* Where a disablement pension is payable in respect of an assessment of less than 100 per cent, and the beneficiary goes into hospital, the pension will be increased to the maximum rate.

NOTE: Unemployability supplement and special hardship allowance will not be payable for the same period.

31. Industrial death benefit.

(*a*) The widow of the deceased will be entitled to death benefit if at her husband's death she was either residing with him or was receiving, or was entitled to receive, periodical payments for her maintenance. She will receive:

(*i*) a weekly pension commencing from the death of her husband for life or until she remarries; or (*ii*) a gratuity payable if she remarries.

A pension will not be payable for any period during which she is cohabiting with a man not her husband: s.67.

(*b*) The widower of the deceased will be entitled to death benefit if at his wife's death he:

(*i*) was being, or would have been, wholly or mainly maintained by her; and

(*ii*) was permanently incapable of self-support.

However, the widower will receive a weekly pension commencing from the death of the deceased and payable for life: s.69.

(*c*) Additional payments shall be made for the children of the deceased's family, dependent parents and relatives, and for a woman having care of the deceased's children.

INDUSTRIAL DISEASES

32. Prescribed industrial diseases. A disease or injury may be prescribed in relation to any employed earners if the Secretary of State for Social Services is satisfied that:

(*a*) it ought to be treated as a risk of their occupations and not as a risk common to all persons; and

(*b*) the attribution of particular cases to the nature of the employment can be established or presumed with certainty.

Certain benefits are provided in respect of any prescribed disease or personal injury (but not an injury caused by an accident arising out of and in the course of his employment) being a disease or injury due to the nature of that employment and developed after 4th July 1948.

Subject to the power to make different provision by regulations, benefits payable in respect of a prescribed industrial disease or injury and the conditions for receipt of benefit will be the same as in the case of personal injury by accident arising out of and in the course of employment.

An example of a prescribed industrial disease is angiosarcoma of the liver. At present there are about fifty prescribed diseases or injuries. Industrial injuries benefits are also paid for pneumoconiosis, byssinosis and occupational deafness. The Pneumoconiosis etc. (Workers' Compensation) Act 1979 makes it possible for a person who has become disabled, due to his employment, by pneumoconiosis, byssinosis or diffuse mesothelioma, to obtain lump sum compensation from the Secretary of State for Employment if his employer has gone out of business and cannot be sued for damages (*see* VIII, **15** and XIV, **53**).

33. Qualifications for benefit. In order to be successful in his claim, the employed earner would have to show that he was suffering from a prescribed disease and that he had been employed at some time since 4th July 1948 in one of the occupations prescribed for that disease or injury. The disease or injury must be due to the nature of the work in that employment. Thus if a claimant is suffering from cramp of the hand or forearm due to repetitive movements, then he would have to show that he had been employed at some time since 4th July 1948 in an occupation requiring prolonged periods of handwriting, typing or other repetitive movements of the finger, hand or arm.

Slightly different rules apply to claimants suffering from pneumoconiosis, byssinosis, or occupational deafness.

ADMINISTRATION OF THE SCHEME

34. Structure of administration. The Social Security Act 1975 maintained the existing structure for running the scheme through the Department of Health and Social Security, which has local offices to deal with individual claims. Claims for benefit are made against the State and not the employer and, unlike common law actions for damages, there is no recourse to the law courts except in limited circumstances. The system includes a number of tribunals to which recourse can be made in cases of dispute. The advantage of administrative tribunals is said to be their comparative speed, informality and cheapness.

The system of adjudication has been amended by the Health and Social Services and Social Security Adjudications Act 1983, s.25 and Sched. 8. There are four main changes.

(*a*) Insurance officers are replaced by adjudication officers. There is to be a Chief Adjudication Officer who will advise adjudication officers and review operating arrangements.

(*b*) National Insurance Local Tribunals and Supplementary Benefit Appeal Tribunals are replaced by Social Security Appeal Tribunals.

(*c*) Provision is made for the appointment of a President, regional chairmen and some full-time chairmen of the new tribunals as well as of the medical appeal tribunals, all of whom must be legally qualified.

(*d*) Medical boards are replaced by "adjudicating medical practitioner(s)" or by a medical appeal tribunal.

35. Adjudication officers. Initially all claims for benefit are made to an adjudication officer. His main task in the case of any claim or question submitted to him is either to decide it in favour of the claimant; or to decide it adversely to the claimant; or to refer it to a social security appeal tribunal. Where a case is referred to a tribunal, notice in writing must be given to the claimant. However, when a claim involves a "special question" it must be referred for determination by the insurance officer to the Secretary of State or, where disablement questions arise, to an adjudicating medical practitioner. "Special" or "principal questions" include:

(*a*) whether a person is an earner and, if he is, into which category of earners he is to be included;

(*b*) whether a person is or was employed in an employed earner's employment;

(*c*) which of two persons satisfying the conditions for an increase of benefit is entitled to the increase, where not more than one of those persons is so entitled;

(*d*) whether the contribution conditions for any benefit are satisfied;

(*e*) certain questions relating to liability for Class 4 contributions;

(*f*) whether the relevant accident has resulted in loss of faculty; and

(*g*) at what degree the extent of disablement resulting from a loss of faculty is to be assessed, and what period is to be taken into account by the assessment; s.93, 1975 Act.

NOTE: As (*f*) and (*g*) are disablement questions they are considered by an adjudicating medical practitioner(s) or a medical appeal tribunal (*see* **41, 42**).

Other questions to be determined by the Secretary of State include whether there can be an increase in the disablement pension to include constant attendance allowance or the exceptionally severe disablement allowance and whether a child, or the family of which the child is a member, is to be treated as included for the calculation of benefit.

Any question of law arising in connection with the determination by the Secretary of State of a "special" or "principal question" may be referred by the Secretary of State, or appealed against by any person aggrieved, to the High Court.

36. Decision of the adjudication officer. An adjudication officer to whom a claim or question is submitted must take it into consideration and, so far as is practicable, dispose of it within fourteen days of its submission to him.

37. Appeal to a social security appeal tribunal. These tribunals consist of:

(*a*) one member drawn from a panel of persons representing employed earners; and

(*b*) one member drawn from a panel composed first of persons representing employers and persons representing earners other than employed earners, and secondly of persons with local knowledge who represent the community; and

(*c*) a person appointed by the Secretary of State to act as chairman. The 1983 Act requires that in future chairmen must be barristers or solicitors of not less than five years' standing. The Health and Social Security Bill 1984 provides that members of a social security tribunal, other than the chairman, must be drawn from a panel of persons having knowledge or experience of conditions in the area, and who are representative of persons living or working in the area. The President, when appointing members, should take into account recommendations from appropriate persons or organisations.

When the adjudication officer has decided a claim or question adversely to the claimant, the claimant may appeal to a tribunal. The claimant must be notified in writing of the adjudicating officer's decision and the reasons for it, and of his right of appeal. The claimant must give notice of appeal within twenty-one days after the date of the decision or within such further times as the chairman of the tribunal may for good cause allow.

NOTE: An appeal will only lie with the leave of the chairman of the tribunal where the adjudicating officer certifies that his decision was based solely on the determination of a "special question" by the Secretary of State or a medical board.

38. Appeal from a social security appeal tribunal to a Commissioner. The Chief Social Security Commissioner and the other Social Security Commissioners are barristers of not less than ten years' standing. Their function is to hear appeals from the decision of a social security appeal tribunal. No appeal shall lie to a Commissioner from a unanimous decision of a tribunal except with the leave of the chairman of that tribunal, or if he refuses with the leave of the Commissioner: Social Security Act 1980, s.15. The Commissioner is not required to give reasons for his decision as to whether leave should be granted.

If it appears to the Chief Social Security Commissioner that an appeal involves a question of law of special difficulty he may direct that the appeal be heard, not by one Commissioner, but by a tribunal of three Commissioners. Where the appeal involves a question of fact of special difficulty the Commissioner may have the assistance of one or more specially qualified assessors. The following persons can appeal.

(*a*) An adjudication officer.
(*b*) The claimant.
(*c*) Trade unions (or any other association which exists to promote the interests and welfare of its members) where:
(*i*) the claimant is a member of the union at the time of the appeal and was so immediately before the question at issue arose;
(*ii*) the question relates in any way to a deceased person who was a member of the union at the time of his death;
(*iii*) the case relates to industrial injuries benefit; and the claimant or, in relation to industrial death benefit, the deceased was a member of the union at the time of the relevant accident.
(*d*) In a case relating to industrial injuries benefit, a person whose right to industrial death benefit may be affected by the decision appealed against.

An appeal must be brought within three months from the date of the decision of the tribunal, or such further period as a Commissioner may in any case for special reasons allow. The appeal shall be brought by giving notice in writing stating the grounds of appeal.

39. Appeal from a Commissioner. An appeal on a question of law shall lie to the Court of Appeal from any decision of a Commissioner. Leave to appeal must be given either by a Commissioner, or if he refuses by the Court: Social Security Act 1980, s.14. The Commissioner is not required to give reasons for his decision as to whether leave should be granted.

40. Review of decisions. Any decision of an adjudication officer, a social security appeal tribunal or a Commissioner may be reviewed at any time by an adjudication officer or, on a reference from an adjudication officer, by a tribunal if:

(*a*) the officer or tribunal is satisfied (and in the case of a decision of a Commissioner, satisfied by fresh evidence) that the decision was based on a mistake as to some material fact; or
(*b*) there has been any relevant change of circumstances since the decision was given; or
(*c*) the decision was based on the determination of a "special

question" which was given in ignorance of, or was based on a mistake as to, some material fact; or

(*d*) the decision was based on the determination of a "disablement question" and:

(*i*) the adjudicating medical practitioner(s) or medical appeal tribunal are satisfied by fresh evidence that the decision was given in consequence of the non-disclosure or misrepresentation by the claimant or any other person of a material fact, or

(*ii*) since the making of the assessment of the extent of the disablement resulting from the relevant loss of faculty, the above medical experts are satisfied that there has been an unforeseen aggravation of the results of the relevant injury, or

(*iii*) where it was decided in a claim for disablement benefit that the relevant accident had not resulted in a loss of faculty but there has been an unforeseen aggravation of the results of the relevant injury.

41. Adjudicating medical practitioners. "Disablement questions" are decided upon by either one or more adjudicating medical practitioner or by a medical appeal tribunal. These questions are referred by an adjudication officer and are as follows:

(*a*) whether the relevant accident has resulted in loss of faculty;

(*b*) at what degree the extent of disablement resulting from a loss of faculty is to be assessed; and

(*c*) what period is to be taken into account by the assessment.

42. Medical appeal tribunals. These consist of a chairman who must be a solicitor or barrister of not less than seven years' standing, and two medical practitioners appointed by the Secretary of State. If a claimant is dissatisfied with the decision of the adjudicating medical practitioner(s) he may appeal in the prescribed manner and within the prescribed time to a medical appeal tribunal. If the Secretary of State notifies the adjudicating officer within the prescribed time that he is of the opinion that any decision of the adjudicating medical practitioner(s) ought to be considered by a medical appeal tribunal, the officer will refer the case to that tribunal for their consideration, and the tribunal may confirm, reverse or vary the decision in whole or in part as on an appeal. The tribunal may refer a question of law to a Commissioner.

43. Social Security Commissioners. An appeal lies to a Commissioner from any decision of a medical appeal tribunal on the ground that the decision is erroneous in point of law at the instance of:

(*a*) the claimant; or

(*b*) a trade union of which the claimant was a member at the time of the relevant accident; or

(*c*) the Secretary of State.

NOTE: No appeal lies without the leave of the chairman of the medical appeal tribunal or of a Commissioner.

44. Appeal from a Commissioner. *See* **38**.

45. Review of decisions. Any decision of an adjudicating medical practitioner(s) or a medical appeal tribunal may be reviewed at any time at the former level if:

(*a*) satisfied by fresh evidence that the decision was given in consequence of the non-disclosure or misrepresentation by the claimant or any other person of a material fact; or

(*b*) satisfied that since the making of the assessment there has been an unforeseen aggravation of the results of the relevant injury. (*see* **40.**)

LAW REFORM (PERSONAL INJURIES) ACT 1948

46. Alternative remedies. The Law Reform (Personal Injuries) Act 1948 provides for circumstances where a person may claim (*a*) under the social security scheme, (*b*) under the Factories Act, and (*c*) at common law, e.g. because of an accident at work.

47. Damages at common law. Where an employee sues his employer for breach of his common law duty (i.e. in contract or in tort) the court may award damages. In tort (*see*, for example, VIII, **15**) the employee may claim damages under two heads as follows.

(*a*) *General damages*, which need not be specially pleaded, represent the damage or loss which the law presumes to have been caused by the defendant's tort, e.g. the injured party's pain and suffering.

(*b*) *Special damages*, which must be specially pleaded, represent the additional loss resulting from the particular circumstances of the case, e.g. the plaintiff's loss of wages.

48. Adjustment of damages. The Law Reform (Personal Injuries) Act provides that where special damages are awarded against loss of wages, the court must take into account, in assessing the sum, any payments made to the plaintiff under the industrial injuries and sickness benefits schemes.

This provision is made because the employer, as well as the employee, has contributed towards the schemes. If the employee were allowed to claim the industrial injuries or sickness benefits in full he would be receiving two payments from the employer to cover the same loss, namely:

(*a*) the portion of the benefits which has been paid into the schemes as a contribution by the employer, and

(*b*) special damages awarded by the court, for example for loss of wages, should the employee succeed in his action against the employer for negligence.

> NOTE: In principle, unemployment benefit may be deducted in mitigation of damages, e.g. for wrongful dismissal, to the extent that it constitutes a net gain to the employee: *see Westwood* v. *Secretary of State for Employment* (1984) H. L.

49. Sum deducted. The Act provides that where special damages are awarded the court must deduct from such sum one-half of the plaintiff's benefits for five years under the industrial injuries and sickness benefit schemes. This sum will be deducted before the amount for contributory negligence should the court find the plaintiff guilty of such negligence.

> EXAMPLE: X suffers injury at work as a result of which he is incapacitated for some months. He brings an action against his employer for negligence at common law. The court awards him general damages of £2,000 and special damages of £500 against loss of earnings. They find that X was guilty of contributory negligence to the extent of 50 per cent of the blame. X will receive £2,000 general damages minus 50 per cent for contributory negligence. This assessment will therefore amount to £1,000. X will also receive £500 as special damages. The value of his industrial disablement benefits amounts to £100. Half of this sum must first be deducted leaving £450. A deduction will then be made for contributory negligence. 50 per cent of £450 comes to £225. The total damages awarded to X will be £1,000 general damages and £225 special damages.

PROGRESS TEST 11

1. Who is required to make contributions into the social security scheme? **(3, 5)**

2. Bill is employed by a dairy as a milkman. In the afternoons he works as a window-cleaner, and employs John to help him in his thriving business. What contributions would Bill be required to pay? **(3)**

3. What conditions must a person satisfy in order to claim unemployment benefit? **(7–9)**

4. When can the standard rate of unemployment benefit be (*a*) reduced, or (*b*) increased? **(8)**

5. For how long can unemployment benefit be paid? **(10)**

6. When can a person be refused unemployment benefit (*a*) for the whole period of unemployment, and (*b*) for a maximum of six weeks? **(11)**

7. What conditions must a person satisfy in order to claim sickness benefit? **(7, 8, 13)**

8. For how long can sickness benefit be paid? **(14)**

9. On what grounds may a person be disqualified from receiving sickness benefit? **(15)**

10. Who is protected under the industrial injuries scheme? **(16, 17)**

11. Define an industrial injury. **(18, 19)**

12. Which accidents are automatically covered by the scheme, subject to evidence to the contrary? **(20)**

13. What must be proved to show that other accidents are covered by the scheme? **(21–23)**

14. When can an employee claim industrial injuries benefit? **(25)**

15. What benefits can be claimed if an employed earner suffers an accident at work? **(2, 7, 26–30)**

16. When can an employee claim industrial injuries benefit as a result of an industrial disease? **(25, 32, 33)**

17. Who determines whether a claimant is entitled to receive social security? **(35)**

18. What questions raised by a claim for disablement benefit must be decided by (*a*) a medical practitioner(s) and, (*b*) the Secretary of State? What appeals procedure is provided? **(35, 41–44)**

19. Describe how a claimant can appeal against the decision of an adjudication officer. **(37, 38, 39)**

20. Who else, apart from the claimant, can appeal against a social security appeal tribunal's decision, and on what grounds? **(38)**

21. In what circumstances may an appeal be made against the decision of a Commissioner? **(39, 44)**

22. Are there any other methods by which the decision of an adjudication officer or tribunal can be altered? **(40)**

23. What effect do social security benefits have on an employee's legal remedies? **(46–49)**

CHAPTER XII

Statutory Control of Working Conditions

HEALTH AND SAFETY AT WORK ETC. ACT 1974

1. The purpose of the Act. The Health and Safety at Work etc. Act 1974 broadly implements the basic recommendations of the Report of the Robens Committee on Safety and Health at Work in 1972. The aim of the Act is to:

(*a*) provide a unified and integrated system of health and safety at work applicable to all workplaces;
(*b*) restate the common law duties of employers and employees in broad terms, which will be enforced by the criminal law; and
(*c*) establish an effective method of providing advice and information, as well as enforcing the Act, by the creation of the Health and Safety Commission, and the Health and Safety Executive.

2. An enabling Act. The Act is an enabling measure superimposed over existing health and safety legislation contained in 31 statutes and 500 subsidiary regulations, known as the relevant statutory provisions. The existing duties under the Factories Act 1961, and the Offices, Shops and Railway Premises Act 1963 remain in force for the time being (*see* XIII and XIV). This is true of many other statutes relating to health and safety at work, e.g. Mines and Quarries Act 1954. The Health and Safety at Work Act 1974 provides for a gradual replacement of existing health and safety requirements by revised and updated provisions, in the form of a system of regulations (*see* **4**) and approved Codes of Practice, which will be supplemented by guidance notes (*see* **7, 8**). There have been approximately 69 sets of general regulations, 3 codes of practice, and 73 sets of guidance notes issued under the Health and Safety at Work etc. Act 1974.

3. EEC directives. In 1978 the Council of Ministers of the EEC approved proposals which aim to achieve the ultimate harmonisation of future laws in the field of safety, health and welfare at work.

There are already EEC directives applicable to this area of law. The United Kingdom is obliged to implement these directives, but before they can become part of UK law they have to be approved by Parliament, as, for example, have the Safety Signs Regulations 1980.

4. Regulations. These have been and will be made by the appropriate minister, usually the Secretary of State for Employment, normally on the basis of proposals submitted by the Health and Safety Commission after consultation with appropriate organisations. Regulations may relate to any of the purposes of Part One of the Act, which is concerned with health and safety and welfare at work, and with the control of dangerous substances and certain emissions into the atmosphere.

Health and safety regulations may, *inter alia*:

(*a*) repeal or modify any of the existing statutory provisions, e.g. the Factories Act 1961;

(*b*) exclude or modify in relation to any specified class of case, any of the general duties (*see* **10**), or any of the existing statutory provisions;

(*c*) make a specified authority or class of authorities responsible for the enforcement of any of the relevant statutory provisions;

(*d*) provide for exemptions from any requirement or prohibition imposed by a relevant statutory provision;

(*e*) specify the persons or classes of persons who, in the event of a contravention of a requirement or prohibition, are guilty of an offence;

(*f*) provide for any specified defence to be available in proceedings for any offence under the relevant statutory provisions;

(*g*) exclude proceedings on indictment in relation to specific offences; and

(*h*) restrict the punishment which can be imposed in relation to specific offences: s.15.

5. Examples. An example of regulations which have come into force are the Regulations on Safety Representatives and Safety Committees. These Regulations prescribe the cases in which recognised trade unions may appoint safety representatives, specify the functions of such representatives, and set out the obligations of employers towards them. The Regulations should be considered together with the relevant Code of Practice and guidance notes (*see* **7**).

Other examples of regulations are those concerned with Safety Signs; the Control of Lead at Work; and the Notification of Accidents and Dangerous Occurrences. These last impose duties on persons responsible for the activities of persons at work and on self-employed persons to report to the enforcing authority under the 1974 Act (*see* **30**) accidents resulting in the death of or major injury to persons arising out of or in connection with that work (*see* XIII, **52** and XIV, **22**).

6. Classification of regulations. Regulations may be:

(*a*) *general*—such as those concerned with the notification of accidents and dangerous occurrences;
(*b*) *limited*—such as regulations concerning chromium plating;
(*c*) *functional*—such as regulations concerning electricity;
(*d*) *industry-related*—such as regulations for dockers.

7. Codes of Practice. Regulations may be supplemented by Codes of Practice or guidance notes (*see* **8**), which are not specifically mentioned in the regulations themselves.

(*a*) *Legal status.* They are not part of the statutory requirements set out in the regulations and are, therefore, not legal rules, but in criminal proceedings the court is required to admit in evidence any provisions of an approved Code of Practice which appear to be relevant. Furthermore, where the court considers that provisions of the Code are relevant to matters which must be proved in order to establish a contravention, failure to observe these provisions is to be taken as proof of those matters unless the court is satisfied that other satisfactory measures were taken.
(*b*) *Use with notices.* In addition, where an improvement or prohibition notice (*see* **33** and **34**) is issued and includes directions specifying remedial measures needed, such directions may be framed by reference to the provisions of an approved Code of Practice, which will then become part of the notice.
(*c*) *Origin of approved Codes.* Approved Codes of Practice will usually be generated by the Health and Safety Commission, the Executive, industry advisory committees set up by the Commission, or possibly in conjunction with such a body as the British Standards Institution. Codes generated elsewhere will not normally be approved by the Commission unless they are felt to be a necessary and suitable form of extension of the law.
(*d*) *Example.* An example of an approved Code of Practice is that on safety representatives, which together with the relevant Regulations (*see* **5**) provide a legal framework within which

employers and trade unions can make agreements for the functioning of safety representatives and safety committees. The Health and Safety Commission regard the relevant Regulations and the Code as essential to the full and effective implementation of the 1974 Act and crucial to the improvement of the health and safety of people at work.

(*e*) *Proposed Codes*. There were at least nine Codes of Practice in the pipeline during 1980, including ones on Lead; Notification of Accidents and Dangerous Occurrences; First Aid; and Safety Signs and Colours.

8. Guidance notes. Guidance notes will usually be issued by the Commission, the Executive, industry advisory committees and industry. They are essentially of practical rather than legal importance and they are available to the general public. They have been divided into the following five groups:

(*a*) medical;
(*b*) environmental hygiene;
(*c*) chemical safety;
(*d*) plant and machinery;
(*e*) general.

An example of guidance notes are those on safety representatives and safety committees which, together with the Code of Practice, offer practical guidance on the Regulations. A further example is the Guidance Notes on Articles and Substances at Work (*see* **16**).

9. Scope of the Act. The Act is concerned with:

(*a*) securing the health and safety of persons at work, whether employers, employees or self-employed persons, but not domestic servants employed in private households;

(*b*) protecting the general public against risks to health and safety arising out of, or in connection with, the activities of persons at work;

(*c*) controlling the keeping and use of dangerous substances, and generally preventing the unlawful acquisition, possession and use of such substances; and

(*d*) controlling the emission into the atmosphere of noxious or offensive substances from prescribed premises.

NOTE: Risks arising out of or in connection with the activities of persons at work will be treated as including risks attributable to the manner of conducting an undertaking, the plant or substances used for the purpose of an undertaking, and the conditions of premises so used or any part of them.

GENERAL DUTIES

10. Introduction. The Act imposes broad general duties on employers and on employees, which will supplement existing common law and statutory duties. These general duties will act as a framework within which to enact more detailed regulations. No civil liability is incurred for breach of the duties mentioned in **11–18**.

11. General duties of employers to their employees. It is the duty of every employer to ensure, so far as is reasonably practicable, the health, safety and welfare at work of all his employees, and in particular that duty extends to:

(*a*) the provision and maintenance of plant and systems of work that are, so far as is reasonably practicable, safe and without risk to health;
(*b*) arrangements for ensuring, so far as is reasonably practicable, safety and absence of risks to health in connection with the use, handling, storage and transport of articles and substances;
(*c*) the provision of information, instruction, training and supervision as is necessary to ensure, so far as is reasonably practicable, the health and safety at work of his employees;
(*d*) so far as is reasonably practicable as regards any place of work under the employer's control, the maintenance of it in a condition that is safe and without risks to health and the provision and maintenance of means of access to and egress from it that are safe and without such risks;
(*e*) the provision and maintenance of a working environment for his employees that is, so far as is reasonably practicable, without risks to health, and adequate as regards facilities and arrangements for their welfare at work: s.2.

12. Further specific duties. An employer is also under a duty to undertake the following.

(*a*) Prepare and revise a written statement of his general policy with respect to the health and safety at work of his employees, and the organisation and arrangements for the time being in force for the carrying out of that policy. This statement should be brought to the notice of his employees. However, employers who employ less than five persons are exempt from this duty.
(*b*) Consult safety representatives appointed by recognised trade unions with a view to the making and maintenance of arrangements which will enable him and his employees to co-operate effectively in promoting and developing measures to ensure the health and

safety at work of the employees, and in checking the effectiveness of such measures.

(*c*) Establish a safety committee, if requested to do so by the safety representatives, having the function of keeping under review the measures taken to ensure the health and safety at work of his employees and such other functions as may be prescribed: s.2 (*see* 5 and 7(*d*)).

In addition, the employer is under a duty not to levy, or permit to be levied, on any employee of his any charge in respect of anything done or provided in pursuance of any specific requirement of the relevant statutory provision: s.9.

13. General duties of employers and self-employed persons to persons other than their employees. It is the duty of every employer and self-employed person to conduct his undertaking in such a way as to ensure, so far as is reasonably practicable, that he (where a self-employed person) and persons not in his employment, who may be affected thereby, are not exposed to risks to their health and safety, and that they are informed about any aspects of his undertaking which might affect their health and safety: s.3.

14. General duties of persons concerned with premises to persons other than their employees. Controllers of premises owe a duty to persons, other than employees, who use those premises as a place of work, or as a place where they may use plant or substances provided for their use there. It is the duty of such a controller to take such measures as are reasonably practicable to ensure that the premises and their means of access are safe and without risk to health: s.4.

15. General duty of controllers of certain premises in relation to harmful emissions into the atmosphere. It is the duty of such persons to use the best practicable means for preventing the emission into the atmosphere from the premises of noxious or offensive substances and for rendering harmless and inoffensive such substances as may be so emitted: s.5.

16. General duties of manufacturers and others as regards articles and substances for use at work.

(*a*) It is the duty of any person who designs, manufactures, imports or supplies any article for use at work:

(*i*) to ensure, so far as is reasonably practicable, that the article is so designed and constructed as to be safe and without risk to health when properly used;

(*ii*) to carry out or arrange for the carrying out of such testing and examination as may be necessary for the performance of the duty imposed on him above;

(*iii*) to take such steps as are necessary to secure that there will be adequate information available about the use of the article, and about any conditions necessary to ensure that when put to that use, it will be safe and without risks to health.

(*b*) It is the duty of any person who undertakes the design or manufacture of any article for use at work to carry out or arrange for the carrying out of any necessary research in order to discover, and so far as is reasonably practicable to eliminate or minimise risks to health and safety.

(*c*) It is the duty of any person who erects or installs any article for use at work to ensure, so far as is reasonably practicable, that there is nothing in the way it was erected or installed which makes it unsafe or a risk to health.

(*d*) It is the duty of any person who manufactures, imports or supplies any substance for use at work:

(*i*) to ensure, so far as is reasonably practicable, that the substance is safe and without risks to health;

(*ii*) to carry out or arrange for the carrying out of such testing and examination as may be necessary to comply with (*i*);

(*iii*) to take such steps as are necessary to secure that there will be adequate information available about the results of any relevant tests which have been carried out relating to the substance, and about any conditions necessary to ensure that it will be safe and without risk to health.

(*e*) It is the duty of any person who undertakes the manufacture of any substance for use at work to carry out or arrange for the carrying out of any necessary research in order to discover, and so far as is reasonably practicable, eliminate or minimise risks to health and safety: s.6.

17. General duties of employees at work. It is the duty of every employee while at work:

(*a*) to take reasonable care for the health and safety of himself and of other persons who may be affected by his acts or omissions at work; and

(*b*) as regards any duty or requirement imposed on his employer, or any other person by or under any of the relevant statutory provisions, to co-operate with him so far as is necessary to enable that duty or requirement to be performed or complied with: s.7.

18. General duty. No person may intentionally or recklessly interfere with or misuse anything provided in the interests of health, safety or welfare in pursuance of any of the relevant statutory provisions: s.8.

THE INSTITUTIONS

19. General. The Health and Safety at Work Act 1974 established the Health and Safety Commission, the Health and Safety Executive and maintained the Employment Medical Advisory Service which was established under the Employment Medical Advisory Service Act 1972. The Commission and the Executive have the power to do anything (except borrow money) which is calculated to facilitate, or is conducive or incidental to, the performance of any of their functions.

20. The Health and Safety Commission. The Commission consists of a Chairman and between six and nine other members who are appointed by the Secretary of State. Three members should be representatives of employers' organisations, and a further three, representatives of employee's organisations. Any other members should be from organisations representing local authorities and other interested bodies.

21. Duties of the Commission. It is the general duty of the Commission to do such things and make such arrangements as it considers appropriate for the general purposes of the Act. In addition, it is the duty of the Commission:

(*a*) to assist and encourage persons concerned with matters relevant to any of the general purposes of the health, safety and welfare provisions;

(*b*) to make appropriate arrangements for the carrying out of research, the publication of the results of research and the provision of relevant training and information, and to encourage others to do likewise;

(*c*) to make appropriate arrangements for securing that government departments, organisations representing employers and employees, and other concerned persons, are provided with an information and advisory service;

(*d*) to submit from time to time such proposals as the Commission considers appropriate for the making of regulations;

(*e*) to submit to the Secretary of State particulars of what it proposes to do for the purpose of performing its functions;

(*f*) to ensure that its activities are in accordance with proposals approved by the Secretary of State; and

(*g*) to give effect to any directions given to it by the Secretary of State: s.11.

22. Advisory Committees. To assist it in its duties, the Commission has set up (with external members) Advisory Committees on, for example, Major Hazards; Asbestos; Toxic Substances; Nuclear Materials; Railways; and the Construction Industry.

23. Powers of the Commission. The Commission may authorise an investigation or, with the consent of the Secretary of State, direct that an inquiry should be held into any accident, occurrence, situation or other matter where the Commission thinks it necessary or expedient to do so: s.14.

The Commission has certain other powers which are concerned with:

(*a*) the transfer of the performance of the function of the Commission, the Executive, central government and public authorities;

(*b*) the provision of other appropriate services and facilities for government departments or public authorities;

(*c*) the appointment of committees to advise the Commission; and

(*d*) the arrangement of appropriate research and the dissemination of information derived from such research: s.13.

24. Control of the Commission. The Secretary of State has certain powers to control the Commission in that he may:

(*a*) approve, with or without modifications, any proposals submitted to him under **21**(*e*) above; and

(*b*) give to the Commission such directions as he thinks fit with respect to its functions, and any other directions which it appears to him requisite or expedient to give in the interests of the safety of the State: s.12.

25. The Health and Safety Executive. The Executive consists of three officers, one of whom will be appointed the Director of the Executive by the Commission with the approval of the Secretary of State. The Executive is composed of the former staffs of the health and safety inspectorates covering factories, mines and quarries, explosives, nuclear installations, alkali works and pipelines. The Executive is responsible together with local authority inspectors for enforcing statutory requirements on safety and health. They continue to administer the provisions of existing legislation and in addition use the new powers and procedures provided under the 1974 Act, including the power for inspectors to issue improvement and prohibition notices (*see* **33** and **34**).

26. Duties of the Executive. In addition to any other functions which may be conferred on the Executive, it is the duty of the Executive:

(*a*) to exercise on behalf of the Commission such of the Commission's functions as the Commission directs it to exercise;
(*b*) to give effect to any directions given to it by the Commission;
(*c*) to provide a Minister of the Crown with information about activities of the Executive with which he is concerned;
(*d*) to provide a Minister of the Crown with relevant expert advice on any matter with which he is concerned; and
(*e*) to make adequate arrangements for the enforcement of relevant statutory provisions: ss.11 and 18.

27. The Employment Medical Advisory Service. This service was established under the Employment Medical Advisory Service Act 1972. It was envisaged that the service would bring together the various categories of doctors employed in industrial medicine. The Health and Safety at Work Act 1974 amended the 1972 Act with regard to the functions and powers of the service.

28. Functions of the Advisory Service. The service is responsible for the following.

(*a*) Informing and advising those concerned with the health of employed persons, on matters concerning the safeguarding and improvement of the health of those persons. In particular, information and advice should be given to the Secretary of State, the Health and Safety Commission, the Manpower Services Commission, employers' and employees' organisations, and occupational health practitioners.
(*b*) Informing and advising employed persons and those seeking training for employment on relevant health matters.

29. Maintenance of the Advisory Service. The Secretary of State is the authority responsible for maintaining the service, but he can make arrangements for this responsibility to be discharged by the

Health and Safety Commission or some other body. Whosoever is responsible for maintaining the service is able to:

(*a*) investigate or organise research into relevant problems of health and safety at work;

(*b*) provide and maintain laboratories and other necessary services; and,

(*c*) appoint fully registered medical practitioners to be employment medical advisers.

ENFORCEMENT PROVISIONS

30. Responsible authority. The Health and Safety Executive is responsible for making adequate arrangements for the enforcement of the relevant statutory provisions, although the Secretary of State may make local authorities or any other authority similarly responsible.

It has been the practice for local authorities to deal with fire regulations and safety in shops in offices. Where the enforcing authority is a local authority, the Commission may make a report to the Secretary of State where it is of the opinion that an investigation should be made as to whether that local authority has failed to perform any of its enforcement functions.

31. Appointment of inspectors. Every enforcing authority may appoint inspectors. The appointment of a person as an inspector must be in writing, and must specify which relevant statutory powers can be exercised by the person appointed. When the inspector seeks to exercise those powers he can be required to produce the written evidence of his appointment.

32. Powers of inspectors. An inspector may exercise the following powers.

(*a*) To enter premises.

(*b*) To take with him a constable if he has reasonable cause to apprehend any serious obstruction in the execution of his duty.

(*c*) To take with him any other duly authorised person.

(*d*) To take with him any necessary equipment or materials.

(*e*) To make any necessary examination and investigation.

(*f*) To direct that the premises should be left undisturbed so that any necessary examination or investigation may take place.

(*g*) To take such measurements and photographs and to make such recordings as may be necessary.

(*h*) To take samples of any articles or substances and the atmosphere.

(*i*) To cause any article or substance found to be dismantled or tested if it is likely to cause danger to health or safety.

(*j*) To take possession of such an article or substance for certain purposes.

(*k*) To require persons to give him relevant information, answer questions, and sign a declaration of the truth of those answers.

(*l*) To require the production of, inspect and take copies of, any relevant books or documents.

(*m*) To require a person to afford him necessary facilities or assistance.

(*n*) Any other power which is necessary to carry into effect any of the relevant statutory provisions: s.20.

In addition the inspector can issue prohibition notices and improvement notices. He can also seize, render harmless or destroy any article or substance which is a cause of imminent danger of serious personal injury. Finally, he may prosecute where there have been offences committed under the relevant statutory provisions.

> NOTE: The inspector's powers are subject to certain limitations. For example, in the exercise of the power described in (*i*) the inspector may be required to exercise his power in the presence of a person who has responsibilities in relation to the premises, and he is required to consult appropriate persons to ascertain what dangers may arise if he exercises his power.

33. Improvement notices. If an inspector is of the opinion that a person is contravening one or more of the relevant statutory provisions or has contravened one or more of those provisions in circumstances which make it likely that the contravention will continue or be repeated, he may serve on that person an improvement notice. The notice should include details of the contravention and require that it be remedied within a specified time: s.21. It may include directions as to measures to be taken to remedy any contravention or matter to which the notice relates (*see Tesco Stores* v. *Edwards* (1977) and XIV, **13**). In 1978, 1979 and 1980 the numbers of improvement notices issued were 12,217, 13,517, 12,625: *Health and Safety Statistics 1980* (1982).

34. Prohibition notices. If an inspector is of the opinion that certain activities will involve a risk of serious personal injury, he may serve a prohibition notice on the person in control of those activities. A prohibition notice should include details of the matters which in the inspector's opinion give rise to such a risk, and of any contravention of any of the relevant statutory provisions. It should also direct that the activities should not be continued under the person on whom the notice is served, unless the contraventions have been remedied: s.22. The notice may include directions as to measures to be taken to remedy any contravention or matter to which the notice relates. In 1978, 1979 and 1980 the numbers of prohibition notices issued were 3,434, 3,674 and 3,238: *Health and Safety Statistics 1980* (1982).

35. Appeal against notices. A person on whom a notice (either improvement or prohibition) is served may appeal to an industrial tribunal, which may either cancel or affirm the notice: s.24.

(*a*) *Affirm with modifications.* If the tribunal affirms the notice it may well do so either in its original form or with such modifications as the tribunal may in the circumstances think fit. However, it appears that the tribunal cannot amend the notice to include an alleged breach of other provisions: *British Airways Board* v. *Henderson* (1979).

(*b*) *Prosecution.* If a prosecution is brought for non-compliance with the improvement or prohibition notice, then a decision of an industrial tribunal is not binding on the criminal court. The prosecution must prove not only that the notice has not been complied with, but also that the requirements of the notice were validly imposed in accordance with the relevant statutory provisions: *Paull* v. *Weymouth and Portland BC* (1979).

(*c*) *Suspension of notices.* The bringing of the appeal will suspend the operation of the notice, but in the case of a prohibition notice it will only be suspended if the tribunal so directs.

(*d*) *Assessors.* One or more assessors may be appointed to hear such appeals.

In 1980 there were 22 appeals heard by a tribunal against the 15,863 notices issued. In four cases the appeal was upheld; in thirteen cases it was dismissed with modification of the notice; and in five cases dismissed completely: *Health and Safety Statistics 1980* (1982).

36. Obtaining and disclosure of information. The Commission may, with the consent of the Secretary of State, serve on any person a notice requiring that person to furnish to the Commission, or the enforcing authority in question, such information which the Commission or the enforcing authority needs for the discharge of its functions. However, no relevant information may be disclosed without the consent of the person by whom it was furnished, with certain exceptions—disclosure to the Commission, the Executive, a government department or any enforcing authority without consent is permissible.

37. Criminal liability. The Act provides that an offence will be committed when there has been a contravention of certain of its provisions: s.33. Prosecutions by or for the Health and Safety Commission enforcement authorities amounted to a total of 2,006 in 1978, 1,584 in 1979 and 1,751 in 1980. The conviction rate is approximately 90 per cent: *Health and Safety Statistics 1980* (1982). Individual employers and bodies corporate (*see* II, **2**) can be held liable for the offences.

(*a*) Examples of the offences are as follows.

(*i*) Failure to discharge one of the duties described in **11** and **12**.

(*ii*) Contravening the duty described in **18**.

(*iii*) Contravening any health and safety regulation.

(*iv*) Contravening any requirement or prohibition imposed by any improvement or a prohibition notice.

(*v*) Intentionally obstructing an inspector in the exercise or performance of his powers or duties.

(*b*) Proceedings for an offence under any of the relevant statutory provisions may mot be instituted except by an inspector or by or with the consent of the Director of Public Prosecutions.

(*c*) The onus is on the accused to prove, where necessary, that it was not practicable or not reasonably practicable to do more than was in fact done to satisfy the statutory duty or requirement, or that there was no better practicable means than was in fact used to satisfy the duty or requirement.

(*d*) Where an offence is committed which is due to the fault of some other person, that other person may be charged with and convicted of the offence.

(*e*) Where an offence is committed by a body corporate, the body corporate as well as any director, manager, secretary or other similar officer may be charged and convicted of the offence.

(*f*) If a person is found guilty of an offence he will be liable on summary conviction to a fine not exceeding £2,000 and (for some offences) on conviction on indictment to imprisonment for a term not exceeding two years, or a fine, or both. The court may, in addition to or instead of imposing any punishment, order the convicted person to take specified steps for remedying the said matters.

38. Civil liability. The Health and Safety at Work Act 1974, s.47 specifically excludes the possibility of any civil action arising from the Act's provisions for safety, health and welfare, and in particular the provisions dealt with in **11–18**. However, these add little to the common law duty of an employer (*see* VIII, **15**), and the Act recognises that certain breaches of a duty imposed by existing statutory provisions are actionable, and will continue to be so. In addition, breach of a duty imposed by health and safety regulations shall, so far as it causes damage, be actionable, except insofar as the regulations provide otherwise. Finally it should be remembered that the object of the 1974 legislation is to provide a system of health and safety at work which prevents accidents, rather than a system which provides sanctions after there has been a contravention of the provisions.

PROGRESS TEST 12

1. What is the aim of the Health and Safety at Work Act 1974? **(1, 9)**
2. How are health and safety laws altered since the passing of the Health and Safety at Work Act 1974? **(2, 4)**
3. What will supplement the health and safety enactments, in order to give practical guidance? What is the legal status of these supplements? **(7, 8)**
4. Describe the general duties owed by employers to their employees under the Act. Do these duties impose civil or criminal liability? **(11, 12, 37, 38)**
5. What duties are owed by whom to (*a*) the general public, (*b*) persons using premises as a place of work, and (*c*) persons using articles at work? Do these duties impose civil or criminal liability on any person? **(13–16, 37, 38)**
6. What are (*a*) the duties, and (*b*) the powers of the Health and Safety Commission? **(21, 23)**
7. What are the duties of the Health and Safety Executive? **(26, 30)**
8. What are the responsibilities of the Employment Medical Advisory Service? **(28)**
9. Who is responsible for enforcing the Act and the relevant statutory provisions? **(30–32)**
10. When can (*a*) an improvement notice, and (*b*) a prohibition notice be served? **(33, 34)**

11. Is the 1974 Act chiefly concerned with providing a system of prevention or with imposing criminal and civil liability? Give examples to illustrate your answer. **(37, 38)**

CHAPTER XIII

Statutory Control of Working Conditions: Factories

FACTORIES ACT 1961

1. Scope of the Act. The Factories Act 1961 is a relevant statutory provision under the Health and Safety at Work Act 1974. This means that the 1961 Act remains in force with some amendments until it is eventually replaced by health and safety regulations which will apply to most workplaces, not only factories.

The 1961 Act only governs working conditions in factories laying down general provisions which are supplemented by detailed regulations which expand particular sections. For example, the Factories (Cleanliness of Walls and Ceilings) Order 1960, as amended in 1974, defined "wash", "walls and ceilings" and other such terms used in s.1 of the Act (*see* **9**).

The Act deals with the following four main aspects of factory employment.

(*a*) Health provisions.
(*b*) Safety provisions.
(*c*) Welfare provisions.
(*d*) The employment of women and young persons. (They are protected by more stringent measures, particularly with regard to the length of working hours.)

It is important to remember that the provisions of the Health and Safety at Work Act 1974 apply to factories, as well as the provisions of the 1961 Act. The institutions and the enforcement provisions applicable to factories are dealt with in the chapter on the 1974 Act (*see* XII).

2. Definition of a factory. The expression "factory" means any premises in which, or within the close or curtilage or precincts of which, persons are employed in manual labour in any process for, or incidental to:

(*a*) the making of any articles or of part of any article;

(*b*) the altering, repairing, ornamenting, finishing, cleaning or washing or the breaking up, or the demolition of any article;

(*c*) the adapting for sale of any article;

(*d*) the slaughtering of cattle, horses and certain other animals; or

(*e*) the confinement of such animals at certain premises (with certain exceptions) while awaiting slaughter at other premises, in a case where the place of confinement is available in connection with those other premises, is not maintained primarily for agricultural purposes and does not form part of premises used for the holding of a market in respect of such animals,

being premises in which, or within the close or curtilage or precincts of which, the work is carried on in the way of trade or for the purposes of gain and to or over which the employer of the persons employed therein has the right of access or control: s.175(1).

3. Other premises. The Act lists certain kinds of premises which are to be regarded as factories, even though they may not fall within the definition in s.175(1). These include the following.

(*a*) Any yard or dry dock where ships or vessels are constructed, repaired or broken up.

(*b*) Any premises in which articles are sorted out preliminary to work in a factory.

(*c*) Any premises where bottles or containers are washed or filled or articles are packed incidentally to the purposes of a factory.

(*d*) Any premises where yarn or cloth is made up or packed.

(*e*) Any laundry which is ancillary to a business or public institution.

(*f*) Any premises in which locomotives or vehicles are constructed or repaired ancillary to a transport, commercial or industrial undertaking.

(*g*) Any premises where printing or bookbinding is carried out as a trade or incidental to a business.

(*h*) Any premises in which dresses or properties for film or theatrical productions are made or repaired.

(*i*) Any premises where films are produced.

(*j*) Any premises in which articles are made or prepared incidentally to carrying on of operations or work of engineering construction.

4. Employed in manual labour. For premises to be classed as a factory, persons must be employed there in manual labour.

(*a*) *Non-manual work on same premises.* Difficulty may arise where occupations of various kinds are found on the same premises. In *Joyce* v. *Boots Cash Chemists (Southern) Ltd.* (1950) it was held that the test to be applied was whether the employment of persons in manual labour was the substantial purpose for which the premises were used. In that case the plaintiff was a porter at the defendant's chemist shop. Five other persons were employed there, but the plaintiff was the only one whose work could be described as manual labour. Since the porter's work was incidental to the main purpose of the premises, the shop was not a factory. (After the passing of the Offices, Shops and Railway Premises Act 1963, the premises would be covered by different provisions.)

(*b*) *What is manual labour?* Another difficulty has arisen in defining what kinds of work are to be regarded as manual labour. Most occupations are composed of both elements to varying degrees. It seems that the test which the courts will apply is whether the work is primarily or predominantly manual or primarily and predominantly intellectual in nature. The test is not always easy to apply.

J.F. Stone Lighting and Radio Ltd. v. *Haygarth* (1966): S was employed as a radio and television engineer. He worked in a room behind a shop which sold televisions, radios and other electrical goods, and was occupied in repairing faults, replacing faulty parts and adjusting sets, all of which he did by hand. The work also required him to diagnose and to locate faults, a task which was sometimes difficult and sometimes easy. During most of his working time he used his knowledge of television and radio sets and electrical equipment but his work with his hands occupied the greater part of his time and was an essential part of what he was engaged to do. HELD: the fact that in doing work with his hands a man used technical knowledge did not prevent that work being manual work, so long as it was not primarily or predominantly work of a different kind (e.g. intellectual activity) to which work with the hands was merely accessory. On the facts of the case, S was a skilled craftsman applying technical knowledge in doing manual work. The premises were, therefore, a factory.

(*c*) *Contract of service.* It is not sufficient that a person is engaged in manual work: he must also be employed under a contract of service. In *Pullen* v. *Prison Commissioners* (1957) an ex-prisoner brought an action against the Prison Commissioners alleging that the tuberculosis he had contracted was the result of the dust to which he had been exposed while working in a prison workshop. It was held that the prison workshop was not a factory within the meaning of the Act since there was no relationship of master and servant, or employment for wages in the case of the prisoner.

5. Adapting for sale. It is a question of fact in each case whether an article is being adapted for sale, but something must be done which makes the article different, or more readily saleable. It has been held that adapting for sale includes the following processes: separating saleable parts of refuse from the bulk; packaging and arranging sweets into boxes; making of wreaths; compressing of waste paper into bundles. However, the following have not been regarded as adapting for sale: the cleaning and cooling of milk; the storage of food by means of refrigeration.

6. By way of trade or for purposes of gain. The courts have held that these words include any manufacture, alteration or adaptation which directly or indirectly results in trading or gain for the occupier.

Stanger v. *Hendon Borough Council* (1948): A consulting engineer tested materials used for building and was paid by the builders who supplied him with the materials. He constructed concrete blocks, which were then tested for durability by a crushing machine. HELD: the premises constituted a factory and the process of making and breaking the blocks was carried on "for the purposes of gain".

Manual work carried on in a technical college does not convert the building into a factory since the work is not by way of trade, nor for purposes of gain by the occupier. The same principle has been applied to work carried out in the kitchen of a hospital: *Wood* v. *LCC* (1941). However, this case has been distinguished in *Bromwich* v. *National Ear Nose and Throat Hospital* (1980) where a hospital workshop was held to be a factory, even though its work was merely incidental to the functioning of the hospital and it had never been treated as a factory by the Health and Safety Executive.

7. Other purposes. A place which is situated within the area of the factory which is used solely for some purpose other than the processes carried out in the factory is not part of the factory. However, this will not apply if the work carried on there is ancillary to the main purpose of the factory. Thus in *Thurogood* v. *Van den Berghs and Jurgens Ltd.* (1951), it was held that a shed where maintenance of machinery used in the factory was carried out was a part of the factory and covered by the Factories Act 1961. However, in *King* v. *Magnatex Ltd.* (1951), a workshop on the factory premises which had been cleared of machines in order to hold a Christmas party ceased to be a factory during that time.

NOTE: A canteen within the precincts of a factory used to feed and entertain persons working there formed part of the factory. This was a purpose incidental to the main aim of the factory: *Luttman* v. *Imperial Chemical Industries Ltd.* (1955). However, a canteen used exclusively for executives and the administrative staff did not form part of the factory premises even though occasional meetings between the management and shop stewards were held there. The purpose to which the building was put was not essential "for the welfare of the industrial workers". It was solely used for some purpose other than processes carried on in the factory: *Thomas* v. *British Thomson-Houston Co. Ltd.* (1953).

8. Other premises. Sections 123–127 specify other premises which are not considered factories as defined by s.175, but which are covered by certain measures in the Factories Act. These include electrical stations; parts of charitable institutions; docks; wharves and quays, warehouses with mechanical power; the loading, unloading and coaling of ships; building operations and works of engineering construction.

HEALTH (GENERAL PROVISIONS)

9. Cleanliness. The requirements are as follows.

(*a*) In general every factory is to be kept in a clean state and free from effluvia arising from any drain, sanitary convenience or nuisance. Accumulations of dirt and refuse must be removed daily by a suitable method from floors and benches of work-rooms and from staircases and passages. The floor of every work-room must be cleaned at least once every week by washing or other effective method.

(*b*) All inside walls and partitions and all ceilings or rooms and passages and staircases must (*i*) where they have a smooth surface be washed with hot water and soap or cleaned by any other approved method every fourteen months, (*ii*) where they are painted in a prescribed manner or varnished be repainted or revarnished periodically as may be prescribed (but at least once every seven years). They must be washed with hot water and soap or cleaned at least once every fourteen months.

(*c*) In any other case they are to be kept whitewashed or colour-washed, which is to be renewed every fourteen months.

These provisions as to methods of cleaning will not apply, except if the inspector so required, to a factory where mechanical means are not used and less than ten persons are employed: s.1 (*see also* **1**).

10. Overcrowding. In general, a factory must not, while work is carried on, be so overcrowded as to cause risk or injury to the health of the persons employed in it. Every person working in a room must be allowed a space of at least 400 ft^3 ($11.3m^3$). In calculating this space, no space more than 14 ft. (4.2m) from the floor may be taken into account. A notice must be placed in each workroom specifying the number of persons who may be employed there, unless the district inspector of factories otherwise allows: s.2.

11. Temperature. Effective provision must be made for securing and maintaining a reasonable temperature in each room, but not by means which will cause injury to persons employed there, for example by the release of fumes. In every workroom where a substantial proportion of work is done sitting and does not involve serious physical effort, a temperature of less than 60°F (16°C) would not be regarded as reasonable after the first hour. At least one thermometer is to be provided in a suitable position in such a room: s.3.

12. Ventilation. Effective and suitable provision must be made for securing and maintaining by the circulation of fresh air in each workroom the adequate ventilation of the room, and for rendering harmless, so far as practicable, all such fumes, dust and other impurities generated in the course of any process or work carried on in the factory as may be injurious to health: s.4.

13. Lighting. Effective provision must be made for securing and maintaining sufficient and suitable lighting, whether natural or artificial, in every part of a factory in which persons are working or passing: s.5.

Thornton v. *Fisher & Ludlow Ltd.* (1968): The plaintiff, a cleaner, was on her way to work in a factory at 6.45 a.m. on a morning in October. She was walking on a factory roadway when she tripped over a coil of wire, fell and was injured. There were sufficient and suitable lights along a wall by the roadway, but they were not turned on. The plaintiff sued for breach of s.5(1) as well as for negligence at common law. HELD: that the defendants were liable to the cleaner because by not ensuring that the lighting was turned on they failed to make "effective provision" for securing and maintaining sufficient lighting in a part of the factory, and were thus in breach of the Act.

All glazed windows and skylights used for lighting of work-rooms must, so far as is practicable, be kept clean on both the inner and outer surfaces and free from obstruction. This measure does not prevent the whitewashing or shading of windows and skylights in order to lessen heat or glare.

14. Drainage of floors. Where any process is carried on which renders the floor liable to be wet to such an extent that the wet is capable of being removed by drainage, effective means must be provided and maintained for draining: s.6.

15. Sanitary conveniences. Sufficient and suitable sanitary conveniences for the persons employed in the factory must be provided, maintained and kept clean. Effective provision must be made for lighting them. Where persons of both sexes are employed, separate accommodation must be provided for each sex: s.7.

NOTE: (1) Enforcement of this section and any regulations made thereunder will be by the district council. (2) The district council will also enforce other health provisions (*see* **9** to **12** and **14**) in respect of any factory in which mechanical power is not used.

16. Medical examinations. Any employment medical adviser (*see* XII, **27–29**) may serve on the occupier of a factory a written notice that he is of the opinion that on certain grounds there ought to be a medical examination of a person employed in the factory. He may insist that the occupier permit such a medical examination.

The grounds on which the employment medical adviser can rely are that:

(*a*) the person's health has been, or is being, injured; or
(*b*) it is possible that the person's health has been, is being, or will be injured,

by reason of the nature of the work he is, or has been called upon to do, or may be called upon to do: s.10A.

It should be noted that the persons concerned can refuse to submit to such an examination.

17. Medical supervision. The Health and Safety Executive may make orders in relation to a particular factory and for a limited period of a maximum of six months requiring reasonable arrangements to be made for the medical supervision of persons employed at the factory where it appears that:

(*a*) cases of illness have occured which they believe to be due to the nature of the work done there; or

(*b*) there may be a risk to the health of the persons employed in a factory because of a new process, or of new substances used in a process, or because of changes in conditions of work; or

(*c*) young persons are employed in work which may cause risk or injury to their health: s.11.

SAFETY (GENERAL PROVISIONS)

18. Fencing of machinery. Sections 12–14 of this Act provide that there is an absolute duty to fence the following:

(*a*) prime movers;
(*b*) transmission machinery;
(*c*) every dangerous part of any machinery.

19. Prime mover. This is machinery such as an engine or motor which provides mechanical energy. Every flywheel directly connected to any prime mover and every moving part of any prime mover must be securely fenced. Electric generators and flywheels connected to them must be securedly fenced unless they are in such a position or of such construction as to be safe to every person employed or working on the premises as it would be if securely fenced: s.12.

20. Transmission machinery. This is machinery by which the motion of a prime mover is transmitted to or received by any machine. Every part of the transmission machinery must be securely fenced unless it is in such a position or of such construction as to be safe to every person employed or working on the premises as it would be if securely fenced. Devices or appliances for promptly cutting off power from transmission machinery must be provided in every room or place where work is carried out. The Health and Safety Executive may, where special circumstances exist, direct that this section does not apply: s.13.

21. Every dangerous part of any machinery. Such parts must be securely fenced unless in such a position or of such construction as to be safe to every person employed or working on the premises as it would be if securely fenced. If such part of a machine cannot by reason of the nature of the operation be secured by means of a fixed guard, it will be sufficient if a device is provided which automatically prevents the operator from coming into contact with that part: s.14.

22. Unfenced machinery. In deciding whether unfenced machinery is safe in accordance with the above tests no account is taken of any person carrying out an examination, lubrication or adjustment of machinery which can only be carried out while the machinery is in motion. This section applies only to persons over 18 and is subject to conditions specified in the regulations: s.15.

23. Construction and maintenance of fencing. All fencing or safeguards provided under ss.12–14 must be of substantial construction, and constantly maintained and kept in position while parts required to be fenced or safeguarded are in motion or use. An exception to this rule is allowed when any such parts are necessarily exposed for examination and for lubrication or adjustment shown by the examination to be immediately necessary, and all such conditions as may be specified in regulations are complied with: s.16.

The phrase "in motion" has been discussed in a number of cases.

(*a*) In *Stanbrook* v. *Waterlow & Sons Ltd.* (1964), it was held that although the movement of a machine was not intended to last for more than a moment of time, yet the machine was in motion for the purpose of s.16 because it was moving at speed, and therefore the defendants were in breach of their statutory duty.

(*b*) However, in *Kelly* v. *John Dale Ltd.* (1965), the machine was not in motion or use within the meaning of the section when a woman supervisor was cleaning a machine and rotating a cylinder gradually by means of an inching button, about every 10 minutes. The defendants were, however, in breach of s.20. This was also held in the case of *Denyer* v. *Charles Skipper & East Ltd.* (1970) (*see* **61**).

(*c*) A narrow construction was also placed on the words in *Mitchell* v. *Westin Ltd.* (1965) in the Court of Appeal, in which an experienced fitter removed a guard off a power-driven lathe in order to do some repairs. In order to tighten some screws, he had to turn the lathe round. He could have done so without switching the machine on, but he did it by switching the machine on and almost simultaneously switching it off. While doing this he leaned his left hand on the machine and caught a forefinger in a nip between two cog wheels. It was held that the lathe was not "in motion" within the meaning of s.16 because there was only an intermittent movement, no evidence of high speed, and no substantial movement comparable to the ordinary working of the lathe. According to Pearson LJ, in deciding whether in a particular case the movement is or is not of such a character that the machinery is "in motion", the factors to be taken into account include the speed of the movement, the duration, the method of starting the machinery and probably to some extent or in some cases also the purpose for which the movement had been instituted.

24. Interpretation by the courts of ss.12–16. The application of these safety measures has been open to judicial consideration in a number of cases, as follows.

(*a*) *"Every dangerous part of every machinery" (s.14).* In *Close* v. *Steel Company of Wales Ltd.* (1961), the House of Lords gave approval to the test that machinery is dangerous if it is "a reasonably foreseeable cause of injury to anybody acting in a way in which a human being may reasonably be expected to act in circumstances which may reasonably be expected to occur".

In *Cross* v. *Midland and Low Moor Iron and Steel Co. Ltd.* (1965) the House of Lords held that this test was to be applied to a machine when it was doing work which it was designed to do; a part of a machine might then become dangerous through the juxtaposition of that part and a piece of material. This decision was applied in the following case.

> *F.E. Callow (Engineers) Ltd.* v. *Johnson* (1971). A horizontal boring bar with a cutting tool in one end was used to bore a workpiece. No guard was provided between the bore and the workpiece. An automatic coolant system was fitted to the machine but the plaintiff found it more convenient to use his own "squeezie" bottle, a practice known to his employers though not approved by them. The plaintiff slipped while reaching for the bottle and caught his hand in the nip between the bore and the rotating workpiece. HELD: (*inter alia*): the boring bar and the rotating workpiece could not be treated in isolation since it became a dangerous part of the machinery when, in the normal working of the machine, it was brought into such close juxtaposition with the workpiece. (Lord Hailsham considered that some of the protection to the workman which at first sight might be thought to be available under s.14 turns out on closer scrutiny to be illusory. For example, there is no obligation to fence a dangerous machine unless it has dangerous parts, nor is there such an obligation to prevent the ejection of flying material from the machine.)

In *Wearing* v. *Pirelli* (1977) the plaintiff was employed by the defendants to work on a machine which moulded and formed rubber for the purpose of making tyres. The machine was defective in that the automatic process had to be assisted by the use of a hand tool. This tool was jerked out of the plaintiff's hand while he was manually engaged in this process and his wrist was injured. The revolving drum which was involved in the process was not fenced and the plaintiff claimed that the defendants were in breach of their statutory duty under s.14(1). It was found that the revolving drum was a dangerous part, but the defendants claimed that the plaintiff's injury was caused by the rubberised coating on the drum, not the drum itself. The House of Lords held that if the incident was looked at in a practical way the injury had been caused by the revolving drum and its fabric covering was an irrelevance.

(*b*) *Reasonable foreseeability.* The test of what is reasonably foreseeable must be applied to the possible behaviour both of employees and of machines. Machinery which is not intrinsically dangerous may become so by reference to the behaviour of an employee. Any behaviour which is reasonably foreseeable would come within the test, so that it will be a question of fact in each case whether the employee should have anticipated the danger. The possibility of careless and inattentive behaviour by employees must be taken into account as must the behaviour of a machine when it is being used in the usual course of working. This point was discussed in *F.E. Callow (Engineers) Ltd.* v. *Johnson* (*see* above) where it was found that once the defendants were aware that their employees were using "squeezies" they could have foreseen that sooner or later someone might slip or overreach himself or some careless operator might get his hand too far inside the workpiece with the danger of being trapped between the boring bar and workpiece.

(*c*) *Duty to fence.* There is an absolute duty to fence *securely* and it is no defence to show that it would not be practicable to fence the machine. If it is not possible to use the machine when it has been fenced, then it should not be used. The Secretary of State has power to modify the strictness of this rule by special regulation under s.76. This has been done, for example, with regard to the fencing of wood-working machinery.

John Summers & Sons Ltd. v. *Frost* (1955): A fitter injured his thumb when it came into contact with a power-driven grinding machine. A fixed guard covered a part only of the grindstone. HELD: a grindstone was a dangerous part of a machine within s.14 and so must be securely fenced even though such fencing rendered it unusable.

Automatic Woodturning Co. v. *Stringer* (1957): S operated a power-driven circular saw being used for cutting lengths of timber. She was provided with a stick to push away the offcuts of timber. While using the push stick her hand came into contact with the saw and she was injured. The saw was fenced in accordance with the Woodworking Machinery Regulations. HELD: the saw as a whole complied with the Woodworking Machinery Regulations and therefore the provisions of s.14 of the Factories Act did not apply.

(*d*) *Standard fencing*. By s.16 of the Act all fencing must be of substantial construction and constantly maintained and kept in position while parts are in motion or use, except where the machine is being examined, lubricated or adjusted. The obligation is to fence securely. The test of reasonable foreseeability, taking into account the possible behaviour of persons employed in deciding what is sufficient fencing, seems to have been modified in the following case.

Millard v. *Serck Tubes Ltd.* (1969): The appellant suffered severe injuries when his hand was dragged into a drilling machine. No accident had ever occurred in this way before. Salmon LJ distinguished between the test to be applied here and the test of foreseeability as applied to deciding if a machine is dangerous. Once it is decided that a machine is dangerous, foreseeability of behaviour is no longer relevant. Since this machine was dangerous it ought to have been fenced *properly* and this had not been done. HELD: the occupier of the factory was liable for breach of the statute.

(*e*) *Extent of duty*. The extent of duty to fence is limited in two ways as follows.

(*i*) The fencing should be such that it prevents the operator from coming into contact with the machine; it need not prevent parts of the machine from flying out. This principle has been supported by the House of Lords in *Close* v. *Steel Company of Wales Ltd.* In *Eaves* v. *Morris Motors Ltd.* (1961), it was stated by Holroyd Pearce LJ that "there is no protection under s.14 against a class of obvious perils caused by dangerous machinery, namely, perils which arise from a dangerous machine ejecting at the worker pieces of material or even pieces of the machinery itself". It follows that there is no duty to fence against material being ejected whilst being worked on. (The Secretary of State may make regulations requiring that materials or articles which are dangerous while in motion in a machine should be fenced.) Nor need the protection extend to preventing an injury resulting from a tool held by a workman coming into contact with a dangerous part of the machinery: *Sparrow* v. *Fairey Aviation Co. Ltd.* (1964).

Close v. *Steel Company of Wales* (1961): C operated an electric drilling machine, the bit of which shattered and a piece entered his eye. HELD: this was not a dangerous part of machinery, since the harm which had been caused by it was not reasonably foreseeable. Where machinery is dangerous, the duty to fence extends to preventing the body of the operator from coming into contact with the machine. It is not necessary to fence so as to prevent fragments of machinery or material from flying out.

(*ii*) The machinery which must be fenced is that which is used in the manufacturing process of a factory. There is no duty to fence machinery which is in a factory for repair or which has been manufactured at the factory.

Parvin v. *Morton Machine Co. Ltd.* (1952): P, an apprentice fitter, was injured while cleaning a dangerous part of a machine which had been manufactured in the factory. This machine, a dough-brake, was unfenced while adjustments were made to it. HELD: the words "any machinery" in s.14 meant machinery used in the factory for production, and there was no duty to fence machinery which had been made there. Applied in *Ballard* v. *Ministry of Defence* (1977).

Another aspect of this duty was discussed by the House of Lords in *Irwin* v. *White, Tomkins and Courage Ltd.* (1964). In that case, the deceased was in charge of installation of machinery at the respondent's mill in Northern Ireland. The installation was not complete and the machinery had not been taken into commercial use. The machinery included seven sack hoists to raise sacks to the first floor and corresponding conveyor belts to remove sacks that had been hoisted. The deceased was killed while running one sack hoist which had been completed. It was held that since the sack hoist was an independent entity of machinery which had been completely installed, it should have been fenced, notwithstanding that the machine had not been taken into commercial use.

The mobility of a piece of machinery does not exclude it from possible inclusion within the terms of the Act. In *British Railway Board* v. *Liptrot* (1967), the respondent was injured when a revolving body of a mobile crane caught and squeezed him against one of the chassis wheels. It was held, *inter alia*, that the crane was part of the factory equipment and its mobility did not exclude it from the scope of s.14; accordingly s.14 applied to dangerous parts of machinery contained in the mobile crane. No distinction was to be drawn between mobility and immobility but between machinery and vehicles.

25. Construction and sale of new machinery. Machinery which is to be driven by mechanical power must not be sold, let on hire, or used unless certain parts are effectively guarded so as to prevent danger: s.17.

26. Dangerous substances.

(*a*) Vessels containing dangerous liquids with edge less than 3 ft (1 m) above the ground must be securely fenced to that height or securely covered. Where such measures are impracticable, all practicable steps must be taken to prevent any person from falling into the vessel.

(*b*) Where a vessel containing a dangerous substance is not securely covered, no ladder, stair or gangway must be placed above, across or inside it which is not at least 18 in (46 cm) wide and securely fenced to a height of at least 3 ft (1 m) and securely fixed: s.18.

27. Hoists and lifts.

(*a*) Every hoist or lift must be of good mechanical construction, sound material and adequate strength and must be properly maintained.

(*b*) Every hoist or lift must be thoroughly examined by a competent person at least once every six months.

(*c*) A report must be entered or attached to a general register within twenty-eight days of examination.

(*d*) Where a fault is discovered a copy of the report must be sent to the district inspector within twenty-eight days.

(*e*) Every hoistway or liftway must be efficiently enclosed so as to prevent any person from falling down the way or coming into contact with the lift.

(*f*) Gates to liftways must be fitted with efficient interlocking or other device to ensure that the gate cannot be opened except when the cage or platform is at the landing.

(*g*) The maximum working load must be marked conspicuously on every hoist or lift: s.22.

28. Hoists and lifts used for carrying people. In addition to these precautions, hoists and lists used to carry people must be equipped with devices to prevent them over-running and from operating unless the access gate is closed: s.23.

29. Teagle openings. Teagle openings or similar doorways used for hoisting or lowering goods must be securely fenced except when in use, and must be provided with secure hand-holds: s.24.

30. Chains, ropes and lifting tackle. With respect to every chain, rope or piece of lifting tackle used for the purpose of raising or lowering people, goods or materials, the following provisions must be complied with.

(*a*) They must be of good construction, sound material, adequate strength and free from patent defect.
(*b*) They must not be used for a load exceeding the specified safe working load.
(*c*) Chains, ropes and lifting tackle must be tested and thoroughly examined by a competent person every six months.
(*d*) No new equipment of this kind (except fibre ropes) may be taken into use for the first time without being tested and certified: s.26.

Ball v. *Richard Thomas and Baldwins* (1968): An overhead crane was used to lift overspill of molten metal known as "scab", off the floor of a steel works. The plaintiff loosened the scab so that the crane could lift it away. As the crane started to lift the scab, on this occasion, the hook straightened or opened dropping the scab, hitting the plaintiff in the face and injuring him. HELD: the operation was one of "raising" materials within the meaning of s.26(1), and, as it had been conceded by the defendant that the hook was not of adequate strength, the employers were in breach of the section.

31. Cranes and other lifting machines.

(*a*) These must be of good construction, sound material, adequate strength and free from patent defect and must be properly maintained.
(*b*) They must be thoroughly examined by a competent person at least once every fourteen months, and the result entered on a register.
(*c*) Where a fault is discovered a copy of the report must be sent to the district inspector within twenty-eight days.
(*d*) The safe working load must be shown and must not be exceeded except for the purpose of a test.

(*e*) No lifting machine may be used for the first time without being tested and certified.

(*f*) Any person working near the wheel track of an overhead crane must be warned of its approach or it must be ensured that the crane does not come within 20 ft (6.1 m) of that place.

(*g*) Any person working above floor level and liable to be struck by a crane or its load must be warned of its approach: s.27.

32. Floors, passages and stairs.

(*a*) All floors, steps, stairs, passages and gangways must be of sound construction, and must be properly maintained and must, as far as is reasonably practicable, be kept free from any obstruction and from any substance likely to cause people to slip.

(*b*) Every staircase must be provided with a handrail which, if the staircase has an open side, must be on that side. Where there are two open sides or the staircase is specially liable to cause accidents, a handrail must be provided on both sides.

(*c*) All openings in floors must be securely fenced except where the nature of the work renders this impracticable.

(*d*) All ladders must be soundly constructed and properly maintained: s.28.

NOTE: (1) The words "of sound construction and properly maintained" in s.28(1) establish an *absolute* duty to maintain the structure of floors, steps, stairs, passages and gangways. The duty does not apply to transient or exceptional conditions such as sudden flooding due to a heavy storm.

(2) There is a further duty in this section to keep floors, steps, stairs, passages and gangways free from any obstruction and from substances likely to cause persons to slip. This duty is to do only that which is *reasonably practicable* and is not absolute in nature. The onus of proof rests on the employer.

Jenkins v. *Allied Ironfounders Ltd.* (1970): The appellant was a labourer at the respondent's factory. Part of his duties were to help two other labourers in decoring castings in the moulding shop. First the castings were removed from the moulding boxes while still hot, and were then put with forty or fifty castings in a heap. When the castings were cold they were moved again, decored, and piled ready for removal. The castings usually had excrescences of scrap (known as "gates"). Some gates got knocked off when the castings were first emptied but most had to be knocked off when the castings were decored. The appellant was helping to move castings from the first pile to the second when he caught his heel in a gate hidden in the sand which covered the floor. The appellant fell and was injured. HELD: that the respondents were not guilty of breach of statutory duty because it was not reasonably practicable to have a system which would have resulted in the removal of the gate before the accident.

33. Safe means of access and place of work. So far as it is reasonably practicable there must be safe means of access to every place at which any person has at any time to work. Every such place must, so far as is reasonably practicable, be made and kept safe for any person working there: s.29.

Nimmo v. *Alexander Cowan & Sons Ltd.* (1968): The appellant was unloading railway wagons filled with bales of pulp. He stood on a bale which tipped, and he fell and was injured. The appellant claimed that the bales were insecurely placed in the wagon, but he did not maintain that it was reasonably practicable for the respondents to make the working place safe. HELD: the obligation of proving that it was not reasonably practicable to make the working place any safer was on the occupiers of the factory, and so the case was properly pleaded.

Woodward v. *Renold* (1980): The employers failed to grit, in icy weather, that area of their car park which was near to a footpath extensively used by their employees to walk up to the work's entrance. The court held that the employers were in breach of s.29, and so were liable in damages to their employee for the injuries she suffered as a result of slipping on the icy car park.

34. Dangerous fumes.

(*a*) Where work has to be done inside a chamber or other confined place, where there are likely to be dangerous fumes (or lack of oxygen) a manhole must be provided in the absence of other adequate means of exit.

(*b*) Unless a confined space has been certified by a responsible person as being safe for entry, no person may enter without wearing suitable breathing apparatus. Where practicable he must also wear a belt with a securely attached rope.

(*c*) Before being certified as safe, effective steps must be taken to prevent further entry of fumes, to remove the source of fumes, and to ensure that the space is adequately ventilated.

(*d*) Apparatus, belts and ropes must be examined at least once a month or as prescribed by a competent person. A sufficient number of persons must be trained in the use of such apparatus: s.30.

35. Explosive and inflammable substances. All practicable steps must be taken to prevent explosions arising out of the presence in a factory of explosive or inflammable dust, gas, vapour or substance: s.31.

36. Steam boilers. The following provisions are contained in ss.32–35, 37, 38, Sched. 6, para 5.

(*a*) Every steam boiler must be of good construction, sound material and adequate strength and free from patent defect.

(*b*) It must have attached to it:

(*i*) a suitable safety valve so as to prevent the boiler being worked at a pressure greater than maximum permissible pressure;

(*ii*) a suitable stop-valve connecting boiler to steam-pipe;

(*iii*) a correct steam pressure gauge or maximum permissible pressure marked on it;

(*iv*) at least one water gauge of transparent material to show water level in the boiler;

(*v*) where the boiler is one of a number, a plate bearing a distinctive number.

(*c*) It must be provided with means for attaching a test pressure gauge.

(*d*) It must, unless externally fixed, be provided with a suitable fusible plug or an efficient low-water alarm device.

(*e*) Steam boilers must be thoroughly inspected by a competent person at least once every fourteen months, and after extensive repairs a report must be attached to the general register.

(*f*) All new boilers must be examined and certified; used boilers must be examined before being taken into use.

37. Air receivers.

(*a*) They must be of sound construction and properly maintained.

(*b*) Requirements similar to those for steam boilers apply.

(*c*) They must be thoroughly cleaned and examined at least once in every period of twenty-six months, by a competent person and the report attached to the general register. For certain constructions, the examination period may be extended, but not beyond four years: ss.36 and 37.

38. Fire precautions. The fire provisions of s.40 have been repealed and replaced by the Fire Precautions Act 1971 which applies to factories, as well as to offices, shops, railway and other premises. Regulations provide that fire certificates from the fire authority are required for all factory (and office, shop and railway) premises in which people are employed to work except:

(*a*) those in which the persons employed at any one time do not exceed twenty; or
(*b*) those in which not more than ten persons are employed other than on the ground floor.

However, a certificate is required even for these exceptions if the building contains two or more of the prescribed premises, e.g. an office and a factory, and the aggregate number of persons employed exceeds those described in (*a*) and (*b*) above, or in the case of factory premises, where explosive or highly flammable materials, which constitute an additional fire risk, are stored or used in the premises.

NOTE: Certain premises must have a fire certificate obtained from the Health and Safety Executive, e.g. premises which can store liquified petroleum gas.

Regulations provide for certain fire precautions to be taken in the smaller factory (and smaller offices, shops and railway) premises which do not require a fire certificate. The precautions are concerned with the means of escape in case of fire and fire-fighting equipment. For example, access and exit doors on to corridors and staircases and other places should open outwards.

39. Fire certificates. Before they issue a fire certificate, the fire authority must be satisfied that:

(*a*) means of escape in case of fire are provided,
(*b*) means of escape can be safely and effectively used at all material times,
(*c*) means of fighting fire are provided for use by the persons in the building,
(*d*) means are provided for giving persons in the premises warning in case of fire, and

are such as may be reasonably required. If the fire authority are not so satisfied, they may inform the applicant of that fact and of the steps which need to be taken before they will issue a fire certificate.

40. Specifications of the fire certificate. The fire certificate must specify:

(*a*) the particular use of the premises which the certificate covers,

(*b*) the means of escape in case of fire,

(*c*) the means by which escape can be safely and effectively used at all material times,

(*d*) the type, number and location of the means of fighting fire, which is provided for use by the persons in the building,

(*e*) the type, number and location of the means with which the relevant building is provided for giving to persons in the premises warning in case of fire, and

(*f*) in the case of factory premises, particulars as to any explosive or highly flammable materials which may be stored or used on the premises.

The fire authority may impose certain additional requirements as they consider appropriate in the circumstances.

The Secretary of State has the power to make regulations about fire precautions necessary on premises requiring a fire certificate.

41. Liability of occupiers and owners. The occupier of premises is generally responsible for applying for a fire certificate and for any contravention of any requirement imposed by the fire certificate. However, in respect of factories (and offices, shops and railway premises) where:

(*a*) the premises are held under a lease or an agreement for a lease, or under a licence, and consist of part of a building all parts of which are in common ownership; or

(*b*) the premises consist of part of a building in which different parts are owned by different persons, then the owner, or owners, is so responsible.

(An occupier of certain premises, chiefly offices, shops and railway premises, but *not* factories, is under a duty to provide those premises with means of escape in case of fire. However, if (*a*) and (*b*) above apply, then the owner, or owners, is under that duty.)

WELFARE (GENERAL PROVISIONS)

42. Supply of drinking water.

(*a*) At suitable points conveniently accessible to all employees, there must be an adequate supply of wholesome drinking water from a public main or from some other source approved by the local authority.

(*b*) Where the water is not laid on it must be contained in suitable vessels, and the supply renewed daily. It should be clearly marked as drinking water.

(*c*) Except where the water is delivered in an upward jet, one or more suitable cups must be provided with facilities for rinsing them: s.57.

43. Washing facilities. Adequate and suitable washing facilities must be provided. These should include the provision of soap and clean towels (or other means of cleansing or drying) and a supply of clean running hot and cold or warm water. Facilities should be conveniently accessible and be kept in a clean and orderly condition: s.58.

44. Accommodation for clothing. Adequate and suitable accommodation for clothing not worn during working hours must be provided. Arrangements for drying such clothing must also be made when reasonably practicable. s.59.

45. Facilities for sitting. Where any employed persons have in the course of their employment reasonable opportunities for sitting without detriment to their work, there must be provided and maintained for their use suitable facilities for sitting sufficient to enable them to take advantage of the opportunities. Where a substantial proportion of any work can be done sitting, suitable seating must be provided and maintained: s.60.

46. First aid.

(*a*) A first-aid box or cupboard of the prescribed standard must be provided, which must be readily accessible. Where more than 150 persons are employed an additional box must be provided for every additional 150 people.

(*b*) Each box or cupboard must be in the charge of a responsible person. In factories where more than fifty people are employed, this person must be trained in first aid, and must always be available during working hours.

(*c*) There must be a notice in every workroom stating the name of the person in charge of the first-aid box or cupboard.

(*d*) If an ambulance room is provided in which all injuries can be treated, the chief inspector may exempt that factory from certain of these requirements: s.61.

SPECIAL HEALTH, SAFETY AND WELFARE PROVISIONS

47. Removal of dust and fumes.

(*a*) All practicable steps must be taken to protect employees against inhalation of dust, fumes or other impurities, arising from a process, which are likely to be injurious or offensive or where there is any substantial quantity of dust of any kind.

(*b*) Where practicable, exhaust appliances must be provided and maintained so as to prevent dust and fumes entering the workroom.

(*c*) No stationary internal combustion engine may be used unless:

(*i*) provision is made to conduct the exhaust gases into the open air; and

(*ii*) the engine is partitioned off from any workroom so as to prevent fumes from entering the room: s.63.

NOTE: (1) *Comparison with s.4.* The effect of s.63 should be compared to that of s.4(1). Devlin J said in *Graham* v.*Cooperative Wholesale Society Ltd.* (1957): "Section 4 is dealing with the circulation of fresh air which gets rid of impurities which come into the air, whereas section 63 is dealing with methods of prevention, of stopping the impurities from ever getting into circulation at all."

(2) *Nature and quantity of dust.* The two parts of s.63(1) impose duties in relation to two types of circumstances: (*i*) where the dust given off is likely to be injurious or offensive; (*ii*) where dust of any kind is given off in substantial quantity.

(3) *Measures must be "practicable".* The duty under s.63 is to take measures which are "practicable". What is practicable depends upon methods of protection which were known to exist at the time of the alleged breach. The onus of proof that injury is a result of a breach of statutory duty lies on the plaintiff.

Richards v. *Highway Ironfounders (West Bromwich) Ltd.* (1955): From 1930 until 1952 the plaintiff was employed in the defendant's factory. The operation of moulding required the use of sand and involved a process known as "knocking out" in which grains of sand had to be knocked out of moulds. Whenever the process took place a substantial quantity of dust was given out. Until about 1950, the dust was not thought to be dangerous but it was then established that after being inhaled over a number of years it was liable to produce silicosis. No steps were taken to protect moulders against inhalation and no exhaust appliances were installed. HELD: since at the time when the plaintiff became seriously affected with silicosis the dust was not known to be injurious, the duty under s.63 did not arise.

48. Meals in dangerous trades.

(*a*) Where poisonous substances are used so as to give rise to dust or fumes, no person may partake of food or drink in that room, nor remain there during meal times.

(*b*) A person must not remain during meal times in a room in which a process gives rise to siliceous or asbestos dust.

(*c*) Suitable provision must be made for these employees to take their meals elsewhere in the factory: s.64.

49. Protection of eyes. The Secretary of State by regulation may specify that certain processes involve special risk of injury to the eyes. Suitable goggles or effective screens must then be provided: s.65.

50. Underground rooms.

(*a*) The district inspector may certify any underground room as unsuitable for work other than for storage purposes or other specified uses.

(*b*) "Unsuitable" means unsuitable as regards height, light or ventilation or on any hygienic ground, or because means of escape in case of fire are not provided: s.69.

51. Lifting excessive weights. A person must not be employed to lift, carry or move any load so heavy as to be likely to cause him injury: s.72. Section 72 requires two questions to be considered. First, was the load in question so heavy as to be likely to cause injury. If so, secondly, was the person in question employed to lift, carry or move it: *per* Lord Dilhorne in *Brown* v. *Allied Ironfounders Ltd.* (1974).

ACCIDENTS AND INDUSTRIAL DISEASES

52. Notification of accidents. The Notification of Accidents and Dangerous Occurrences Regulations 1980, made under the Health and Safety at Work etc. Act 1974, now impose duties on persons responsible for the activities of persons at work and on self-employed persons to report to the enforcing authority (*see* XII, **30**) accidents resulting in the death of or major injury to persons arising out of or in connection with that work. The duty to notify is applicable to all places of work, not just factories.

The employer is required to keep records of accidents and dangerous occurrences arising out of and in connection with work. It is a defence for an employer or other responsible person to show that he was not aware of the accident or occurrence and that he had taken all reasonable steps to have all notifiable accidents and dangerous occurrences brought to his notice. A breach of these regulations is a criminal offence under the Health and Safety at Work etc. Act 1974, s.33 (*see* XII, **37**).

53. Notification of industrial diseases.

(*a*) Every medical practitioner attending a patient whom he believes to be suffering from lead, phosphorous, arsenical or mercurial poisoning or anthrax contracted in any factory, must immediately inform the Health and Safety Executive: s.82.

(*b*) Where any of the above-mentioned diseases occurs in a factory, the occupier must immediately inform the inspector and the employment medical adviser in charge of the area in which the factory is situated: s.82.

(*c*) The statutory list of diseases has been extended by regulation to include toxic jaundice, toxic anaemia, ulceration and others (*see* also XI).

(*d*) The Industrial Diseases (Notification) Act 1981 provides for regulations to be made concerning the notification and certification of death and the recording of information relating to industrial disease.

EMPLOYMENT OF WOMEN AND YOUNG PERSONS

54. Working hours. The Factories Act 1961 contains no restriction as to the length of hours of work of men. However, women, and young persons of either sex under the age of 18, must not work longer than the hours set down by the statute. The Act imposes the following general conditions of work for women and young persons.

(*a*) Total hours of work excluding intervals allowed for meals and rest must not exceed nine in any day nor exceed forty-eight in any week (forty-four hours for a young person under the age of 16).

(*b*) The period of employment must not exceed eleven hours in any day and must not begin earlier than 7 a.m., nor end later than

6 p.m., for young persons under 16 years, and 8 p.m. in other cases. Work must end at 1 p.m. on Saturday afternoons.

(*c*) The maximum continuous spell of work must not be longer than four-and-a-half hours without a break of at least thirty minutes. However, the spell of work may be extended to five hours if at least ten minutes' break is allowed during this time.

(*d*) The period worked and the meal and rest periods allowed must be the same for all women and young people employed. However, a young person under the age of 16 may finish work earlier.

(*e*) No woman or young person must work during meal and rest periods: s.86.

55. Notice of working hours. A notice of hours of work for each day for women and young persons must be posted in the factory, together with the meal and rest intervals: s.88.

NOTE: (1) Different periods of employment and different intervals may be fixed for different days of the week. (2) The district inspector must be informed of any changes in these hours, which cannot be made more frequently than once every three months.

56. Overtime. Pressure of work in a factory may be eased by the overtime employment, within limits, of women and young persons over 16 years of age, subject to the following conditions contained in ss.89–100.

(*a*) The total hours worked per day must not exceed ten (or ten-and-a-half where a five-day week is operated). These hours must be within a maximum period of twelve hours, that is, between 7 a.m. and 9 p.m. or 8 p.m. for young persons.

(*b*) The overtime worked must not exceed an allowance of 100 hours per year for any factory nor six hours in any week. This allowance does not vary with the number of women or young persons so employed.

(*c*) The period during which overtime is worked must not exceed twenty-five weeks in any year.

(*d*) The Secretary of State may make regulations altering in certain circumstances the factory allowance of overtime and substituting a personal allowance. The personal allowance must not exceed seventy-five hours per year for a woman and fifty hours per year for a young person.

(*e*) In factories subject to a seasonal pressure the Secretary of State may by regulation increase the hours of work of women but not for longer than eight weeks in any year. The allowance for a factory may be increased to an aggregate not exceeding 150 hours, but no young person may work for more than 100 hours.

(*f*) The Secretary of State may by regulation allow employment in different parts of a factory or in different processes to be regarded as employment in different factories for the purpose of reckoning hours of overtime: s.89.

57. Shift work. The Health and Safety Executive may, on application of the occupier, authorise the employment of women and young persons of 16 and over on shifts between 6 a.m. and 10 p.m. and up to 2 p.m. on Saturdays. Generally the shifts must not exceed eight hours in length. A secret ballot must be held to ascertain the consent of the majority of the employees concerned: s.97.

58. Exceptions. Women in responsible positions of management are not covered by these provisions: s.95. Also, the Health and Safety Executive has power to suspend certain of these provisions in the event of an emergency to avoid serious interference with the ordinary work of the factory: s.96.

59. Exemption orders. Where an application is made to the Secretary of State, he may, when satisfied that it is desirable in the public interest, to maintain or increase efficiency of industry or transport, exempt the employment of women and young persons from the provisions as to working hours: s.117.

Exemption orders may be special or general.

(*a*) *Special exemption orders* apply only to particular classes of employment.

(*b*) *General exemption orders* extend to the employment of persons generally, and may be made only on:

(*i*) the application of a joint industrial council or similar body,

(*ii*) the application of a wages council,

(*iii*) the joint application of an organisation which appears to represent employers and one representing workmen, or

(*iv*) the application of an organisation representative of employers or employees after consultation with the other organisations.

NOTE: The importance of the provisions relating to the employment of young persons under 16 has diminished since the school-leaving age was raised to 16 in 1972.

HEALTH AND SAFETY PROVISIONS FOR WOMEN AND YOUNG PERSONS

60. Certificate of fitness. Where an inspector is of the opinion that the employment of a young person is prejudicial to his health, he may require the occupier of the factory to discontinue the employment of the young person unless the appointed factory doctor or an employment medical adviser has certified that the young person is fit for work: s.119.

NOTE: The occupier of a factory is under a duty to give written notice of the employment of a young person to the local careers office within seven days of the start of the employment. The notice should state the name of the occupier, the address of the factory, the fact of the young person's employment, the date, and information about the young person such as name, date of birth, address and address of his or her school: s.119A.

61. Cleaning of machinery. A woman or young person must not clean any part of a prime mover or transmission machinery which is in motion; nor any part of any machinery if there is a risk of injury from a moving part of that machine or any adjacent machinery: s.20.

Denyer v. *Charles Skipper & East Ltd.* (1970): While the rollers of a lithographic printing machine were being cleaned, the main current of the machine was turned off. When one length of a roller had been cleaned, it had to be turned by means of an inching button to expose another part for cleaning. When pressing the inching button with his left hand, the plaintiff, a youth of 17, put his right hand too close to the roller so that it was dragged in with the cleaning rag, and he was injured. HELD: the defendants were liable for damages for breach of s.20 since the operation exposed him to risk of injury and the rollers, when being inched, were moving parts of the machinery.

62. Training and supervision. A young person must not work any machine prescribed as dangerous by the Secretary of State unless:

(*a*) he has received sufficient training in the work; or
(*b*) he is under adequate supervision by a person with experience of the machine: s.21.

63. Prohibition of employment. The Act prohibits the employment of women and young persons as follows.

(*a*) *Female young persons* must not be employed where certain processes involving melting or blowing glass, or the evaporation of brine, are being carried out: s.73.

(*b*) *Women and young persons* may not be employed in certain processes connected with the manufacture of lead, or the use of lead compounds: ss.74 and 75.

MISCELLANEOUS PROVISIONS

64. Posting of abstract of Act and notices. At the principal entrances of a factory the following must be kept posted.

(*a*) The prescribed abstract of the Factories Act 1961.

(*b*) A notice of the address of the district inspector and the superintending inspector for the division.

(*c*) A notice of the name and address of the employment medical adviser in charge of the area in which the factory is situated.

(*d*) A notice specifying the clock, if any, by which periods of employment and intervals are regulated.

(*e*) Every notice and document required by the Act to be posted in the factory: s.138.

(*f*) Copies of all regulations in force in the factory: s.139.

65. General register. A general register must be kept in every factory in which the following particulars are entered.

(*a*) The prescribed particulars as to young persons employed in the factory.

(*b*) The prescribed particulars as to washing, whitewashing and painting of the factory.

(*c*) The prescribed particulars as to every accident and case of industrial disease occurring in the factory of which notice is to be sent to an inspector.

(*d*) Particulars of exceptions under certain sections of the Act of which the occupier has availed himself.

(*e*) All reports and particulars required by the Act to be entered or attached.

(*f*) Particulars of other matters as the Secretary of State may prescribe: s.140.

OBSERVANCE AND ADMINISTRATION OF THE ACT

66. Duty to observe the provisions of the Act. This duty falls primarily on the occupier of the factory, who may or may not be the owner of the factory: s.155. However, occupiers will have a defence if they can show that they took all reasonable steps to prevent a breach, but they could be liable under a different provision in a different capacity, e.g. as an employer (*see Davies* v. *Camerons Industrial Services* (1980)). In certain circumstances the duty falls on the owner of the factory, or the owner of a machine, or on the employer, as follows.

(*a*) *Liability of owner.* The owner (whether or not he is the occupier) of a tenement factory will be liable for certain contraventions of the Act. A tenement factory is one in which the owner supplies mechanical power to occupiers of different parts of the same premises. Where parts of the same building are let off as separate factories, the owner will again be liable in certain circumstances: ss.121, 122.

(*b*) *Liability of owner of a machine.* The owner or hirer of a machine may be deemed the occupier of the factory for any offence committed to a person employed on the machine who is in the employment of the owner or hirer of the machine: s.163. (*See also* **41** for liability to take fire precautions.)

67. Criminal and civil liability. A person in breach of a duty imposed by the Act is always liable to a prosecution under the criminal law: he may *also* have incurred a civil liability for breach of statutory duty which could result in damages being awarded against him. In addition, an occupier of premises, or an employer, or a manufacturer, may be liable in damages for breaches of other duties imposed by the law of tort, such as the employer's duty of care (*see Lineker* v. *Raleigh Industries* (1980) and *see* VIII, **15**), occupier's liability or negligence (*see*, for example, *Hill* v. *James Crowe (Cases) Ltd* (1978)) or imposed by the terms of a contract.

With regard to civil liability for breach of the provisions of the Factories Act 1961, broadly speaking the position is as follows.

(*a*) *Safety provisions.* A civil right of action is allowed to an employee to claim damages where he has suffered loss due to any breach of a duty imposed by the safety provisions in ss. 12–56 of the Act.

(*b*) *Health and welfare provisions.* There is no clear rule whether the parts of the Act relating to health (ss.1–11) and welfare (ss.57–62) give rise to civil actions or to criminal proceedings only. As regards the health provisions of the Act there have been a number of decisions in which a civil action was allowed, though the point has not been fully discussed by the courts. There is no general rule as to whether a civil action will be allowed for breach of a welfare provision. Each section must be considered separately. In

McCarthy v. *Daily Mirror Newspapers Ltd.* (1949) an action was allowed on what is now s.59(1) of the 1961 Act. In Part IV of the Act, which deals with special provisions as to health, safety and welfare, a right of action will depend upon whether the section is concerned to protect health or safety.

68. The administration of the Act. The Health and Safety Executive is responsible for the enforcement of the provisions of the Act, which in practice is chiefly carried out by Her Majesty's Factory Inspectorate. In 1980 the Factory Inspectorate issued 5,970 enforcement (prohibition or improvement) notices (*see* XII, **33**, **34**). By 31st December 1980, 3,960 had been complied with, 16 had been withdrawn, 20 had led to prosecution, on 103 no further action was taken, and 1,871 were unresolved. In the same year there were 1,297 cases heard involving 2,438 breaches of the Factories Act 1961, which resulted in 2,227 convictions. The average fine for each breach amounted to £170: *Health and Safety Statistics 1980* (1982).

PROGRESS TEST 14

1. What is the relationship between the Health and Safety at Work Act 1974 and the Factories Act 1961? **(1**; XII, **2)**
2. What aspects of working conditions in factories are governed by the Factories Act 1961? **(1)**
3. How is a factory defined by s.175 of the Factories Act 1961? **(2, 3)**
4. What difficulties have arisen in connection with the phrase "employed in manual labour"? **(4)**
5. To what extent are the occupier's purposes relevant to the definition of a factory? **(6)**
6. Some premises situated within the factory complex may be excluded from the general definition of a factory. On what grounds may this be the case? **(7)**
7. Outline the main provisions of the Factories Act with regard to health. **(9–17)**
8. List the main provisions of the Factories Act with regard to safety. **(18–41)**
9. What machinery must be fenced in accordance with the Factories Act? **(18–21)**
10. How have the courts interpreted ss.12–16? **(24)**
11. Discuss the various duties contained in s.28 **(32)**
12. When are fire certificates required for a factory, and under the provisions of which Act? **(38)**

13. In which matters must a fire authority be satisfied before they will grant a fire certificate for a factory? **(39)**

14. Who is responsible for making an application for a fire certificate? Is an occupier or owner of a factory under a duty to provide the factory with means of escape in case of fire? **(41)**

15. Outline the general principles of the Act with regard to welfare. **(42–46)**

16. What is meant by "all practicable steps" in relation to the duty to remove dust and fumes under s.63? Cite any relevant cases. **(47)**

17. When should accidents and industrial diseases be notified, and to whom? **(52, 53)**

18. What provisions are set out in the Act in relation to women and young persons under 18 with regard to (*a*) employment, and (*b*) health and safety? **(54–63)**

19. Who is responsible for the enforcement of the Factories Act 1961? (1, **68**; XII, **30**)

CHAPTER XIV

Statutory Control of Working Conditions: Offices, Shops and Railway Premises

OFFICES, SHOPS AND RAILWAY PREMISES ACT 1963

1. Scope of the Act. The Offices, Shops and Railway Premises Act 1963 is a relevant statutory provision under the Health and Safety at Work Act 1974. This means that the 1963 Act remains in force with some amendments until it is eventually replaced by health and safety regulations which will apply to most workplaces, not just those covered by the 1963 Act. Thus regulations (*see* XII, **4**), codes of practice and guidance notes (*see* XII, **7, 8**) issued under the 1974 Act are applicable where relevant to offices, shops and railway premises.

The 1963 Act applies, with certain exceptions, to offices, shops and railway premises where persons are employed to work. The protection of the Act is generally not confined to protecting those injured in the course of their employment: *Westwood* v. *Post Office* (1974).

(*a*) *Offices.* Office premises means a building or part of a building which is solely or principally used as an office or for office purposes. A room, if its area is separate and definable even though not substantial, may be part of a building and therefore office premises: *Oxfordshire County Council* v. *Chancellor, Masters and Scholars of Oxford University* (1980). Office purposes include the purposes of administration, clerical work, handling money, and telephone and telegraph operating. Clerical work includes writing, book-keeping, sorting papers, filing, typing, duplicating, machine calculating, drawing, and the editorial preparation of matter for publication.

(*b*) *Shops.* The term shop premises is defined to include a building or part of a building which is not a shop but of which the sole or principal use is the carrying on there of retail trade or business. Thus the Act would cover libraries from which books were lent for profit, and restaurants selling food or drink for immediate consumption.

(*c*) *Railway premises.* The term railway premises means a building occupied by railway undertakers for purposes of the railway undertaking carried on by them and situate in the immediate vicinity of the permanent way: s.1.

NOTE: (1) Staff canteen are included premises. (2) The Shops Act 1950, Part II deals with, *inter alia*, conditions of employment in shops. It is not a relevant statutory provision under the Health and Safety at Work etc. Act 1974.

It is important to remember that the provisions of the 1974 Act apply to offices, shops and railway premises, as well as the provisions of the 1963 Act. The institutions and enforcement provisions applicable to these premises are mainly dealt with in XII.

2. Exceptions. Although the Act applies to most offices, shops and railway buildings, there are certain exceptions. These excepted premises include the following.

(*a*) Premises where self-employed persons work. The Act applies only to premises where a person is employed under a contract of service or apprenticeship.

(*b*) Premises where only certain of the employer's relatives work.

(*c*) Dwellings of outworkers.

(*d*) Premises where employees normally work no longer than a total of twenty-one hours per week.

(*e*) Premises occupied for a temporary purpose which is six months in the case of a moveable structure and six weeks in other cases.

HEALTH, SAFETY AND WELFARE PROVISIONS

3. Cleanliness. All premises and all furniture, furnishings and fittings must be kept in a clean state. No dirt or refuse must be allowed to accumulate, and the floors and steps must be cleaned not less than once a week by washing or where suitable by sweeping or other method: s.4.

4. Overcrowding. A room in which people are working must not be overcrowded so as to cause a risk of injury to health. In determining whether a room is overcrowded regard must be had not only to the number of people but also to the space in the room occupied by furniture, furnishings, and other things. The room must be of such a size as to allow 40 ft^2 (3.7 m^2) of floor space or 400 ft^3 (11.3 m^3) of air space per person: s.5.

5. Temperature. Effective provision must be made to ensure that a reasonable temperature is secured and maintained in every room. No method of heating which might result in the escape of fumes likely to be injurious or offensive may be used. Where a substantial proportion of the work does not involve severe physical effort, a temperature of not less than 16°C (60.8°F) after the first hour is deemed a reasonable temperature. In addition, a thermometer must be provided in a conspicuous place on each floor of the premises: s.6.

6. Ventilation. Effective and suitable provision must be made for securing the ventilation of every room by the circulation of adequate supplies of fresh or artificially purified air: s.7. The Health and Safety Executive has issued a guidance note on how to fulfil the requirements of this provision.

7. Lighting. Suitable and sufficient lighting, whether natural or artificial, must be provided for every part of the premises. Windows and skylights used for lighting must be, so far as is reasonably practicable, kept clean and free from obstruction. However, windows and skylights may be whitewashed to mitigate glare. All apparatus for producing artificial light must be properly maintained: s.8.

8. Sanitary conveniences. Suitable and sufficient sanitary conveniences must be provided at conveniently accessible places. They must be kept clean and properly maintained and effective provision must be made for lighting and ventilating them: s.9.

A toilet in a flat above a shop was considered by an industrial tribunal to be "conveniently accessible" to women working in the shop: *A. C. Davis & Sons* v. *Environmental Health Department of Leeds City Council* (1976).

9. Washing facilities. Suitable and sufficient washing facilities must be provided including a supply of clean, running hot and cold water or clean running warm water, and soap and clean towels or other suitable means of cleaning and drying. Effective means of lighting must be provided and be kept clean and all apparatus must be kept clean: s.10.

10. Drinking water. An adequate supply of wholesome drinking water must be provided. Where a supply of water is not piped, it must be contained in suitable vessels and must be renewed daily. Where water is supplied other than in a jet, a supply of drinking vessels must be provided of a kind to be discarded after use or other vessels together with facilities for rinsing them in clean water: s.11.

11. Accommodation for clothing. Suitable and sufficient provision must be made for clothing not worn during working hours to be hung up or otherwise accommodated. Such arrangements as are reasonably practicable must be made for drying clothing: s.12.

12. Seating arrangements. Where persons have in the course of their work reasonable opportunities for sitting without detriment to their work, suitable facilities must be provided. The employer must permit employees to use facilities provided whenever this does not interfere with their work: s.13.

NOTE: On shop premises where customers resort, the number of seats must not be less than one for every three persons employed.

13. Sedentary work. Seats of a suitable design, construction and dimension must be provided for workers whose work is done sitting down. A foot rest must be provided if the employee cannot comfortably support his feet without one: s.14.

An industrial tribunal considered that Tesco Stores were in contravention of s.14 because the seating they provided for their check-out point operators had no foot rests, was unsuitable in design, not being adjustable in height, having no back rest or swivel facility and was generally uncomfortable. The improvement notices would be affirmed and modified to add a requirement that the chairs should be able to swivel. Tesco Stores' argument that practicability had to be borne in mind in the light of the Health and Safety at Work Act 1974, s.2 (*see* XII, **11**) was not relevant to s.14 of the 1963 Act: *Tesco Stores* v. *Edwards* (1977).

14. Eating facilities. Where persons employed in shops eat meals there, suitable and sufficient facilities for eating them must be provided: s.15.

15. Floors, passages and stairs. All floors, stairs, steps, passages and gangways must be soundly constructed and properly maintained and must, so far as is reasonably practicable, be kept free from obstructions and slippery substances. A substantial handrail must be provided for every staircase: if the staircase has an open side, it must be on that side. Where there are two sides or where there is a particular risk of accidents, a handrail or handholds must be provided on both sides: s.16.

16. Fencing of machinery. The provisions of s.17 are similar to those of the Factories Act 1961 (*see* XIII, **18**).

17. Cleaning of machinery. No young person (that is, below 18 years) may clean any machinery if this exposes him to the risk of injury from a moving part of any adjacent machinery: s.18.

18. Training and supervision. No person must work at any machine prescribed as dangerous unless he has been fully instructed as to the dangers arising, and the precautions to be observed, and has received sufficient training in the work or is under adequate supervision by a person experienced in the use of the machine: s.19.

19. Prohibition of heavy work. No person should be required to lift, carry or move a load so heavy as to be likely to cause injury to him: s.23.

20. First aid. A first-aid box or cupboard must be provided which is readily accessible to employees. It must contain only first-aid requisites. Where more than 150 persons are employed, an additional box or cupboard must be provided for every 150 persons employed or a fraction of that number. Where more than 150 persons are employed the person in charge of the first-aid box or cupboard must be trained in first-aid treatment in accordance with orders made by the Department of Employment. A notice giving the name of the trained persons must be displayed so as to be easily read by employees.

21. Fire precautions. The provisions under the Offices, Shops and Railway Premises Act 1963 have been replaced by those under the Fire Precautions Act 1971, and subsequent regulations, which also apply to factories (*see* XIII, **38–41**).

22. Notification of accidents. This is governed by the Notification of Accidents and Dangerous Occurrences Regulations 1980 (*see* XIII, **52**).

23. Exemptions. The enforcing authority has power to exempt individual premises from the provisions of the Act, where by reason of special circumstances it would not be reasonably practicable to require compliance. These provisions relate to room space, temperature, sanitary conveniences and requirements as to running water.

An application for exemption must be accompanied by a certificate stating that a notice has been posted on the premises. The notice should contain the following statements.

(*a*) That an application for exemption is being made.
(*b*) The requirement from which the exemption is being sought.
(*c*) The period for which the exemption is being sought.
(*d*) The name and address of the authority to which application is being made.
(*e*) That written representations may be made to that authority within fourteen days beginning with the day upon which the notice was first posted: s.46.

OBSERVANCE AND ADMINISTRATION OF THE ACT

24. Duty to observe the provisions of the Act. This duty falls primarily on the occupier of the premises. However, in certain circumstances the duty falls on the employer of any persons employed on the premises, or on the owner of the premises, or on other persons.

25. Liability of occupier. In general, the occupier will be responsible for observing the Act in a building occupied solely by him.

26. Liability of employer. The actual employer of persons working on premises may have responsibilities under the Act if he is different from the occupier of those premises. For example, by s.13(3) it is the duty of the employer to permit employees to make use of sitting facilities.

27. Liability of the owner. The owner of a building is liable for observing certain provisions where the building is let to a number of occupiers, or where part only of a building is leased to an occupier. In such cases the owner of the building is liable as follows.

(*a*) *Common parts.* By s.42 of the Act the owner is responsible for complying with certain requirements in the "common parts" of the building. The owner must ensure that these parts are kept in a clean state, that suitable lighting is maintained, and that all floors, stairs, steps, passages and gangways are of sound construction and properly maintained.

(*b*) *Sanitary conveniences and washing facilities.* The owner is responsible for providing sanitary conveniences and washing facilities in accordance with ss.9 and 10 of the Act. He is *not* responsible for cleaning sanitary conveniences and washing facilities, nor for providing means of cleaning or drying where these are not provided solely for use by the employees of a single occupier.

(*c*) *Fire precautions.* See XIII, 41.

28. Summary of responsibilities. The following table shows how responsibility is shared between owners and occupiers in a building let to a number of occupiers or where part only of a building is leased to an occupier.

	Responsibility allocated to:	
	Occupier	*Owner*
(1) Common parts (cleaning, lighting, safety).		X
(2) Provision of sanitary conveniences and washing facilities (including maintenance, lighting and ventilation, as required).		X
(3) Cleaning of sanitary conveniences and washing facilities provided for joint use by two or more occupiers.		X
(4) Cleaning of sanitary conveniences and washing facilities provided for sole use of one occupier.	X	
(5) Provision of soap and towels or other means of cleaning and drying.	X	

29. Liability of owners in plural ownership. A building may be divided into different parts owned by different persons. Each owner is responsible for the part owned by him. (*See* also XIII, **41** for fire precautions.)

30. Defences. Where a person is prosecuted under the Act it is a defence for him to show that he used all due diligence to comply with the provisions: s.67 (But *see* **13**.)

31. The administration of the Act. This is in the hands of the

Health and Safety Executive and local authorities. (The fire precautions are enforced by local fire authorities.)

The Health and Safety Executive will be responsible for the enforcement of the provisions. In practice the Act is enforced mainly by local authorities, but also partly by the Factory Inspectorate, HM Inspectorate of Mines and Quarries, and the Railway Inspectorate. It is provided that the local authority will be the enforcing authority where certain specified activities are the main activities carried on in those premises. Examples of such specified activities are as follows.

(*a*) The sale or storage of goods for retail or wholesale distribution other than, for example, on premises controlled or occupied by a railway undertaking.

(*b*) Office activities.

(*c*) Catering services.

(*d*) The provision of residential accommodation.

(*e*) Consumer services provided in shop premises except dry cleaning or radio and television repairs.

(*f*) Dry cleaning in coin-operated units in launderettes and similar premises.

In 1979 local authorities (other than fire) obtained 122 convictions under the Offices, Shops and Railway Premises Act 1963 and 120 under the Health and Safety at Work etc. Act 1974. In 1980 the figures were 250 and 240 respectively. In 1979 local authorities issued approximately 1,160 prohibition and 6,114 improvement notices. In 1980 the approximate figures were 1,003 and 6,223 respectively: *Health and Safety Statistics 1980* (1982).

PROGRESS TEST 14

1. What is the relationship between the Health and Safety at Work Act 1974 and the Offices, Shops and Railway Premises Act 1963? **(1; XII, 2)**

2. Which premises are subject to the Offices, Shops and Railway Premises Act 1963? Mention any exceptions. **(1, 2)**

3. What provision does the 1963 Act make for the following: (*a*) cleanliness, (*b*) overcrowding, (*c*) temperature and ventilation, (*d*) lighting, and (*e*) sanitary and washing facilities? **(3–9)**

4. What are the rules as to the fencing, cleaning and use of machinery? **(16–18; XIII, 18)**

5. Which Act makes provision for fire precautions in offices, shops and railway premises? Is there any difference between the duties imposed on an occupier/owner of factory premises and that

imposed on the occupier/owner of offices, shops and railway premises? (**21**; XIII, **38–41**)

6. In what circumstances must accidents be notified? Who must give the notification to the appropriate authority? (**22**; XII, **30**; XIII, **52**)

7. May premises be exempted from the provisions of the Act? (**23**)

8. Explain the liability of (*a*) the occupier, (*b*) the employer, and (*c*) the owner of premises covered by the Act. What are the provisions as to common parts and plural ownership? (**24–29**; XII, **37**, **38**)

9. Who is responsible for the administration and enforcement of the Act? (**31**; XII, **30**)

APPENDIX I

Examination Technique

1. Two types of question. A student preparing for a law examination must train himself to answer the following two kinds of question.

(*a*) *Textbook questions*, i.e. those requiring exposition or discussion of a particular topic.

(*b*) *Problems*, i.e. those requiring the application of legal principles to a given situation.

2. Textbook questions. These are designed to test the student's knowledge and understanding of the subject. Such questions require the statement, criticism, or discussion of principles. Here are some points for guidance.

(*a*) *Read the question carefully.* In any examination, there are always students who fail to do this. Underline any parts of the question which seem to you to be significant. Notice particularly what you are told to do.

(*b*) *Make an outline of your answer.* In order to do this, you must try to see exactly what the examiner wants. If the question is widely drawn you will need a widely drawn plan. If the question is narrowly drawn, you will need a narrowly drawn plan. Make sure that the aim and scope of your plan exactly satisfy the question. It is at this stage that you must settle what goes into your answer. Your outline plan will probably consist of four or five key sentences arranged in logical sequence. (Each of these key sentences will probably develop into a paragraph of your final answer.) Jot down the names of cases and statutes you wish to cite.

(*c*) *Write an answer based on the plan.* Stick to the plan and try to set out the answer in an attractive way. Let the plan "show through" the answer so that your work has an obvious shape to it. If you think that subheadings will help to underline the form of your answer, then delineate them clearly (e.g. by numbering and underlining them).

(*d*) *Express yourself with clarity and precision.* Your style of writing is personal, but in law examinations it is usually best to aim at simplicity. Never use a long sentence when a shorter one will do. Never use a long sentence when the ideas contained in it can be more simply expressed in two or three short sentences. Keep close to the line of argument in your outline plan. Above all, do not "waffle": the examiner will always recognise this for what it is, and it will gain you no marks.

3 Problems. These questions are designed to discover whether the student can (*i*) recognise the legal principles which are applicable to the given situation, and (*ii*) apply these principles. Here are some points for guidance.

(*a*) *Read the problem carefully.* Be sure that you have considered all the facts stated. Do not bother how these facts could be proved: just accept them as facts. Notice what the instructions are. If for instance, you are asked to "advise X" you should carry out these instructions exactly.

(*b*) *Decide what principles should be applied.*

(*c*) *Make an outline plan of your answer.* This should consist of the principles briefly stated, the sequence being such as to allow you to bring out the relationship between these principles, e.g. where you need to apply a rule which is an exception to the general rule, state the general rule and follow it with the exception; also, where two conflicting rules seem to apply, state both rules. Jot down the names of cases and statutes to be cited. Complete your plan by making a *brief note* of the result when relevant principles are applied to the case in question.

(*d*) *Write an answer based on the plan.* Aim at a *concise* statement of the rules applicable, and give an authority for each rule stated if you can: the name of a case is usually sufficient. Do not launch out on a long rigmarole about the facts of cited cases. The examiner is looking mainly for an ability to solve legal problems, not trying to test your memory as to facts of cases.

When your summary of the law applicable is complete, come immediately to the solution of the problem. A good problem frequently has no definite answer; therefore you should deal in possibilities rather than certainties. Your advice should take the form "If so-and-so then so-and-so, but if so-and-so then so-and-so." The examiner does not expect you to reach a hundred per cent correct solution; he wants you to display a lawyerly ability to suggest possible answers to a hypothetical case.

APPENDIX II

Specimen Examination Questions

The following sample examination questions have been selected from past papers of the Institute of Chartered Secretaries and Administrators (ICSA), the Institute of Legal Executives (ILEX) and the Institute of Cost and Management Accountants (ICMA). The ICSA Industrial Law paper (renamed Industrial Law and Practice in 1982) requires five questions to be answered in three hours. The ICSA English Business Law paper requires six questions to be answered in that time, as does the ILEX Commercial Law paper in the Fellowship Examination. The ICMA Business Law paper in the Foundation Stage (Section B) requires five questions to be answered in three hours.

1. Oliver delivers goods to Arthur, his agent, with instructions that they be sold for not less than £800.

Consider the legal position of the parties in each of the following situations:

(*a*) Arthur sells the goods to Percy for £700;

(*b*) Arthur buys the goods himself for £800 and sends the money to Oliver. Shortly afterwards Arthur sells to Percy for £900;

(*c*) Arthur sells the goods to Percy for £850. Percy feels that he has obtained a bargain and gives Arthur a present of £20.

(ICMA, Foundation Stage, Business Law)

2. (*a*) Explain the meaning of the expression "undisclosed principal" as it is used in the law of agency. In what circumstances, if any, may an undisclosed principal sue on a contract which his agent has conducted without mentioning the agency?

(*b*) Describe the duties which an agent owes to his principal.

(ICSA, Part 2, English Business Law)

3. What are the principal legal differences between:

(*a*) a partnership;
(*b*) an unincorporated association; and
(*c*) an incorporated association?

(ICSA, Part 2, English Business Law)

4. (*a*) Who is a holder in due course of a bill of exchange?

(*b*) Consider the legal position in the following cases:

(*i*) B draws a cheque payable to D. It is stolen by F who forges D's endorsement and transfers it to H who cashes it.

(*ii*) M draws a cheque crossed "not negotiable" in favour of P. P endorses it in blank. The cheque is stolen from P by T who transfers it to X for value.

(ILEX, Fellowship Examination, Commercial Law)

5. Define (*a*) a bill of exchange; (*b*) a cheque; and (*c*) a holder in due course.

(ICSA, Part 2, English Business Law)

6. (*a*) What terms as to quality or fitness for purpose are implied by law in a contract for the sale of goods? To what extent, if at all, is it possible for a seller to exclude liability for the breach of such terms?

(*b*) In the course of his employment with the Radon Company, Watkins was sent to take delivery of a machine which the company was buying from the Metalwork Company. Watkins examined the machine superficially and failed to notice that an important working part was defective. He took delivery and, due to the faulty part, the machine did not work. The Radon Company wish to know their rights, if any, against the Metalwork Company. Advise them.

(ICSA, Part 2, English Business Law)

7. (*a*) Why is it important to know precisely when property passes in goods from the seller to the buyer?

(*b*) Fred ordered 100 cases of wine from Len who had just received a shipment of 10,000 cases. Len loaded the wine into a van for delivery to Fred but both the wine and van were stolen when Len's driver entered a shop to buy a packet of cigarettes for himself. Len now seeks payment for the wine from Fred.

Advise Fred.

(ILEX, Fellowship Examination, Commercial Law)

8. Fred buys a toaster from a retail store. Inside the toaster box is a Manufacturer's Guarantee in which the manufacturer promises to replace all faulty parts free of charge for parts and labour. The promise is expressed to be in substitution for all other rights against the manufacturer or retailer. When Fred uses the toaster for the first time it explodes injuring his face. The toaster is ruined.

Advise Fred of his rights, if any, against:

(*a*) the retailer, and

(*b*) the manufacturer.

(ILEX, Fellowship Examination, Commercial Law)

9. On 1st April 1977 Tom bought a three-piece suite from G. Ltd on hire-purchase terms. After ten weeks the suite developed a squeak and two days later the settee collapsed. Advise Tom.

(ILEX, Fellowship Examination, Commercial Law)

10. In the Consumer Credit Act 1974 what is meant by:
(*a*) a personal credit agreement;
(*b*) an extortionate bargain;
(*c*) a cancellable agreement?

(ILEX, Fellowship Examination, Commercial Law)

11. (*a*) Your company manufactures television sets and uses a standard form of contract for the sale of both the sets and the spare parts. The contract is at present being revised and consideration is being given to the inclusion of a clause providing for arbitration in the event of a dispute.

Draft a report outlining the effects of such a clause, and any advantages or disadvantages of including it.

(*b*) To what extent, if at all, may a commercial dispute be referred to arbitration in the absence of a clause to this effect in the contract?

(ICMA, Foundation Stage, Business Law)

12. Explain what is meant by an arbitration agreement. In what circumstances is the High Court empowered to remove an arbitrator or an umpire or to set aside an award? Outline the law relating to judicial review of arbitration awards.

(ICSA, Part 2, English Business Law)

13. (*a*) A change in the law may necessitate some new provision for the settlement of disputes. What are the advantages of making such provisions a reference to some tribunal instead of leaving it to the courts?

(*b*) Indicate which court or tribunal would settle the following matters and any provisions existing for an appeal:

(*i*) a claim for industrial injuries benefits which has been rejected by the local insurance officer;

(*ii*) a dispute concerning an alleged restrictive trade agreement.

(ICMA, Foundation Stage, Business Law)

14. How does the law determine whether a person is an employee or not?

(ICSA, Part 3, Industrial Law and Practice)

15. What basic terms of a contract of service are now fixed by law?

How does an employee discover the principal terms of his contract of service?

(ICSA, Part 3, Industrial Law)

16. B is going to work. The company for whom he works have arranged with the local municipality to run an early bus service from near his home and running past the factory. The bus driver is careless one day, swerves and hits a lamp standard. B is injured.

Explain how B would get financial compensation.

(ICSA, Part 3, Industrial Law)

17. (*a*) When may an employer be held vicariously liable for wrongful acts committed by an employee?

(*b*) Road Contractors Limited has a contract to repair a section of motorway and requires two specialised pieces of equipment, vehicle A and vehicle B. Vehicle A is required for the duration of the work and is hired from X Limited, which also provides a driver-operator. Vehicle B is required for one specific task and a contract is made with Y Limited for the purpose of this task. The two vehicles collide because of the driver's negligence and, as a result of the accident, David, a stranger, who is driving along that part of the motorway which is still open, is injured.

To what extent is Road Contractors Limited liable for David's injuries?

(ICMA, Foundation Stage, Business Law)

18. Draft a paper for line managers setting out clearly the principal heads of law that protect a woman from discrimination. Include a section setting out the rights of a woman who becomes pregnant.

(ICSA, Part 3, Industrial Law and Practice)

19. Individual rights now set out in the Employment Protection (Consolidation) Act 1978 include (*a*) time off for certain activities; and (*b*) guarantee payments. Write a note setting out and explaining the provisions.

(ICSA, Part 3, Industrial Law and Practice)

20. A has been of the opinion that his manager wants to get rid of him. Several times he has been asked to do things outside the normal range of his job. Now he feels that there is a concerted policy of needless criticism. Assume that A is correct. Advise him what would be the legal consequences of his leaving.

(ICSA, Part 3, Industrial Law)

21. Ann is one of three shop stewards working for L. Ltd. During working hours they meet to discuss possible industrial

action over a pay claim. Because Ann has been sacked for attending the meeting, the other two shop stewards and all the work-force walk out. After three days the work-force returns to work but the company refuses to take the remaining two shop stewards back.

Advise (*a*) Ann, and (*b*) the two shop stewards.

(ILEX, Fellowship Examination, Commercial Law)

22. Draft a memorandum to Heads of Department setting out the principal legal rules of redundancy so that they can address meetings at which a reduction of 10 per cent in staff can be announced. The aim should be to provide a brief clear statement upon those matters which you feel all staff need to know.

(ICSA, Part 3, Industrial Law and Practice)

23. Explain the term "secondary action". How is this concept used to regulate liability for strikes?

(ICSA, Part 3, Industrial Law and Practice)

24. Mark and John work as bakers on the night shift for S. Ltd., at the Liverpool bakery. As a result of a decline in the volume of confectionery sold, Mark and John are given notice that the night shift is being closed and they are both offered alternative work. Mark is offered a job as a baker on the day shift at the same bakery but will no longer receive the night shift premium. John is offered similar work on the same financial terms on the night shift with an associated company in a small town 18 miles outside Liverpool. Advise (*a*) Mark, and (*b*) John.

(ILEX, Fellowship Examination, Commercial Law)

25. Your company has a factory employing 5,000 workers. Orders have fallen away and it is proposed to make 200 workers redundant. You are asked for advice on the possible legal implications of this proposal. You are asked particularly whether your company may keep the decision secret until the last moment for fear of industrial action and whether it is possible to use the opportunity to get rid of some alleged "trouble-makers" and poor workers.

Draft an appropriate report.

(ICMA, Foundation Stage, Business Law)

26. Collective relationships depend upon the availability of methods of solving disputes. Outline the principal methods and say how they are provided by law in the UK.

(ICSA, Part 3, Industrial Law)

27. P is a member of a trade union. He is active politically. His trade union branch fine him because he has said something they feel is offensive. He was not called to the branch meeting at which his

case was considered. He refuses to pay the fine and is expelled. His firm operates a closed shop and P is warned about the future of his job.

Advise him. *(ICSA, Part 3, Industrial Law)*

28. D. is a trade union shop steward. He is having difficulty getting the company to pay what he regards as appropriate shift payments. He therefore issues two threats.

(*a*) He tells the company for whom he works that he will persuade his members to withdraw their labour.

(*b*) He tells a haulage contractor who supplies vital components that in that event he will call out the union members who drive the lorries to stop supplies reaching his firm.

Discuss the implications of these threats.

(ICSA, Part 3, Industrial Law)

29. The Health and Safety at Work Act 1974 provides for prohibition notices and improvement notices. Explain what these are and how they are used. Can they be challenged?

(ICSA, Part 3, Industrial Law and Practice)

30. Roger is driving a loaded fork-lift truck in a factory when unexpectedly the load shifts and Roger loses his balance, falling against the rotating blades of a cutting machine. He loses three fingers of his right hand. Advise Roger of the legal position (*a*) at common law, (*b*) under the Factories Act 1961, and (*c*) under the Health and Safety at Work etc. Act 1974.

(ILEX, Fellowship Examination, Commercial Law)

31. (*a*) The law which attempts to ensure occupational safety may sometimes be broken if greater output is likely to result. Upon whom will liability fall if such a breach is discovered?

(*b*) Which authorities are responsible for the administration and enforcement of the law relating to occupational safety? Outline the powers and duties of such authorities.

(ICMA, Foundation Stage, Business Law)

32. A works for B. & Company as a machinist. He has been properly trained. He should wear goggles when running his machine. In damp weather they steam up and he pushes them on to his forehead. This is a fairly common practice. One day he gets a serious injury to his eye from a piece of metal thrown from the machine.

Discuss the liability of of B. & Company. When A is fit to return what should B. & Company do in respect of his safety?

(ICSA, Part 3, Industrial Law).

Index

CASES IN INCOME TAX LAW

HENRY TOCH

This CASEBOOK is relevant to all students and practitioners of income tax law. May be used independently or in conjuction with the HANDBOOK *Income Tax 1983/84.* Recommended by the Society of Company and Commercial Accountants.

CASES IN TORT

L.A.J. ARMOUR & G.H. SAMUEL

This CASEBOOK is designed for those studying the subject at various levels ranging from business studies, accounting and other professional courses to law degree courses. The text is divided into three Parts: General Principles, Particular Liabilities and Particular Interests. Each chapter has an introductory commentary which puts the cases in context and provides a sketch of the legal issues. "This book is 'par excellence' a book for the student or layman who wishes to pinpoint, with the minimum of fuss and delay, the important judgments and cases in the law of tort." *Law Society's Gazette*

COMPANY LAW

M.C. OLIVER

Since this well-established HANDBOOK was first published in 1966, there has been an almost uninterrupted flow of company law legislation. The maze of company law which exists, formulated and amended by the five Companies Acts, can seem daunting to the student whose examination syllabus requires a knowledge of the subject. To this end the author has sought to present the key facts, in their entirety, in a way which renders the subject interesting and easily assimilable. As a teacher herself, she is well placed to understand the difficulties experienced by many students and this comparatively simple presentation of an immensely technical subject will undoubtedly help to eliminate these problems.

"To pack into a pocket-sized book . . . the wealth of detail required, at least for examination purposes, of aspiring company secretaries, accountants and students of business management is no mean achievement in itself; add to this the bonus of progress tests at the end of each chapter, a selection of test papers and the author's comforting advice on learning and examination technique, and the reasons for the book's continuing popularity are clear." *The Solicitors' Journal* Recommended by numerous professional bodies, including the Institute of Bankers, the Institute of Commercial Management, the Institute of Cost and Management Accountants and the Association of Cost and Executive Accountants.

Mary Oliver was formerly Dean of the Faculty of Law and lecturer in company law at the City of London Polytechnic.

CONSTITUTIONAL AND ADMINISTRATIVE LAW

I.N. STEVENS

The subject of constitutional and administrative law can often seem baffling to the law student who tends to find its rather vague and cumbersome principles difficult to grasp. The aim of this HANDBOOK is to present the salient points with the minimum of complication. The author has not neglected classical constitutional theory, but has avoided excessively general and politically-oriented discussion.

In spite of the concise presentation of the facts, the book is more than an introduction — wherever possible fundamental principles are stated as formulated in judicial decisions rather than in abstract terms. By this means, and also by reference to the interaction between Government (the legislature) and the Courts (the executive), it is hoped that the student will find the facts are more readily understood and assimilated.

No prior knowledge of the subject is assumed, and the book will prove suitable for the first year law students, and also to university, polytechnic, professional and "A" Level students preparing for examinations in politics or government. ". . . an essential handbook for law and administration students." *Teaching Politics*

CONSUMER CREDIT

R.G. LAWSON

The Consumer Credit Act 1974 is one of the most important and most complicated pieces of legislation of recent years. This HANDBOOK provides the student with a concise and clear discussion of the subject, and will be useful both as an introduction and as a revision source.

CONSUMER LAW

M.J. LEDER

This HANDBOOK provides a concise but comprehensive survey of the diverse elements of consumer law, a subject which is being included in an increasing number of courses. It is intended primarily for the use of undergraduates on law degree and mixed degree courses, and for prospective solicitors preparing for the new Law Society final examinations. In addition it should be of considerable interest to business studies and accountancy students, and to anyone whose studies or work involves a consideration of the legal aspects of consumer problems. ". . . an excellent introduction to the subject." *The City of London Law Review*

CORPORATION TAX

B.S. TOPPLE

This HANDBOOK assumes no prior knowledge of taxation on the reader's part. It provides a basic introduction to the principles of company taxation, with chapters covering capital allowances and losses, the treatment of income tax and close companies. The author gives typical examples of firms' accounts in the text to illustrate each point. ". . . difficult to recommend a better book for a basic introduction to the subject. *Accountancy* Recommended by the Association of International Accountants, the Institute of Taxation and the Institute of Cost and Management Accountants.

LABOUR LAW

M. WRIGHT

This HANDBOOK is intended for all those preparing for examinations in labour law or industrial law, whether at university, polytechnic, college or professional level. It will also be useful to the general reader needing a concise statement of the main rules relating to employment and industrial relations. Contents include chapters on administration of labour law, the contract of employment, regulation of remuneration, trade unions, discrimination, termination of employment, safety and welfare, and the laws of collective bargaining and industrial conflict. This reprint takes full account of the provisions of the 1982 Employment Act.